Troublesome Border

Troublesome Border

Revised Edition

Oscar J. Martínez

The University of Arizona Press
Tucson

To Jamie, Gabriel, Daniel, David, and Andrés

The University of Arizona Press
© 2006 The Arizona Board of Regents
First edition published 1988
Manufactured in the United States of America on acid-free,
archival-quality paper.

www.uapress.arizona.edu

Library of Congress Cataloging-in-Publication Data

Martínez, Oscar J. (Oscar Jáquez), 1943–
    Troublesome border / Oscar J. Martínez.— Rev. ed.
        p. cm.
    Includes bibliographical references and index.
    ISBN-13: 978-0-8165-2557-7 (pbk. : alk. paper)
    ISBN-10: 0-8165-2557-9 (pbk. : alk. paper)
    1. Mexican-American Border Region—History.
    2. Mexican-American Border Region. I. Title.
    F786.M42 2006
    972'.1—dc22

                        2005033433

This book was originally published as part of the PROFMEX
(The Consortium of U.S. Research Programs for Mexico)
monograph series, under the editorship of Michael C. Meyer.

Publication of this book is made possible in part by the pro-
ceeds of a permanent endowment created with the assistance
of a Challenge Grant from the National Endowment for the
Humanities, a federal agency.

14 13 12 11 10   8 7 6 5 4 3 2

Contents

Maps

Tables

Preface

This book uses conflict as a unifying theme to examine historical and contemporary relationships in the U.S.–Mexico borderlands. Well into the twentieth century Mexico and the United States faced many troublesome issues at the border that often erupted into armed confrontation. Settling the final boundary between the two countries in itself caused long-term contentiousness, leaving a legacy of bitterness on both sides, particularly in Mexico. Unauthorized armed incursions from the United States into Mexico for the purpose of fomenting insurrection and detaching land from the latter country likewise created serious friction. The border partitioned a distinguishable geographic and cultural region inhabited by Indians and Mexicans, creating untold predicaments for both groups. Indian raids across the border became a source of international strife that lasted until the 1880s. For Mexicans who remained south of the boundary as well as for those who became Mexican Americans by virtue of their incorporation into the United States the border shaped frontier lifestyles that differed markedly from those of the mainstream societies in each nation.

Much of this book is historical in its coverage, but current-day border issues such as rapid population growth, environmental problems, undocumented migration, drug trafficking, and violence receive prominent attention as well. The book concludes with general comments that place the U.S.–Mexico border experience in perspective.

My intent is not to present a comprehensive history of the borderlands; rather, I examine selected topics that illuminate past and contemporary relationships in the region. Although much of the interaction between the two countries and among the different ethnic groups has been characterized by contentiousness, I do not wish to suggest that conflict has governed the lives of border people. Far from that; peaceful relations have prevailed over the course of history. Yet strife has been a persistent fact of life in the region, and my interest is in identifying its roots and in tracing its evolution.

The idea for this book occurred to me in the mid-1970s, when I was preparing to teach a course on the history of the U.S.–Mexico border at the University of Texas at El Paso. As I searched the literature for background information I became aware of the myriad controversies that existed at the frontier. I found numerous works on conflict and many other border topics, but few attempts had been made to synthesize or to interpret events and processes. Since the publication of the first edition of *Troublesome Border* in 1988, studies have appeared that offer historical overviews of the region. Yet the emphases are different from what is found here.[1] My purpose in both the original and revised editions has been to examine border history from various perspectives and to trace problems that confront contemporary border society. This is a topical history rather than a traditional chronological treatment. It offers an alternative, nontraditional way to examine some of the complexities of border history.

Since 1988 many dramatic developments have occurred that warranted the publication of a revised edition. Aware of the use of the book as a teaching tool, I became increasingly conscious of the fact that information pertaining to numerous critical issues in the political, economic, and social arenas had been rendered out of date by transformational events. I felt compelled to chronicle and interpret the extraordinary new circumstances that once again have changed the border region in fundamental ways.

At the turn of the twenty-first century the rapid expansion of the border population and of the region's economy continued as before. That was expected, but here is a quick list of astonishing things that have happened since 1988 that few people could have anticipated. Mexico's northern borderlands led the political struggle that in 2000 ended the stranglehold that the ruling party, the PRI, had maintained over our neighboring country since 1929. In 1994 the United States and Mexico enacted a historic treaty, the North American Free Trade Agreement (NAFTA), a document that formally recognized the intense economic interdependence and growing integration between the two countries, especially along the border. While NAFTA produced winners and losers as trade rose along the border, the agreement also introduced novel institutional approaches to dealing with labor, environmental, and water-related infrastructure issues. By the 1990s drug trafficking had assumed unprecedented gravity and notoriety along the border as cartels emerged to handle smuggling operations into the United States. That subjected the region to horrific levels of lawlessness and violence, making security the number one concern of residents in the Mexican border cities. In the United States the terrorist attacks of September 11, 2001, prompted a renewed outcry for greater militarization of the southern border. The threat of terrorism and concerns about security measures became two issues inextricably linked in border-related discussions in Washington, D.C. With respect to migration, in the 1990s U.S. officials implemented "blockades" in urban areas that effectively drove undocumented migrants to isolated locations where multiple dangers awaited them as they attempted to cross the border. That new policy inevitably led to hundreds of tragic deaths from exposure every year, especially in the desert areas of Arizona.

Though it seems that all the recent news about the borderlands has been bad, that is not so. In the case of Indians, some tribes became beneficiaries of favorable developments, at least materially speaking. In the late 1980s the U.S. government permitted the operation of gaming casinos on Indian reservations, ushering in unprecedented economic opportunities for historically marginalized peoples. Of course, Indians have had to face new social challenges that gaming activity has introduced into their communities.

In preparing the revised edition I incorporated updated information on the above developments in respective chapters. At the same time I took a fresh look at the whole book, making revisions and stylistic changes throughout where appropriate. Chapter 7, a new addition, emphasizes the impact of drug trafficking on the border; the first edition had little information on the drug trade. Chapter 7 also includes an updated section on migration, a theme that I previously discussed in another part of the book.

My interpretations about the borderlands have not changed. If anything, they have been strengthened. I am more convinced than ever of the special nature of the border region and, in particular, the area's overwhelming vulnerability to external forces. Dependence has been the overriding defining feature in the lives of borderlanders, especially on the Mexican side. The urgent and perplexing problems of the border continue to present great challenges to both countries.

Part of the first edition was written during 1981–82, while I was a fellow at the Center for Advanced Study in the Behavioral Sciences (CASBS) at Stanford, California. I gratefully acknowledge the financial support provided at that time by the CASBS, the National Research Council, the Andrew W. Mellon Foundation, and the National Endowment for the Humanities. I remain especially grateful to the staff at the CASBS for extending editorial, library, secretarial, and word-processing assistance but most of all for making my stay at Stanford exceedingly pleasant and memorable. It would take a page to list those at the CASBS who extended kindness and help to me and my family; to all, *muchísimas gracias*. James W. Wilkie, Anne Holder, and the late Larry McConville provided valuable editorial suggestions that improved the work in numerous ways. Thinking back to my years at UT El Paso, I fondly and gratefully recall the assistance rendered by the staff of the Center for Inter-American and Border Studies, which I directed from 1982 to 1987. Carmen García, Mary Mendoza, Nancy Gavaldón, Rose Torres, and the late Isabel Robles all helped to prepare the original manuscript for publication.

Finally, the revised edition has benefited from comments made by anonymous readers, and I express my sincere appreciation to them.

Troublesome Border

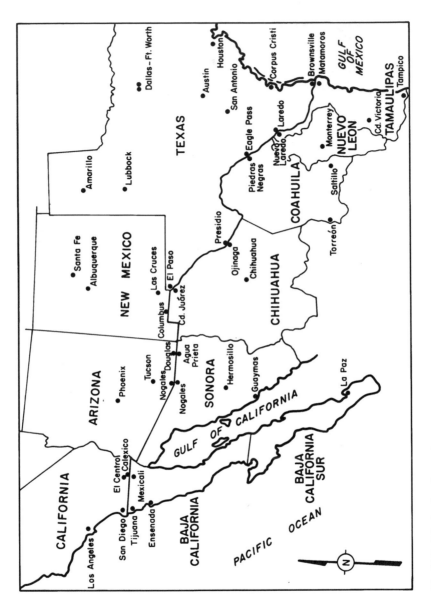

The U.S.–Mexico border region.

Introduction

Scholars and journalists in the United States have long characterized the U.S.–Mexico border as a deeply troubled region with a multitude of problems, a perception widely shared by leaders as well as ordinary people.[1] The border strip between the Texas Gulf and the Pacific has been associated with international disputes, banditry, racial strife, uncontrolled illegal migration, large-scale smuggling of drugs, and corrupt behavior of officials and has become an alleged haven for unassimilated and separatist-prone people (i.e., Mexican Americans in the Southwest).[2] Preoccupation with the border situation reached a new high after the terrorist attacks on the World Trade Center in New York City on September 11, 2001. Since then, many stories in the U.S. national print media and network television have framed traditional controversial issues such as migration and drugs in the context of potential infiltration of terrorists into the United States through a border that is perceived to be "out of control."[3]

U.S. residents are largely unaware that Mexicans also view their northern border with concern and at times even alarm. Historically, the northern zone has been seen as having economic interests, customs, and traditions vastly different from other parts of Mexico. Border communities such as Ciudad Juárez and Tijuana have long been subjected to heavy criticism from Mexico City and other interior areas for their close ties to the United States, a country viewed with apprehension and suspicion by the Mexican citizenry. Frontier Mexicans have been accused of succumbing to *agringamiento* (Euro-Americanization) and of focusing too much of their energies on foreign-oriented economic activities. Border tourism in particular has come under attack for allegedly cultivating a permissive moral climate in order to lure U.S. dollars. Major binational issues such as undocumented migration, drug smuggling, and, more recently, terrorism have been equally worrisome for Mexicans.

Thus, whether viewed from the north or the south, the border is perceived as a highly problematic area. Yet what often appears to people in the United States and Mexico as a breakdown of institutions, social systems, and legal structures at the Rio Grande is in many respects the normal functioning of the border. By nature, border zones, especially those that are far removed from the core, spawn independence, rebellion, cultural deviation, disorder, and even lawlessness. The U.S.–Mexico border fits within that universal scheme.

The history of countless nations illustrates how borderlands regions frequently depart from the norms of interior zones and how they develop institutional patterns and interests quite separate from those at the centers of power. Isolation, weak institutions, lax administration, and a different economic orientation prompt people on the periphery to develop homemade approaches to their problems and unconventional means of carrying on mutually beneficial relationships across an international boundary.[4] Borderlanders view the boundary and the function it is supposed to serve in terms fundamentally different from those of their compatriots in interior regions. If national laws appear unjust or are viewed as impractical in a border context, it becomes culturally acceptable to work around them or ignore them altogether. Lacking an educated understanding of the unique conditions at the periphery, the mainstream society is constantly irritated at the deviant behavior found at the border and is perpetually concerned about the problems the zone generates for the nation-state. Indeed, the historical record confirms that the border has been a persevering headache for both countries, although the degree of aggravation over the years has depended on the nature of the issues under dispute (table I.1).

Essential to understanding the many conflicts that the United States and Mexico have experienced at their common border is an awareness of the process by which the boundary was determined and the many difficulties that both countries have encountered in preserving the integrity of the dividing line. This theme is the focus of chapters 1 and 2. In the history of the relations between the two nations no other issue has caused so much controversy, bitterness, and outright confrontation. Border delimitation is, of course, an age-old problem in the relations between neighboring states. For centuries nations have competed and fought over territorial possessions, and in cases where strong countries abut weak ones, the latter commonly have had to yield lands to ambitious or aggressive neighbors. History demonstrates that few boundaries have been created as a result of peaceful negotiations; power politics, military pressures, and warfare have been the determining factors in most cases.[5] Besides governmental attempts to enlarge the national domain by force, in many cases zealous citizens have, on their own, undertaken unlawful incursions intended to detach the possessions of neighboring countries. Such was the experience of the United States and Mexico.

An issue related to the delimitation and maintenance of borders is the impact that those processes have on people who reside in what becomes the "borderlands." In the broadest sense the U.S.–Mexico boundary partitioned a distinguishable geographic and cultural region inhabited by Indians and Mexicans. The consequences of that momentous development constitute the focus of chapters 3, 4, and 5. Fundamentally, the experience of these groups parallels that of other peoples in other parts of the world whose homelands have been segmented by the redrawing of borders. Power politics, the driving force of border delimitation, have always had little regard for preexisting

Table I.1 Conflict Levels for Selected Border Issues

Issue	Period of Intensity	National (U.S./ Mexico)	Regional (U.S./ Mexico)	Local (U.S./ Mexico)
		Conflict Level[a]		
Territorial integrity				
Boundary delimitation[b]	1821–54	4 / 4	4 / 4	2 / 2
Boundary maintenance[c]	1884–1963	2 / 4		2–3 / 2–3
Filibustering	1820s–1900s	2 / 4	2 / 4	2 / 2–3
Indian depredations	1840s–80s	4 / 4	4 / 4	4 / 4
Irredentism[d]	1915–16	2–4 / 1	4 / 1	4 / 1
Economic integrity				
Trade protectionism	1848–present	1 / 2	1 / 1	2–3 / 2–3
Mexican free zones	1848–1905, 1937–present	2 / 2	1 / 2	2–3 / 1
Smuggling	1848–present	2–3 / 2	1–2 / 1	1 / 1
Sociocultural issues				
Banditry	1848–1920	2–3 / 2–3	4 / 4	4 / 4
Racial strife	1848–present	1–2 / 2	2–4 / 1	2–4 / 1–2
Land claims[e]	1836–1900s	1–2 / 1–2	2–4 / 1	2–4 / 1–2
Migration	1900–present	4 / 2	4 / 1–2	2–4 / 1–3
Drug trafficking	1960s–present	4 / 3	4 / 3	4 / 3
Violence/crime	1980s–present	4 / 4	4 / 4	4 / 4
Environmental issues				
Water allocation	1890–present	2 / 3	1 / 1	2–3 / 2–3
Water contamination	1950s–present	2–3 / 3	1 / 1	2–3 / 3
Air pollution	1960s–present	2 / 2	1 / 1	3 / 2
Sewage spills	1970s–present	2 / 1	2 / 1	4 / 3
Boundary flow				
Transportation	1970s–present	1 / 1	1 / 1	2–3 / 2–3
Fences, towers, etc.	1930s–present	1–3 / 2–3	1–3 / 1–3	2–3 / 2–4
Bridge incidents	1920s–present	1–2 / 1–2	1–3 / 1–3	2–4 / 2–4

[a]Conflict levels

1	low	3	occasionally intense
2	moderate	4	intense

[b]The process by which the boundary was established, that is, conflict over territoriality.
[c]The process of maintaining the physical stability of the boundary, for example, control of the shifting Rio Grande.
[d]An attempt by some frontier Mexicans to promote rebellion in south Texas against established Anglo authority for the purpose of establishing a new political order.
[e]On the U.S. side, land claims involved Chicano/Hispano attempts to assert or reclaim rights to Spanish and Mexican land grants, especially in New Mexico.

cultural entities that lie in territories targeted for partitioning. Throughout history the imposition of arbitrary boundaries has forced millions of people to migrate or to switch political loyalties, learn new languages, and function in alien cultural environments. Instances of natural ethnographical situations seriously disrupted by artificial borders abound in the African continent, and examples of culturally distinct populations absorbed against their will into alien sovereign states through the process of territorial expansionism may be found almost anywhere in the world.[6] In the case of the Indians of northern Mexico and the U.S. Southwest the infiltration of foreigners into their homelands began with the arrival of Spaniards in the sixteenth century. The establishment of the permanent international border in the mid-nineteenth century brought increased pressures from waves of European American and Mexican immigrants, but, just as important, it imposed restrictions on the mobility of those Indians who lived in the vicinity of the line of demarcation. Unaccustomed to such restraints, certain tribes ignored the boundary altogether, triggering many local problems and seriously upsetting relations between the United States and Mexico.

For the Mexican-origin population the new border brought a set of dilemmas and predicaments typical of the experiences of groups who reside on the periphery of nation-states and who are subjected to international forces beyond their control. Mexican Americans, or Chicanos/as (those living permanently north of the border), and Mexicans (those living or originating south of the border) felt deeply the impact of the boundary in the formation of their lifestyles, attitudes, and cultural orientations. Although the border separated Mexican Americans politically from Mexico, physical proximity kept them tied to their roots culturally and socially. Those continuing links to the motherland shaped to a significant degree their marginality within U.S. society. Their compatriots across the Rio Grande or on Mexican soil found themselves insulated from American political domination but not from economic and cultural influences; that reality, coupled with sheer geographic remoteness from the core of the nation, assured that the *norteños/as* (northerners) and *fronterizos/as* (borderlanders) would develop societal patterns distinct from the rest of Mexico.[7] Thus the presence of the border played a fundamental role in converting border Chicanos/as and Mexicans into entities that stood apart from the mainstream societies of each nation.

Those who negotiated the boundary in the 1840s could hardly have anticipated the human consequences of their decision. The Mexican government did attempt to maintain the cultural integrity of the Rio Grande region by proposing that the line of demarcation be drawn to the north of that stream so that a buffer zone would shield the remaining Mexican frontier from further American advances. But it was the U.S. government that dictated the terms of the division of the northern Mexican territories, and the Euro-American negotiators, consumed by a spirit of aggressive expansionism, did not take into consideration how the local populations would fare. The Euro-American approach to determining the border with Mexico contrasted sharply with policies followed during the period of the formation of internal U.S. state and territorial boundaries, when the human factor received eminent consideration. During those earlier determinations population centers were seen as nuclear areas, or cores, from which to calculate where boundaries would be drawn in outward directions at appropriate distances. Guided by the principle that boundaries should only separate people who were already living apart, boundary makers conscientiously avoided lines that would split naturally congregated populations. The drawing of state and territorial borders that resulted from the famous Compromise of 1850 well illustrates the weight assigned to the interests of people.[8] Unfortunately, Indians and Mexicans native to the U.S.–Mexico border area did not receive such considerations.

Chapter 6 examines border issues related to growth, with emphasis on rapid population expansion, ecological problems, environmental pollution, and human conflict spawned by the intense binational interaction in the region. The border communities have become increasingly crowded in recent decades, spawning intense competition for space and resources between the adjoining populations. Fundamentally, it is the boundary itself that acts as the agent of friction, given that it obstructs the normal movement of people and products. Because of the interference with the natural order of things, conflictive situations develop continuously. Fortunately, these tension-generating circumstances at the frontier are well enough understood by local people, especially decision makers, and many conflicts are diffused through the use of time-tested informal mechanisms that often circumvent national laws.

However, major problems that have an effect on interior zones are much harder to resolve informally because of overwhelming pressures that emanate from the core areas. International migration and drug smuggling are two such issues, and their impact on the border is addressed in chapter 7. Federal officials, in their quest to "control" the international line by stopping "invasions" of foreigners and the influx of banned substances, often dictate policies and make laws frequently detrimental to the welfare of the border communities. The constant struggle between local needs and national "interests" represents a basic element in the complex periphery-core heritage of the border frontier.

Viewed in the context of U.S.–Mexico relations, the border has occupied a preeminent place in countless disagreements and agreements entered into by the two countries. It is not an exaggeration to say that border issues have overshadowed all other binational concerns since the two neighbors began to negotiate with each other as independent nations. Over time, four distinct phases have become apparent in the role played by the border in that bilateral relationship. The first phase began with the initial contact between Spain and England in contested territories of North America and ended with the signing of the Adams-Onís Treaty in 1819, which demarcated the line between the United States and New Spain. Those years produced an infiltration of English people and residents of the United States into Spanish territory, filibustering, and aggressive U.S. diplomacy calculated to alter the boundary. In the second phase Mexico, after its successful drive for independence from Spain, assumed the challenge of containing the aggressive U.S. advance on the northern frontier, but to no avail. Between the 1820s and early 1850s the borderlands witnessed the Texas rebellion of 1836, the U.S.–Mexico War of 1846–48, and the signing of the border-altering Guadalupe Hidalgo and Gadsden treaties (1848 and 1853, respectively), both of which were highly favorable to the United States. The third phase, lasting from 1853 to 1920, saw chronic transboundary encounters that almost produced international warfare on numerous occasions. Intense nationalistic feelings arising out of continuous violations of the integrity of the border combined with racial strife north of the Rio Grande to create an explosive climate in the border communities. Perhaps the most difficult era was the 1910s, when the Mexican Revolution raged throughout northern Mexico and spilled across the boundary. The fourth phase began in 1920 and continues to the present. By the end of the Revolution friction over border violence had ceased to be a major concern between the two countries. Armed invasions of each other's territory ended, significantly reducing the nationalistic feelings that had reached fever proportions in the 1910s. Henceforth the two governments sought to solve their problems, some of which actually arose from disagreements unrelated to the border, through diplomatic negotiation rather than through direct confrontation. The new approach reflected profound changes that had transpired in the border region and in each nation's core by the first quarter of the twentieth century, including the end of U.S. territorial expansionism, reduced isolation of the frontier, the onset of modernization, a rise in population in the periphery, the founding of new border cities, the beginning of long-term political stability in modern Mexico, and an improved framework for solving international conflicts.

1 Whither the Boundary?

Fixing the limits of territorial jurisdiction between neighboring countries can be a complicated process that may involve conflict. A line that is not precisely and permanently determined at an early stage of contact may provide a source of contention for generations. Examples abound of nations that have engaged in prolonged and frustrated border negotiations, culminating in many cases in acrimonious diplomacy or outright warfare. The case of the United States and Mexico fits this pattern, although the problems associated with boundary delimitation and territorial sovereignty are largely historical rather than contemporary.

The lengthy story of the establishment of the U.S.–Mexico boundary began when Spain, France, and England competed for possessions in North America. Upon achieving independence Mexico and the United States inherited the territorial disputes of their former colonial masters. Yet European Americans added a crucial ingredient to the process—national expansionism—that triggered bitter and long-lasting struggles. The ideology of "Manifest Destiny," which held that God favored the conquest of western lands, helped to justify territorial aggression against Mexico. Once set, the boundary's location significantly shaped the destiny of each nation. But many problems remained to be worked out because of the legacy of strife associated with the creation of that boundary and because the line itself had built-in imperfections. Numerous refinements of the border became necessary, and even in the second half of the twentieth century U.S. and Mexican diplomats continued to address technical difficulties pertaining to boundary location.

European Disputation and the Louisiana Controversy

Penetration of North America by the European powers began in the early sixteenth century, when Spaniards explored lands from Florida to California and then established permanent colonies in a wide arc that became known as the "Spanish Borderlands." In the seventeenth century the French began their expansion into the continent via the St. Lawrence River Valley to the Great Lakes region, the Ohio River Valley, and the Mississippi River Valley. The English, having established colonies on the Atlantic Coast, gradually moved west and south. Once contact was made on the frontier the European powers maneuvered to establish territorial claims on the basis of prior explorations, occupation, and alliances with Indians.

France constantly tested Spanish claims during the first half of the eighteenth century, particularly in Texas. The Spanish-French rivalry ended in 1763, when the Treaty of Paris removed the French from continental North America, allowing Spain to acquire Louisiana and to move its eastern boundary to the Mississippi River. But as France stepped out England stepped in, threatening Spanish territory along the northern Mississippi and on the northern Pacific Coast. Spain faced the monumental task of defending a vast frontier. It responded by blazing new trails, establishing new settlements, and befriending Indians who could serve as a buffer against the English. When the United States won its political freedom, it continued the British tradition of contesting Spain's claims by probing into Florida and the western lands.[1] The danger posed to Spain by the new nation is exemplified by the following statement, which appeared in a U.S. publication in 1786: "Two thousand brave [European] Americans . . . , animated with resentment against those troublesome neighbors [the Spaniards], and having in object the conquest of the richest country in the world, would complete in a few weeks, from their arrival at the Natchez, the reduction of West Florida and Louisiana, in spite of all the Spanish efforts to resist us. Another army of about the same number of men . . . would carry the war into the very heart of Mexico."[2] The aggression advocated in that statement was more widely supported in the mid-nineteenth century, when the United States indeed "would carry the war into the very heart of Mexico."

In the late eighteenth century competition for the Indian trade and for territorial control kept the Upper Mississippi and Upper Missouri river valleys in constant turmoil. A pattern soon developed whereby Spaniards would move forward to repel the British and British American penetration but would eventually be forced to fall back, resulting in gradual effective recession of the Spanish frontier.[3] As the nineteenth century began the situation became more confused as Louisiana changed hands and the United States became a confirmed expansionist country. In 1800 Charles IV of Spain, in return for certain Italian lands, ceded Louisiana to Napoleon Bonaparte under a treaty that failed to specify the precise extent of the Louisiana territory. Three years later Napoleon, unable to occupy his new acquisition and fearing that it might fall into English hands, sold Louisiana to the United States. This transaction violated a prior French pledge to Spain that Louisiana would not be sold without consultation with the Spanish, but that did not concern Napoleon or the United States. Further, the land transfer followed precedent by leaving territorial limits very unclear, thus assuring a prolonged border conflict between the United States and Spain.

Once the treaty of cession from France was signed, President Thomas Jefferson expressed the view that Louisiana included all western lands to the Rio Grande. Under this interpretation old Spanish settlements such as San Antonio and Santa Fe had suddenly become U.S. cities! To substantiate his claim on Texas Jefferson cited French settlement of the Gulf Coast in the seventeenth century and the trade monopoly given by Louis XIV to one of his subjects in 1712 over territory extending as far as New Mexico. Spain, armed with maps and other historical evidence, countered that France's presence had been ephemeral and that those areas had long been colonized, settled, and administered as Spanish territory.[4] When appeals and negotiation failed to advance the U.S. position, Jefferson pushed his claims by sending exploring parties beyond the Mississippi. The Lewis and Clark Expedition of 1804 was particularly important in giving impetus to U.S. hunger for more western land. In Lower Louisiana a border conflict nearly triggered hostilities, but these were avoided through the signing of the Neutral Ground Agreement, which applied to the area between the Arroyo Hondo and the Sabine River. In West Florida U.S. intrusions and seizure of land kept Spaniards constantly on the defensive. Anxiety was also high in New Mexico, where U.S. citizens repeatedly penetrated the marginal local defenses.[5]

For many years the United States persisted in its efforts to convince Spain to give up Texas, offering alternative borders from the Sabine to the Rio Grande. The dispute over the Louisiana border was finally settled in 1819, when Secretary of State John Quincy Adams and Spanish minister Luis de Onís concluded a treaty that fixed the border between the United States and Spain along an irregular line beginning at the Sabine, proceeding north to the forty-second parallel, and from there to the Pacific. Spain acknowledged U.S. ownership of East Florida and gave up claims on the Pacific north of the forty-second parallel. The Spaniards, however, refused to accede to Adams's demand that Texas be placed under U.S. jurisdiction. The treaty of 1819, which was ratified in 1821, concluded another phase of Spain's long struggle to hold onto its colonies.[6] Once again Spain's borderlands had been compressed, but U.S. expansionists were still not satisfied. Feeling that the United States should not have given up Texas, to which European Americans were "entitled" by "prior ownership," many expansionists would press for the "reannexation" of that province in subsequent years.

U.S. Expansion into Mexico

With independence achieved in 1821, Mexico inherited from Spain the challenge of safeguarding the vast northern frontier. More population was needed to strengthen the defenses of California and Texas particularly. Following policies begun by Spain, Mexico in the 1820s allowed the entry into Texas of large numbers of immigrants from the United States in order to further populate that sparsely settled province. Anxious to settle in the fertile Texas lands, these European Americans expediently swore allegiance to Mexican laws, religion, and customs. Within a short time Mexico would realize what a volatile situation it had unwittingly created within its own borders. Powerful forces would converge on the periphery and lead to armed conflict and loss of vast territories to the United States.

The isolation of Texas, New Mexico, and California from the rest of Mexico and the inability of the central government in Mexico City to effec-

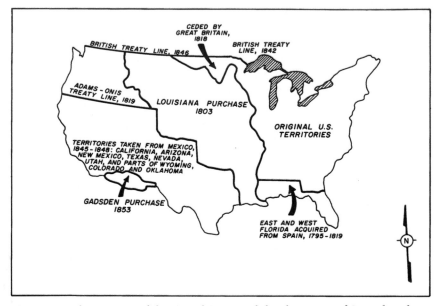

The territorial expansion of the United States and the absorption of Spanish and Mexican territories, 1795–1853.

tively govern and attend to the needs of norteños/as fostered regionalist tendencies and even separatist movements on the northern frontier.[7] That situation played into the hands of U.S. expansionists who coveted those provinces. Once the philosophy of Manifest Destiny took firm hold in the European American mind the outcome seemed clear: sooner or later the United States would detach and annex Mexico's northern territories.

Mexico's apprehensions about threats to its northern frontier surfaced during initial contacts with U.S. officials. From earlier Spanish reports Mexicans knew that European Americans desired to expand their borders to the west and south. Onís had warned as early as 1812 that the U.S. government was prepared to use intrigue and to foment trouble in order to absorb Texas, Nuevo Santander, Coahuila, New Mexico, part of Nueva Viscaya, and Sonora.[8] Another Spanish diplomat had stated in 1820 that U.S. expansionists believed they were destined to extend their dominion "to the Isthmus of Panama, and . . . over all the regions of the new world." Mexican envoys to Washington quickly got a taste of the U.S. territorial ambition reported earlier by the Spaniards. "[European] Americans will be our own sworn enemies," stated a Mexican diplomat in 1822, "and foreseeing this we ought to treat them as such from the present day." In 1823 another Mexican official noted that the European American desire for Texas was so strong that U.S. troops might soon be ordered there.[9]

Rather than attempting to acquire Texas by force, however, the United

States in the 1820s and 1830s adopted a policy of seeking to persuade Mexico to sell that province along with adjacent territories, but Mexico proved unreceptive. Joel R. Poinsett, who would become the first U.S. minister to Mexico, first met as a private citizen in 1822 with a representative of Agustín de Iturbide's government to discuss the U.S. desire to alter the border created by the Adams-Onís Treaty. When he became minister in 1825, Poinsett expressed the European American interest in fixing the border so that New Mexico, California, and parts of Nuevo León, Coahuila, Sonora, and Baja California would be transferred to the United States. An unskilled diplomat, Poinsett simply aroused Mexican suspicions and made no headway. Two years later, under instructions from President John Quincy Adams, Poinsett offered to buy Texas. In 1829, one year after both countries had signed a treaty affirming the boundary established by the Adams-Onís Treaty of 1819, President Martin Van Buren instructed Poinsett to renew the offer for Texas. Poinsett was to suggest options for a new border and was to offer up to $5 million for the line most advantageous to the United States.[10] Before he could act, however, Poinsett was relieved of his post, and for the next six years Anthony Butler represented the United States in Mexico. Butler, politically inept and an unprincipled expansionist, tried various means of acquiring Texas, including threats and the attempted bribery of high officials. By 1835 Mexico City had arranged for his recall.[11]

The use of dollar diplomacy to detach Texas from Mexico became moot in 1836, when European Americans in Texas, assisted by U.S. funds and volunteers as well as some Mexican Texans, staged a successful insurrection against a Mexican government weakened by political instability and economic disarray. The rebels widely assumed that the United States would soon annex the independent Republic of Texas, but sectional rivalry delayed that event until 1845. When the annexation finally occurred, Mexico interpreted it as a serious and hostile act by the United States, for Mexico still considered Texas part of its national domain.

By late 1845 relations between the two countries had seriously deteriorated. Not only had the United States taken Texas; it was also adamantly claiming that the province extended to the Rio Grande. In December U.S. envoy John C. Slidell traveled to Mexico to discuss the boundary and to negotiate other matters, in particular, pending damage claims submitted by U.S. citizens who suffered losses in Mexico during periods of political instability.[12] The timing, however, proved unfavorable for such delicate bargaining. The Mexican government refused to receive Slidell, and President James Polk interpreted this refusal as an insult to the United States. By early 1846 Polk had ordered U.S. troops to proceed to the Rio Grande, thereby setting the stage for direct confrontation. Mexico had tolerated U.S. military control of territory north of the Nueces River while the status of Texas remained uncertain, but the advance across that stream constituted a flagrant act of aggression because Mexicans viewed Texas as extending no farther than the Nueces.

On April 24 a skirmish between U.S. and Mexican troops resulted in the death of some European Americans, and Polk immediately declared war on the grounds that Mexicans had "shed American blood upon American soil." Polk sidestepped the issue of U.S. provocation: after all, U.S. troops had penetrated disputed territory. What is more, even before the skirmish occurred the United States had blockaded the Rio Grande. For the next two years the two countries fought a war that ended with the occupation of Mexico and the signing of the Treaty of Guadalupe Hidalgo in February 1848, by which Mexico ceded half of its territory to the United States.[13]

The incident seized on by Polk as justification for declaring war illustrates the determination of U.S. expansionists to sustain the claim that the territory of the United States extended to the Rio Grande. The declaration of the Texans in 1836 that their new republic extended that far and the agreement signed that same year by President Antonio López de Santa Anna while a prisoner at San Jacinto, which implicitly recognized Texan jurisdiction to the Rio Grande, lent plausibility to that claim. To expansionists it hardly mattered that the Texas declaration constituted a unilateral action or that the Mexican Congress, the only treaty-making entity under Mexico's constitution, repudiated the Santa Anna agreement.[14] Polk chose to ignore the vast documentation that undermined his claim to the Rio Grande boundary, relying instead on the weak and biased research of contemporary expansionists. Spain had clearly defined the Nueces River as the southern border of Texas, and Mexico had never given Texas jurisdiction over the strip between the Nueces and the Rio Grande. Over the years, responsibility for the Nueces strip had rested with the state of Tamaulipas. Mexicans clearly had physical possession of the disputed territory, with settlements well established on the northern bank of the Rio Grande.[15] Most maps and atlases published during the period, including European ones, showed Texas extending no farther than the Nueces. Even Stephen F. Austin, the "father of Texas," recognized that border in three maps he prepared in the 1820s, and national leaders such as John Quincy Adams and Andrew Jackson concurred.[16]

Many European Americans who were knowledgeable about the border issue condemned Polk for starting the war and then labeling Mexico as the provocateur.[17] Members of Congress, editors, intellectuals, and other influentials viewed Polk as a liar and as the instigator of national aggression calculated to end in the absorption of land belonging to a weak neighbor. John C. Calhoun, who refused to vote on the war bill, felt that Polk had created hysteria and had used stampede tactics to obtain support. Calhoun believed that less than 10 percent of Congress would have voted with Polk if they had had time to examine the documents closely. Abraham Lincoln felt Polk waged "a war of conquest." If expansionists had not coveted Mexico's northern provinces, the dispute would have been settled "in an amicable manner," said Lincoln.[18] Once the war was in progress, however, many of its critics supported it on the principle of "country first, right or wrong."

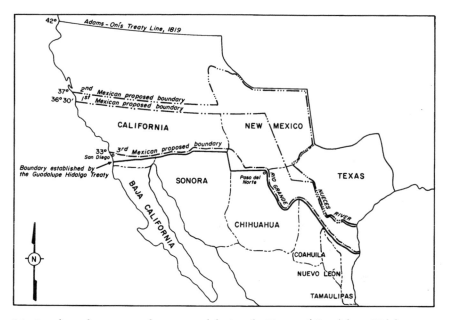

Mexican boundary proposals presented during the Treaty of Guadalupe Hidalgo boundary negotiations in 1847. (Based on Prescott, *Boundaries and Frontiers*, 81)

Dissent notwithstanding, the United States took the war deep into Mexico, forcing its neighbor to negotiate a drastic change in the border. The draft treaty carried by U.S. State Department representative Nicholas Trist called for the acquisition of New Mexico, Alta California, and Baja California and for the establishment of U.S. rights across the Isthmus of Tehuantepec.[19] If Mexico agreed to these terms, $30 million would be paid; if not, lesser sums would be offered for less territory. By then Mexico was resigned to the loss of large amounts of northern land but struggled for the best terms possible under the circumstances. Thus Mexico rejected the Tehuantepec provision and insisted that in any transfer of territory in its northwest a Mexican land connection between Baja California and Sonora be maintained. Mexico also proposed the creation of a neutral buffer zone between the Nueces and the Rio Grande, hoping thus to keep European Americans at a distance and to exert better control of smuggling. Trist agreed to the buffer strip and to a line along the thirty-third parallel, which would have placed San Diego, California, in Mexican territory. Unhappy with those terms, Trist's superiors in Washington not only rejected the compromise but ordered Trist home. Disobeying orders, Trist remained in Mexico and continued negotiations, though he lacked the authority to do so. By December 1847 Mexico had withdrawn the buffer idea, instead proposing that a line be drawn one league north of the Rio Grande but still insisting on the land connection that would

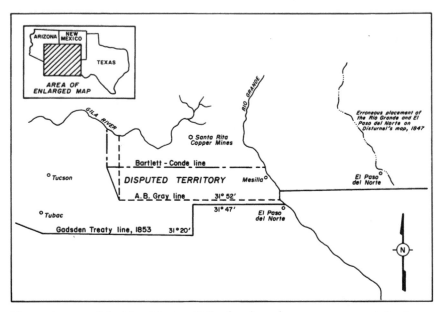

The settlement of the New Mexico–Chihuahua boundary controversy, 1848–1853

keep San Diego in Mexican territory. Further talks followed as the pressure mounted on Mexico. Finally, it agreed to the Rio Grande as the eastern half of the border and to a line across the desert from Paso del Norte (present-day Ciudad Juárez) to the Pacific as the western half, placing San Diego in U.S. hands.[20]

Exulting in the strong bargaining position of the United States, many expansionists criticized their government for seeking only a portion of Mexico. Instead, they argued, all of Mexico should be seized. Providence had willed the fall of Mexico, they reasoned, and higher duty demanded that the United States rescue the Mexicans from their "depraved" and "backward" state. Thus adherents of this view, affected by Manifest Destiny and the psychology of war and impatient with the prolonged negotiations, launched a crusade that seriously threatened the future existence of Mexico as a republic. Support for the "all Mexico" idea spread quickly among members of Polk's cabinet, in both chambers of Congress, in the military, in the press, and among other influential sectors of U.S. society.[21] No doubt this ominous development motivated the Mexicans to "seize the opportunity" to part with their northern territories before Washington dismembered their country altogether. In February 1848 the negotiators signed a peace treaty, and Trist quickly forwarded it to Polk.

The unexpected arrival of that document, known as the Treaty of Guadalupe Hidalgo, abruptly halted the "all Mexico" drive. Despite Trist's dubious status, Polk accepted the treaty since it fulfilled his original territorial desires and U.S. domestic political considerations dictated a termination of the war. By then, serious resistance to the campaign to absorb Mexico had developed among Polk's political opponents, including opponents of slavery, proponents of peace, and race-conscious elements who had apprehensions about admitting nonwhites to the Union. Southerners especially expressed anxiety over the prospect of extending U.S. citizenship to dark-skinned Mexicans, whom they deemed as inferior and incapable of self-government. For example, in his bitter denunciations of the "all Mexico" movement John C. Calhoun frequently buttressed his position with racial arguments.[22]

Many historians are convinced that if negotiations had dragged on much longer, the "all Mexico" movement would have prevailed. Fate took an unexpected turn, however, and Mexico continued to exist.[23] Nevertheless, U.S. expansionism up to 1848 had cost Mexico half of its territory, including Texas, New Mexico, Arizona, California, Nevada, and Utah and portions of Wyoming, Colorado, Kansas, and Oklahoma. In part to mitigate the appearance of outright landgrabbing, the United States paid Mexico $15 million for this vast domain and assumed old claims of its citizens against Mexico, valued at just over $3 million. Never before or since has the United States negotiated a treaty that yielded so much and cost so little. President James Polk clearly recognized the significance of the newly acquired lands, stating that they would "add more to the strength and wealth of the nation than any which have preceded them since the adoption of the Constitution."[24] The border question, however, was far from settled.

Article V of the Treaty of Guadalupe Hidalgo provided for the surveying and marking of the boundary by two separate commissions representing the interests of each nation. Following their appointment in 1850, the Mexican and U.S. commissioners managed to lay out the western portion of the boundary, but controversy erupted when they attempted to establish the dividing line between New Mexico and Chihuahua. The treaty described the boundary of southern New Mexico only as a line that ran "north of the town called Paso" without specifying distance.[25] Lacking precise information concerning the exact location of Paso del Norte, a crucial landmark, and unable to find an accurate map, the treaty negotiators had used an erroneous one that placed the town 34 miles north and 130 miles east of its true location.

It was up to the commissioners to decide exactly where the line should be drawn. The Mexicans proposed a line from the Rio Grande to the Gila River that would leave the Santa Rita del Cobre mines and the fertile Mesilla Valley in Mexico; the U.S. contingent countered with a line that not only would place that valuable real estate in the United States but would assure a much-desired pathway for a proposed railroad route to the Pacific. Commissioners Pedro García Conde and John Russell Bartlett compromised by agreeing on a boundary that would leave the Mesilla Valley in Mexico but place the Santa Rita mines in the United States and include enough territory for the railroad route. Expansionists in Washington rejected that agreement, however,

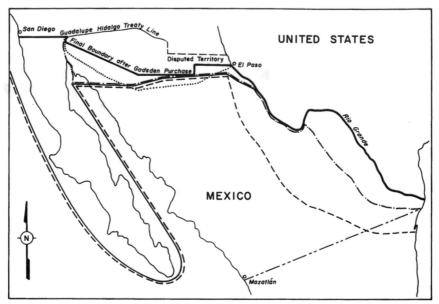

U.S. boundary proposals during the Gadsden Treaty negotiation and ratification process of 1853. Under instructions, James Gadsden presented the following options to Mexican negotiators:

- – – – – –   The line most desired by President Franklin Pierce. Proposed cash payment to Mexico: $50 million.
- ⋅ ⋅ – ⋅ — ⋅ — ⋅ —   The second most desired line by President Pierce. Proposed cash payment: $35 million.
- —————   Third line designated by President Pierce. Proposed cash payment: $30 million.
- ⋯⋯⋯⋯⋯   The line agreed upon by Gadsden and Mexican negotiators.
- – – — ⋅ ⋅ —   The line proposed by Senator William McKendree Gwin before ratification of the Gadsden Treaty.

(Based on Garber, *Gadsden Treaty*, 90–93, and Zorrilla, *Historia*, 1:352–53)

arguing that the best railroad path had been surrendered. Several members of the U.S. Boundary Commission, including the principal surveyor, refused to give their approval as well. The issue became embroiled in Washington politics, with the result that the Conde-Bartlett pact was declared null and void. Moreover, by late 1852 the U.S. Boundary Commission itself had been disbanded, although a new one was created the following year to survey the Rio Grande from Paso del Norte to the Gulf.

The presence of settlers in the disputed territory made resolution of the New Mexico–Chihuahua boundary even more difficult. Around 1850 approximately two thousand people from New Mexico and the El Paso area who wished to remain subjects of Mexico had founded the town of Mesilla in what they believed was Chihuahua territory. New Mexico Governor William

Carr Lane, however, claimed Mesilla was within U.S. jurisdiction and even insisted in 1852 that those settlers had petitioned for U.S. citizenship. When Lane sought to assert U.S. control over Mesilla, Governor Angel Trías of Chihuahua responded by mobilizing Mexican troops at the frontier. Both governors issued strong warnings regarding the possible use of force to bring justice on behalf of each nation's interests. Once again, armed confrontation over disputed land seemed imminent between the United States and Mexico, but a determination to resolve the matter through negotiations eventually prevailed. Lane, whose impetuous actions had contributed significantly to bringing about the crisis, unintentionally helped matters by resigning the New Mexico governorship for reasons unrelated to the border controversy.

Confrontation at the New Mexico–Chihuahua frontier gave way to hard bargaining in Mexico City with the arrival in 1853 of newly appointed U.S. Minister James Gadsden. This envoy had instructions to reach a settlement on the border question, to seek abrogation of Article XI of the Treaty of Guadalupe Hidalgo (which bound the United States to prevent Indian raids into Mexico), to seek restoration of normal commercial relations between the two countries, and to establish U.S. transit rights through the Isthmus of Tehuantepec.[26] Seeing the troubled state of affairs in Mexico, Gadsden grasped the opportunity to pressure the Mexican government into parting with more of its northern territories. His maneuvers recalled those of his offensive predecessors who had previously attempted to alter the border. In a letter to the Department of State Gadsden asked whether money could be made available if circumstances favored the immediate acquisition of Sonora and Chihuahua and more territory later. Gadsden wished to establish a more "perfect" and "durable" border that would start at the Gulf of Mexico a short distance south of the Rio Grande and extend westward to the Pacific to include Baja California within the United States. In conversations with President Antonio López de Santa Anna he proposed a line that would follow mountains and deserts, noting that to make that possible Mexico would need to sell two or more of its frontier states.[27]

Apparently, Gadsden undertook the preceding initiatives on his own, but in October he received secret instructions from Washington to propose to Mexico four alternative boundaries along with differing sums of money for the purchase of land. The Franklin Pierce administration favored the option that called for the annexation of Coahuila, Chihuahua, Sonora, and Baja California in exchange for $50 million. The other proposals included less territory and of course carried smaller price tags, but in all cases the United States sought at a minimum the acquisition of favorable terrain for a railroad route to the Pacific and a port on the Gulf of California. Before presenting these proposals formally to the Mexicans, Gadsden revealed his aggressive expansionists tendencies in a letter to Foreign Minister Manuel Díaz de Bonilla. Gadsden had learned that Mexico was seeking an alliance with European powers in case of conflict with the United States, and he warned

Díaz de Bonilla that any European meddling would only hasten the inevitable absorption of a sizable part of northern Mexico into the United States. It would be wiser for Mexico, advised Gadsden, to avoid that possibility by consummating the sale of the additional territory.[28] This attempt at intimidation illustrates the contempt for Mexico then widely felt in the United States. Washington knew it had the upper hand. Santa Anna needed funds desperately to prop up his teetering regime, and Gadsden conveniently stepped in to offer the dictator a financial deal.

But the Mexican negotiators proved tougher than Gadsden had anticipated. They resisted the U.S. plan for the cession of several northern states, conceding only the minimum amount of land required for the desired railroad route. After considerable hard bargaining the two sides signed a treaty in December 1853 known as the Gadsden Treaty. Its major features included (1) payment of $15 million to Mexico in exchange for the Mesilla strip, (2) U.S. assumption of U.S. claims against Mexico (amounting to about $5 million), (3) abrogation of Article XI of the Treaty of Guadalupe Hidalgo, (4) affirmation of U.S. navigation rights in the Gulf of California and on the Colorado and Brazos rivers, and (5) the promise of mutual cooperation to suppress filibustering expeditions.[29] The terms were hardly unfavorable to the United States, yet many European Americans had come to expect greater concessions from Mexico. Opposition to the treaty burst forth among members of the Pierce administration, the Senate, and prominent private interests.

In a heated Senate debate that lasted three months the document underwent considerable alteration. Ironically, on the border question the final document provided for the acquisition of less territory than the agreement negotiated by Gadsden. Several senators did attempt to drive the border deeper into Mexico, but each time their amendments failed. Finally, Senator James M. Mason of Virginia offered the decisive compromise on the boundary, but even then the treaty failed on the first vote of the full Senate. Passage came only when the treaty was amended to give the United States transit and other privileges across the Isthmus of Tehuantepec, including the right to intervene on behalf of U.S. investors.[30] The Mexican government received the revised document with considerable displeasure, but it was in no position to reject it. Nonacceptance could bring war with the United States. Besides, Santa Anna was predisposed to cooperate because he needed funds immediately to fight an insurrection in the state of Guerrero. Thus Mexico reluctantly accepted the new U.S. Senate–imposed terms, which included (1) payment of $10 million for the ceded land instead of the $15 million agreed upon originally, (2) removal of the clause concerning U.S. assumption of claims against Mexico, and (3) elimination of the provision that bound the United States to formally cooperate in suppressing filibustering expeditions into Mexican territory.

Santa Anna's acceptance of the Gadsden Treaty provided his enemies with additional ammunition to use against him, and within a year he was overthrown and eliminated from Mexican politics. Once again Mexico faced pain-

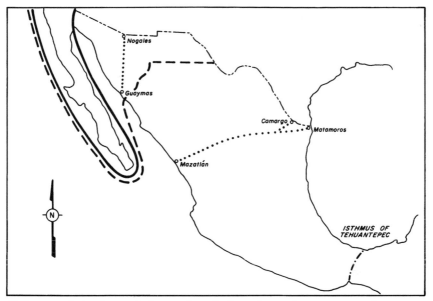

U.S. proposals in 1857 and 1859 to alter the boundary and to secure transit privileges in northern Mexico and in the Isthmus of Tehuantepec.

======= Offers presented to Mexico by the Buchanan administration in 1857 to bring about a change in the border.

················ Routes over which the United States would have transit privileges, as provided by the negotiated (but never ratified) McLane-Ocampo Treaty of 1859.

_.._._.._._ The Isthmus of Tehuantepec route, over which the United States had obtained transit privileges as part of the Gadsden Treaty. Further rights were sought through the McLane-Ocampo Treaty.

(Based on Zorrilla, *Historia de las relaciones*, 1:368–69, 376–78, 393–94)

ful introspection as it tried to determine the causes of the loss of additional territory. Another distasteful agreement had been forced on the nation to accommodate foreign designs and intrigues of its own opportunistic leaders. Fears remained that the country would be further dismembered, for the U.S. government continued to seek more border "adjustments," while many European Americans joined adventurers from other lands in filibustering expeditions against Mexico's northern provinces. The actions of the filibusters, which gave Mexico many headaches but did not result in the loss of land, are treated in chapter 2.

U.S. Attempts to Purchase Additional Mexican Lands
The United States made additional efforts to acquire Mexican territory during the 1850s. Following the established pattern, such attempts came particularly

when the United States perceived a weakness in the Mexican regime in power, such as a need for official external recognition, a need for funds, or both.

In 1857 President James B. Buchanan instructed U.S. Minister to Mexico John Forsyth to propose to the Ignacio Comonfort government a plan for the transfer of parts of Chihuahua and Sonora and the entire Baja California peninsula to the United States. The purpose of this acquisition would be to allow private interests to build a railroad from the Rio Grande to the Sonora coast. Forsyth resurrected the old notion of the need for a more "natural" border between the two nations "to preserve the cordial relations that exist." The U.S. approach to maintaining good relations, observes Mexican historian Luis G. Zorrilla, meant that "for harmony to exist between the two neighbors it was necessary that one kept feeding the other, each time between shorter intervals." The Mexican government rejected Forsyth's offer. In early 1858 Forsyth tried to obtain the desired change in the border along with additional concessions in the Isthmus of Tehuantepec from the Felix Zuloaga administration, but the Mexican answer was still no. Undeterred and obsessed with the issue, Forsyth at one point told the Ministry of Foreign Relations that sooner or later, through the inscrutable designs of the Creator, his country would obtain the territory that had been denied him. Forsyth urged his government to take vigorous measures, including the seizing of Sonora, since "American blood [had been] spilled near its line," and demanding of Mexico that it "give us what we ask for in return for the manifest benefits we propose to confer upon you for it, or we will take it." A short time later the Mexican government asked Washington to remove Forsyth from Mexico; he had become persona non grata.[31]

Having failed to convince Mexico to accede to U.S. designs and exasperated over personal injuries suffered by U.S. citizens in Mexico, Buchanan then proposed to the U.S. Congress the creation of a protectorate in Chihuahua and Sonora under the guise of defending both European Americans and Mexicans against Indian depredations and general lawlessness. The idea of occupying Mexico "for her own good" and for the protection of U.S. interests had been raised in early 1858 by then–U.S. senator Sam Houston, who introduced a resolution in Congress calling for the creation of a committee to determine "whether or not it is expedient for the government of the United States to declare and maintain a protectorate over the so called republic of Mexico." Buchanan's plan failed to win congressional support owing to partisan and sectional considerations, aversion to granting too much power to the executive, and the perceived greater receptivity to U.S. aims when Benito Juárez rose to power. Houston, however, continued to promote direct intervention independent of Washington once he returned to Texas and assumed the governorship. According to Walter Prescott Webb, Houston planned to engage the services of warring Indians and even some Mexicans, including Tamaulipas leader and sometime social bandit Juan Nepomucena "Cheno" Cortina, adding a bizarre twist to the scheme. Only a lack of funds kept Houston from acting on his plan, says Webb.[32]

The United States saw its next opportunity to wrest concessions when the exiled Benito Juárez government struggled to survive in Veracruz during the devastating civil conflict known as the War of the Reform. Juárez stood to benefit from U.S. recognition because he desperately needed loans and other external assistance. After a special U.S. agent reported favorably on the Juárez regime, Buchanan named Robert McLane as minister to Mexico and authorized him to recognize Juárez. These preliminaries and formalities completed, McLane began negotiations for a treaty that would encompass cession of Baja California, more concessions in Tehuantepec, transit rights in Sonora, intervention rights in the transit areas, and resolution of claims against Mexico. Opposition within the Juárez government to altering the border prevented the cession of any territory, but McLane managed to win some extraordinary concessions nonetheless. By the terms of the McLane-Ocampo Treaty of 1859, Mexico agreed to grant the United States perpetual transit rights in Tehuantepec and across northern Mexico, including the prerogative to use military force to protect persons and property in those areas. In turn, the Juárez government would receive $4 million, half of which would be used for settling claims. Although highly favorable to the United States, the treaty met with defeat in the U.S. Senate. Since the treaty was discussed in executive session, it is not known precisely why the Senate rejected it, but apparently the possibility that slavery would be extended into northern Mexico motivated many to vote against it.[33]

In the 1860s Confederate leaders turned toward Mexico in their quest for new territory in which to expand slavery. Their interest in absorbing part or all of Mexico is revealed in statements made shortly before the outbreak of the Civil War. "We must have Sonora and Chihuahua," wrote one prominent military official. "With Sonora and Chihuahua we gain Southern [Baja] California, and by a railroad to Guaymas render our state of Texas the great highway of nations." When those dreams failed to materialize Southerners sought to establish colonies with the cooperation of the French, who then ruled Mexico through Maximilian, archduke of Austria and emperor of Mexico, but such schemes also ended in failure.[34]

Although many European Americans would continue to entertain hopes of further acquisitions of Mexican lands, following the Civil War the U.S. government's compulsion to seek negotiated "adjustments" of the border faded. Henceforth border disputes centered on maintaining the integrity of the established boundary. Technical questions over the exact location of the border, particularly confusion caused by shifts in the Rio Grande, would replace the old concern over which part of Mexico would next be annexed by the United States. There would still be controversy, but the character and level of animosity would differ significantly from that of earlier periods when the specter of land transfer poisoned the relations between the two countries.

Refinement of the Border

Although U.S. expansionists used the notion of a "natural" boundary as a pretext for acquisition of Mexican territory, the failure to find an imposing physical barrier to divide the two countries guaranteed pronounced ambiguity regarding the chosen line. The Rio Grande in particular was certain to sow confusion and discord because of the river's unpredictability. Article V of the Treaty of Guadalupe Hidalgo specified that the boundary would follow the middle of that river; where more than one channel existed, the deepest one would prevail. It is difficult enough to identify "the middle" of any river; in the case of the Rio Grande the problem was compounded by the river's tendency to overrun its banks and open up new meandering channels, frequently leaving detached tracts of land to the north or south of the original border. At times these shifts displaced only a few acres of rather inconsequential land, but on other occasions the affected terrain had considerable value because of its fertility or location at or near populated areas. Conflict over border placement was thus predictable, but by reason of the region's isolation and early sparse population the problems that emerged after the signing of the Treaty of Guadalupe Hidalgo in 1848 and the Gadsden Treaty in 1853 did not assume importance until much later.

The most significant dispute arising from the shifting Rio Grande involved a tract of land in El Paso–Ciudad Juárez known as the Chamizal, named for the desert grass chamiso, which grew there. In the 1850s and 1860s a series of floods caused the river to move southward, leaving some Mexican land on the northern bank. Testimony from residents taken later indicated that torrential rains in 1864 had caused most of the river movement. The United States, assuming the boundary had changed with the shifting of the river, exercised jurisdiction over the tract, prompting Mexico to question the legality of that action in 1867. In the years that followed Mexico made repeated attempts to resolve the problem, but U.S. preoccupation with domestic issues and Washington's nonrecognition of certain Mexican regimes delayed discussion of the issue.[35]

In 1884 consideration of jurisdictional rights over Morteritos Island at the Texas-Tamaulipas border led to a treaty whereby both nations agreed that the boundary would change if a gradual shift in the river took place but would remain intact when "the force of the current" cut a new bed or produced a new channel.[36] To implement the new rule and to address other matters related to border placement, an ad hoc International Border Commission was created in 1889. The commission was made a permanent body in 1900 after it became evident that border concerns would surface with regularity.[37] The commission tackled a series of ticklish problems in the next few years, but the Chamizal dispute was not one of them. Mexico felt the 1884 agreement did not apply in that case because the correct boundary of El Paso–Ciudad Juárez was the one determined in the original Rio Grande survey in 1852. With a solution indefinitely postponed, the Chamizal would become more perplexing as the years passed.

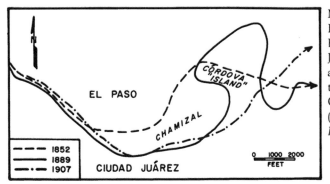

Movement of the Rio Grande in El Paso–Ciudad Juárez, 1852–1907, and the location of the Chamizal and Córdova tracts. (Based on Mueller, *Restless River*, 66)

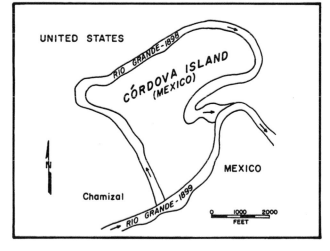

Córdova "Island," created in 1899 with the digging of an artificial cutoff intended to reduce flooding and to increase efficiency in water flow. (Based on Mueller, *Restless River*, 74)

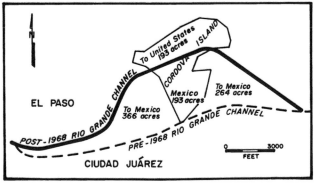

The Chamizal settlement. The Chamizal Treaty of 1963 resulted in the relocation of the Rio Grande and the exchange of lands between Mexico and the United States. (Based on Mueller, *Restless River*, 102)

Meanwhile, the commission discovered discrepancies in that portion of the border established by the Gadsden Treaty. The monuments that marked the line had been placed incorrectly, resulting in a land loss for Mexico of approximately 210,000 acres. The terrain in question included some agricultural land and mineral resources, prompting Mexico to insist on several occasions on rectification of the line. But the United States refused to go along, maintaining that both nations had previously agreed to the permanence of the Gadsden Treaty line; besides, argued U.S. officials, the disputed tract lay in an isolated, uninhabitable, and generally useless region and thus would not justify the expense of moving the monuments. Mexico reluctantly resigned itself to another distasteful U.S. policy decision.[38]

During the 1890s the International Border Commission spent considerable time identifying small parcels of land, called *bancos*, that the meandering Rio Grande had detached from each country in the Texas-Tamaulipas border region. A study identified fifty-eight bancos from Camargo–Rio Grande City to the Gulf. The two sides found a practical solution to the problem of exercising legal jurisdiction over these tracts, signing a convention in 1905 that modified the 1884 treaty to allow for rectification of the border simultaneously with an exchange of bancos. To expeditiously eliminate the bancos the revised treaty purposely assumed that all changes in the course of the river that had created bancos had been caused by slow erosion, even if that had not been the case; therefore, consistent with the principle of the 1884 pact, the boundary would change as well. All bancos on the southern bank went to Mexico, and all those on the northern bank went to the United States. The original boundary would prevail only in those cases where the size of the tract exceeded 250 hectares or where the tract had a population of over two hundred persons. Local residents could retain their original nationality or become citizens of the nation exercising jurisdiction over their locality.[39] In 1910 an additional thirty-one bancos were formally reassigned on the same basis, and through 1970 the total number of boundary changes that followed the precedent established in 1905 amounted to 247 and involved the exchange of thousands of acres.[40]

The commission's inability to resolve the Chamizal dispute and a related though less significant controversy in the Ojinaga-Presidio area marred somewhat the accord reached on the bancos and other issues at the turn of the century. The Chamizal overshadowed other differences because of its location in a prominent binational urban setting. As El Paso–Ciudad Juárez grew in size and importance the land in question increased in value, thus causing both the material and the symbolic stakes to rise. Mexico submitted its first formal claim to the Chamizal in 1895, but despite subsequent meetings and lengthy correspondence nothing concrete materialized until 1910. That year both countries signed a Convention of Arbitration that referred the dispute to an Arbitration Commission comprised of a U.S. representative, a Mexican representative, and a neutral Canadian jurist. The basic question addressed to this body involved determining whether the change in the course of the river had been due to slow and gradual erosion or to sudden and violent movement, or avulsion. Mexico and Canada concluded that avulsion had caused the shift and therefore the boundary should revert to the 1864 position, when that movement took place. The Arbitration Commission proceeded to grant Mexico title to the land south of the 1864 channel and the United States title to the land north of that channel. The United States refused to abide by the decision, however, despite the fact that it had agreed in Article III of the convention that the commission's decision, "whether rendered unanimously or by majority vote of the Commissioners[,] shall be final and conclusive upon both governments and without appeal."[41]

The United States based its rejection of the commission's decision on the following grounds: (1) the guidelines of the arbitration agreement did not empower the commission to divide the disputed land; (2) the commission identified a process of channel change, namely, rapid erosion, that was not covered by the 1884 treaty; and (3) the 1864 channel could not be identified with precision. Clearly, the United States had made a painstaking search for technicalities to justify rejection of the decision. Mexico deeply resented that action, but its only recourse was to protest and continue to press for recognition of its claim.[42]

In the decades that followed various administrations discussed the issue. In 1932 talks over the need to rectify the meandering Rio Grande in the El Paso–Ciudad Juárez area presented an opportunity to resolve the dispute, but continuing differences in interpretations led to the Chamizal's exclusion from the Treaty of Rectification, signed in 1933. As a result of that treaty a small but important portion of the Rio Grande was straightened and stabilized through the construction of river levees. Attendant to the rectification was an exchange of equal portions of land between the two countries.[43]

The Chamizal problem came up for discussion again in the 1940s and 1950s, but no progress was made. Finally, during the administration of John F. Kennedy the matter was settled. Having that diplomatic sore spot lurking in the background was inconsistent with Kennedy's policy of improving relations with Latin America through the newly established Alliance for Progress. Kennedy considered the decision of the United States not to accept the 1911 Arbitration Commission's finding a mistake, and in 1963 he signed a treaty that essentially gave effect to that panel's decision. By 1968 both countries had opened a new concrete-lined river channel and completed an exchange of lands. Mexico received 630 acres and the United States 193 acres. A century of misunderstanding and bitterness over a parcel of land had ended.

Seven years after the signing of the Chamizal pact both countries entered into a comprehensive agreement to resolve pending and future problems connected with changes in the Rio Grande and the Colorado River. Situations had arisen that could not be adequately addressed under existing treaties and conventions, suggesting a need to develop more specific criteria for identifying and handling border shifts. Thus the Treaty of 1970 introduced more detailed and rigorous guidelines, superseding agreements contained in previous accords. Additionally, the new treaty (1) resolved the pending Ojinaga-Presidio dispute over a parcel of land in favor of Mexico; (2) transferred the Horcón and Morteritos tracts near Brownsville to Mexico in exchange for an equal amount of land transferred to the United States near Reynosa, Tamaulipas; (3) assigned eleven river bancos to Mexico and eight to the United States; and (4) set a permanent maritime boundary from the mouth of the Rio Grande 12 miles into the Gulf of Mexico. Thus this important document settled existing differences and wisely provided the mechanisms for dealing with future problems.[44]

Summary and Conclusion

The experience of Mexico and the United States in establishing and maintaining their common boundary reveals how complex that process can be between neighboring countries. In setting the location of the border developments were influenced significantly by the disparity in the strength of the two countries. Try as it might, the weaker party could not repel the expansionist advances of its neighbor, which considered the addition of western territories an aspect of its Manifest Destiny. Mexico, a nation long burdened by neocolonial structures and conflicts, inherited a tradition of a receding northern frontier, while the United States, an emerging world power, first followed the English practice of contesting the possessions of others and then unfolded its own formula for overcoming resistance: the use of dollar diplomacy backed by the threat of force. Through purchase, annexation, and conquest the United States acquired Florida, Louisiana, Texas, New Mexico, Arizona, Nevada, California, and Utah and parts of Wyoming, Colorado, Kansas, and Oklahoma, all at the expense of Spain and Mexico. With the natural resources, superb ports, and other riches thus acquired, the United States assured itself a future of economic and military prominence. Conversely, having lost some of its most valuable assets, Mexico could look forward to diminished wealth, a scarcity of agricultural land, and limited economic growth. Thus the location of the boundary truly helped shape the destiny of each nation.

Boundary troubles also left a legacy of hatred, bitterness, and suspicion between the two neighbors. Mexicans deeply resented the pressure tactics and crude behavior of some U.S. representatives who were obsessed with "adjusting" the boundary. The offensive behavior of Joel R. Poinsett, Anthony Butler, James Gadsden, John Forsyth, and others grew out of feelings of superiority and contempt for Mexicans. Washington was especially intolerant of the political instability that reigned in Mexico because it complicated and slowed down diplomatic negotiations. Well cemented during the years of intense conflict, the U.S. disdain toward Mexico continued for many decades and gave rise to countless misunderstandings.

Mexico was especially frustrated by the behavior of Washington legislators, particularly members of the Senate, who constantly amended pains-

takingly negotiated settlements, usually to the further detriment of N
The Mexicans found irritating the repeated U.S. attempts to change ………
treaties in order to accommodate the insatiable appetite for land, to gain new
concessions, or to win release from existing obligations the United States did
not want to meet. One of the most distressing experiences came at the critical moment of the negotiations over the all-important Treaty of Guadalupe
Hidalgo, when Mexicans found themselves dangerously close to losing their
nationhood. Little wonder that Mexicans came to lament their geographic
position, "so far from God, so close to the United States," and hardly surprising that many felt that between Mexico and the United States "the best thing
is the desert."

History makes it clear why the Rio Grande became half the boundary,
but, given the subsequent cost to each nation and to the people who have
made the area their home, a high price was paid for that choice. Scholars
familiar with the workings of international boundaries agree that rivers
often make poor boundaries. Fertile river valleys attract people; boundaries serve to divide them. Rivers of subhumid zones such as the Rio Grande
are often erratic, giving rise to border maintenance problems. Contention
over the Chamizal, water disputes, and other issues associated with the Rio
Grande, the Colorado River, and the Tijuana River helped to keep alive for
several generations the painful historical reality of how the boundary came
to be. European Americans easily could, and often did, forget the events of
1848 and 1853, but Mexicans understandably found it much more difficult
to do so. The late-nineteenth- and early-twentieth-century disagreements
over the exact location of the border heightened the Mexicans' recollection of
the earlier tragic years. Unquestionably, the memory of the border "adjustments" figured prominently in the attitudes, perceptions, and policies adopted by Mexico toward the United States for generations and indeed influence
events to this day.

2 Marked Frontier

The expansionism practiced by nineteenth-century U.S. governments tells only part of the story of Manifest Destiny. Invasions of Spanish and Mexican territories by independent adventurers constitute a parallel process that gave impetus to official attempts to push U.S. boundaries westward and southward. Organized outside the law on U.S. soil and directed at neighbors who had peaceful relations with the United States, such attacks became known as "filibustering." The exploits of William Walker and other filibusters of the 1850s are familiar to students of U.S.–Mexican relations, but less well known are the activities of self-appointed "liberators," revolutionary agents, and would-be colonizers of earlier and later epochs.

This chapter highlights major filibustering and pseudofilibustering incidents that occurred from the early nineteenth century through the first quarter of the twentieth century. The persistence of conspiratorial activity and unauthorized expeditions for such an extended period illustrates the intensity of that aggressive desire in U.S. society to detach lands belonging to neighboring nations. Cuba, Central America, and Mexico were three areas "marked" for conquest by ambitious men who ignored tenets of national sovereignty to further dreams of personal aggrandizement. Northern Mexico, a receding frontier, long remained isolated and unprotected, thus inviting foreign infiltration and attack. So many plots and incursions took place that a comprehensive account here is impossible; thus narration of major episodes only will be given in the text, with some additional information in the notes.

Filibustering, 1800–1858
U.S. frontiersmen increased the pace of infiltration of Spanish territory once the United States achieved its independence from England. Settlers drifted into East and West Florida, traders and trappers penetrated Texas and New Mexico, and sea merchants docked along the California coast. The U.S. government became very interested in getting information about these territories from its wandering citizens, and reports dribbled into Washington. Given Spain's preoccupation with foreign threats to its borderlands, a large number of infiltrators were arrested, jailed, or had property confiscated. Often, capricious Spanish frontier officials applied the law harshly, reinforcing the long-standing U.S. antipathy toward Spaniards and their hold on desirable lands in the continent. That discontent led to widespread disregard for Spanish regulations and to an attitude among the more aggressive frontier elements that

Spanish territory was fair game for privateering and filibustering. Whether schemes succeeded or failed depended on many factors, including the political climate south of the border and the military strength of the perpetrators. To illustrate the different motives and tendencies of the earliest filibusters, brief descriptions of the adventures of Philip Nolan, Zebulon Montgomery Pike, Bernardo Gutiérrez de Lara, Augustus W. Magee, and James Long are given in this section.

Nolan and Pike may be thought of as "precursors" of filibustering who fulfilled the important task of gathering intelligence for their country. In 1797 Nolan submitted a report to Thomas Jefferson through Gen. James Wilkinson, commander of U.S. western forces, that contained observations on northeast Texas accumulated during Nolan's travels. Three years later Nolan undertook an expedition into Texas ostensibly to round up and sell horses, but his prolonged stay and penetration as far as the Brazos River aroused the suspicion of the Spaniards, who killed him and imprisoned his men. During the planning phase of the Texas adventure Nolan had maintained communication with General Wilkinson, leading to speculation that Wilkinson supported Nolan's scheme or had influenced him in some way. For years Wilkinson was associated with various shady operations, some of which involved violation of Spanish territorial sovereignty. The extent of his participation in filibustering is difficult to determine, however, because he carefully avoided overt ties to the activities of the conspirators.

Pike's mysterious trek into Spanish lands took place in 1806. Wilkinson had ordered Pike to escort Osage and Pawnee Indians to their homeland and to explore parts of the Arkansas and Red rivers, but Pike kept going westward and eventually crossed the border into Spanish territory. Interestingly, Wilkinson's son accompanied Pike's party for part of the trip. Although aware that Spanish officials from New Mexico and Texas had been alerted to his wanderings, Pike advanced through the Rockies into the Upper Rio Grande region. From there a member of the party who was familiar with the area traveled to Santa Fe, ostensibly to settle a business matter with a French trader, but instructions from Pike reveal that he had a spying mission as well. When troops commanded by Bartolomé Fernández met the intruders, Pike feigned embarrassment, explaining that he thought he was on the Red River. Unconvinced, the Spaniards arrested Pike's party and took them to Chihuahua City by way of Santa Fe. Pike cleverly made friends with the Spanish authorities, and they eventually permitted him to return to the United States via Texas. Contrary to Wilkinson's advice to be cautious about revealing details of his trip, Pike wrote a report from memory that stimulated widespread interest in the territories he had visited.[1]

The Bernardo Gutiérrez de Lara–Augustus W. Magee expedition into Texas in 1813 exemplifies the subversion by foreigners of a genuine effort to aid Mexico's independence movement against Spain, with the outsiders' motive being the takeover of Texas. Gutiérrez de Lara, a Mexican, began his odyssey in the United States in 1811 as an agent of Miguel Hidalgo y Costilla, seeking aid from the U.S. government to further the rebellion against Spain. Gutiérrez de Lara found receptivity in Washington, but the terms offered by the Monroe administration, essentially U.S. occupation and control of Texas, were unacceptable. Gutiérrez de Lara then sought private assistance in New Orleans, a city that bustled with exiles, adventurers, mercenaries, and privateers of all shades. With the help of the U.S. consul, William Shaler, he organized a force of several hundred Mexicans, European Americans, and men of various other nationalities. Magee resigned as a colonel in the U.S. Army to become the coleader of the expedition, but his participation was cut short when he died in a battle at Goliad in 1812, whereupon his command passed to Samuel Kemper. The rebels seized San Antonio in April 1813, and a joint Kemper–Gutiérrez de Lara declaration of independence for Texas followed. According to Mexican historian Luis G. Zorrilla, mastermind William Shaler then decided to replace Gutiérrez de Lara because the latter's loyalty to Mexico presented an obstacle to U.S. intentions of taking Texas. José Álvarez de Toledo, a Dominican adventurer who dreamed of forming a federation of free states in the Caribbean, replaced Gutiérrez de Lara. But the internal intrigues and dissensions took their toll, and following defeats at the hands of the Spanish army the movement collapsed in late 1813.[2]

The desire among some frontier European Americans to "liberate" Texas on their own and convert it into an independent country is illustrated by the incursions of James Long and his followers. Long, married to the niece of General Wilkinson, had become acquainted with intrigues along the border. Like many other European Americans he had objected adamantly to the signing of the Adams-Onís Treaty, by which the United States had acknowledged Spanish possession of Texas. After holding a protest meeting Long led fifty to seventy-five residents of Natchez, Mississippi, to Texas, where the invaders proclaimed that province a "free republic" in June 1819. Jean Lafitte, the famous pirate, turned down Long's invitation to join the movement, but veteran rebel Bernardo Gutiérrez de Lara responded in the affirmative, giving hope to Long that Mexicans in Texas would welcome the "liberating" forces. Within a few months, however, Spanish troops drove the intruders out of Nacogdoches. Long refused to give up, however, and organized another incursion with the pretext of seeking to help Mexico gain its independence from Spain. On their way to Goliad Long's forces received word that Mexico had at last defeated the Spaniards and independence had become a reality. That eliminated the justification for their presence in Texas, but when asked by the Mexicans to leave they refused. Finally, they surrendered at Goliad; Long was imprisoned and later shot in Mexico City in 1822.[3]

Long and the other European American filibusters of the 1810s were aided significantly by the failure of the U.S. government to enforce its neutrality laws. Despite repeated Spanish protestations, Washington refused to take effective measures to curb the activities of filibusters, allowing them to organize and launch incursions from U.S. territory. European Americans overwhelmingly supported the cause of the Latin Americans against the Spanish Crown during the wars of independence; thus little enthusiasm existed in the United States for helping Spain retain its New World possessions. On the other hand, Washington avoided giving independence fighters any overt assistance for fear of risking direct conflict with the Spaniards. The chosen policy was to proclaim neutrality but do little to hinder those using U.S. ports and land to plan expeditions into Spanish territory, which pleased the anti-Spanish elements and played well into the hands of ambitious expansionists and adventurers.[4]

Following Mexican independence in 1821, conditions changed on the Texas frontier. Overt filibustering activity declined largely because liberal immigration policies enacted in Mexico City allowed thousands of European Americans to settle in Texas. But the steady, pronounced immigration, both legal and illegal, soon overwhelmed the native *tejanos/as* and undermined Mexico's hold on the province. A preview of future troubles with the restless newcomers unfolded in December 1826, when thirty Texans seized a fort in Nacogdoches and proclaimed the "Republic of Fredonia." But that rebellion proved to be short-lived, for within two months the Mexican militia had driven the rebels across the border into the United States. Less than a decade later, however, the foreigners hatched the well-known independence movement that not only led to the creation of the Republic of Texas but inspired secessionism elsewhere and spawned imperialistic designs on additional Mexican territories.

One separatist movement in 1839–40 along Mexico's northeastern frontier sought to establish a "Republic of the Rio Grande," to be composed of South Texas, Nuevo León, Tamaulipas, Coahuila, Durango, and New Mexico. Gen. Antonio Canales, the commander of the operation, moved freely across the international boundary, raising funds and recruiting followers. The rebels started with a thousand men under arms, including a company of Texans. They were able to capture Victoria, the capital of Tamaulipas, along with various Mexican border towns; they also came close to taking Matamoros, Monterrey, and Saltillo. The high point for the Rio Grande insurgents came in January 1840, when delegates from throughout the region proclaimed a government, drafted a constitution, and selected Laredo, Texas, as their capital. Local Mexicans who despised the centralist regime in Mexico City hailed the new republic with cheers and the ringing of bells. But the dream of a mighty borderlands nation vanished as tactical mistakes on the battlefield and internal dissension triggered confusion and desertions. By the fall of 1840 the movement had been stopped by federal troops. The Mexican rebel forces scattered, and the Texas volunteers dejectedly returned home.[5]

Shortly after the collapse of the Rio Grande republic the Texans sent an expedition into New Mexico ostensibly to promote trade, but the real intention was to attach that province to Texas. Texas President Mirabeau Lamar claimed all lands north and east of the Rio Grande as part of the Texas domain, basing his position on the old argument that the Rio Grande constituted the true boundary of Texas, an interpretation rejected by the New Mexicans. When the nearly three hundred armed Texas "merchants" arrived in New Mexico in mid-1841, they were promptly arrested and taken to Mexico City for imprisonment. Mistreatment of the Texans engendered increased hatred toward Mexicans. Some prisoners managed to escape, and within a year the Mexican government released the rest. For many years thereafter distrust and bitterness characterized relations between New Mexicans and Texans.[6]

By the mid-1840s the annexation of Mexico's northern frontier had become the cornerstone of European American Manifest Destiny. President James W. Polk is well known as the central figure among the expansionists who forced Mexico to agree, by treaty, to give up part of its territory following the U.S.–Mexico War of 1846–48. Prior to the conflict Polk's efforts to bring about the desired land transfer included the use of secret agents in Texas and California, some of whom attempted to provoke armed conflict with Mexico. In May 1845, just prior to the annexation of Texas to the United States, Commodore Robert F. Stockton arrived in Galveston with a squadron of U.S. naval vessels, prepared to start a war on the Texas-Mexico border. A wealthy man, Stockton planned to finance an army of at least two thousand men who would invade Matamoros under the leadership of Maj. Gen. Sidney Sherman, the chief officer of the militia of Texas. That act would trigger conflict between Texas and Mexico and obligate the United States, which was in the process of annexing Texas, to extend "protection" to its new subjects. U.S. participation in the war would ensure victory and lead to the acquisition of Mexican territory, including the much-desired province of California. The plan did not materialize, however, because Anson Jones, then president of Texas, flatly refused to "manufacture a war for the United States." Evidence suggests strongly that Polk knew about and approved the Stockton intrigue, but the link to Washington remains a subject of debate among historians.[7]

Stockton's scheme was actually a variation of a plan advocated in late 1844 by Duff Green, a prominent Democrat and the U.S. consul at Galveston during the last days of the John Tyler administration. Apparently acting on his own initiative, Green wanted to organize Plains Indians under a Texas-chartered corporation for the purpose of invading northern Mexico. Thus when the time arrived to annex Texas to the United States additional, newly conquered Mexican territory could be absorbed as well. In his zeal to enlist the support of the Texans Green acted in an aggressive and offensive manner, even attempting to bribe Anson Jones and other officials. That behavior earned him notoriety and doomed his plan.[8]

Although Texas was the undisputed center of conspiracies against Mexico, similar intrigues unfolded in California. Six months before the outbreak of war between the United States and Mexico U.S. Consul Thomas O. Larkin secretly assumed the role of Polk's "confidential agent," charged with promoting the peaceful secession of California and subsequent voluntary adherence to the United States. But Larkin's mission was upstaged by the "Bear Flag" Rebellion, which broke out in the early summer of 1846. The central figure in that insurrection was John Charles Frémont, the famous western explorer, military officer, and presidential candidate. Frémont had led a "surveying" party into California in December 1845, but in March 1846 Mexican authorities, suspicious of his motives, forced him to leave. As Frémont and his fellow "scientists" traveled toward Oregon, an agent of Polk and Larkin delivered a secret message to them, whereupon they quickly turned southward. Many historians believe that Frémont received instructions from Polk to assist in the impending U.S. conquest of California, but lack of conclusive documentation makes it difficult to know if that was the case.[9] Under official orders or acting on his own, upon his return to California Frémont took charge of an armed movement started by U.S. settlers in June 1846. At Sonoma the rebels proclaimed the "California Republic," with a "bear flag" as their standard. Fighting native Californians along the way, the rebels marched to San Francisco, where Frémont commanded the newly organized California Battalion of American Volunteers. On July 7, however, Frémont's "republic" dissolved as Commodore John D. Sloat officially invaded California on behalf of the United States as part of the war with Mexico.

The aggression of the United States against its southern neighbor in the 1840s yielded lands that European Americans had coveted for years, accomplishing and validating what frontier expansionists outside of Texas had been unable to do. The relative ease with which the United States detached Mexico's frontier provinces encouraged countless adventurers to think that independent invasions would stand a good chance of succeeding; their hopes for support among their countrymen rose with the repeated pronouncements by prominent European Americans for further territorial acquisitions, even after the signing of the Treaty of Guadalupe Hidalgo in 1848.

Filibusters of the Late Nineteenth Century

The years immediately following the U.S.–Mexico War have been called the golden age of filibustering.[10] Men seeking fortune or power cast their eyes on the resource-rich and thinly populated northern tier of Mexican states. War veterans, forty-niners, and miscellaneous travelers during the late 1840s and early 1850s had portrayed that region in colorful, exotic, and economically attractive terms. Great opportunities existed just beyond the new border; further, European Americans felt that local Mexicans could easily be won over to the idea of alignment with Yankees because they would be "liberated" from political tyrants and protected from the disorder that prevailed in Mexico's northern frontier. Indeed, banditry, smuggling, and Indian depredations had kept the residents of Tamaulipas, Nuevo León, Coahuila, Chihuahua, and Sonora in a state of turmoil for many years.[11]

Northern Mexicans found the Indian danger the most troublesome and

vexing problem because it contributed to the abandonment of existing settlements and discouraged prospective colonists from the interior from moving
northward. The California gold rush acted as a further drain on the limited
population in Sonora, as evidenced by the departure of over ten thousand
sonorenses (residents of Sonora) despite official attempts to dissuade them.
Even soldiers deserted their garrisons, leaving the region badly exposed to
Indian attacks. Adding to the dilemma was the inability or unwillingness
on the part of the United States to police the border in accordance with the
Treaty of Guadalupe Hidalgo. Thus those settlers who remained in Sonora
and other neglected areas did so at considerable personal risk.[12]

The Mexican government found it exceedingly difficult to provide the
northern frontier with added protection because it was hampered by inces-
sant internal strife and lack of revenues. Nevertheless, national leaders offered
various proposals between 1848 and 1852 that provided for the establishment
of military-civilian colonies throughout northern Mexico. A particularly detailed plan presented by Sonora leader Mariano Paredes in 1850 called for
granting many benefits to new settlers and for developing comprehensive
commercial activity in undeveloped zones. Paredes hoped that Sonora would
become strong enough "to serve as a barrier to the avaricious neighbor that
lies in wait and does not hide his ambition for the fertile and extensive terrain that he visits daily and which he knows contains equal or more precious
metals than those mined in Upper California; this neighbor will wait quietly
until he thinks the day is at hand, and on that day he will turn into a monster,
attracting opportunities from all parts of the world."[13] Paredes and others
urged that Mexico seek European immigrants to populate the northern frontier. One highly respected senator stated that Mexico needed a population of
25 million, with large numbers concentrated in the north.[14]

Despite official endorsement of the colonization proposals, the effort did
not get very far. Only a few of the contemplated colonies were established.
and within a short period most of these disintegrated. The failure is explained
by poor planning, lack of resources, delays, and hesitation on the part of colonists to move to the boundary area. With its defenses weakened and its
population thinned by out-migration, northern Mexico became an attractive
target for European Americans and others who thought little of violating
another nation's territorial integrity.[15]

The filibustering phenomenon, which is the focus of this chapter, needs to
be distinguished from the smaller but far more frequent incursions that were
prompted by such motives as personal revenge, punishment of Indians, recovery of runaway slaves, theft, and smuggling. The commission sent by the
Mexican government to investigate conditions along the northeast border
in the 1870s documented constant small-scale attacks on Mexican citizens,
towns, and farms from 1848 forward.[16] (Of course, such forays took place
in the opposite direction as well, as evidenced by the investigations of U.S.
congressional committees.[17] But it was Mexico alone that had to contend with

the other far more dangerous intrusions, those large-scale, well-financed expeditions meant to detach parts of the national domain.)

Along the Texas-Mexico border in the early 1850s economic considerations provided a pretext for U.S. merchants to become heavily involved in an invasion of Tamaulipas that had overtones of a secessionist movement. The Texans resented stiff enforcement of Mexican tariff regulations, which cut into their profitable smuggling operations. Mexican border businessmen likewise desired less government restrictions on trade. In 1849 a faction backed by business interests proclaimed the independence of the "Republic of Sierra Madre," but that insurrection degenerated into an assault on the Matamoros customhouse and attempted recovery of confiscated contraband at Mier. The second phase of the Sierra Madre episode occurred the following year when Texas sympathizer José María Carvajal led a revolt against the Mexican government. With financial support and volunteers from both sides of the border Carvajal attacked Camargo and Matamoros, but eventually he withdrew north of the Rio Grande. An easing of the Mexican tariff regulations stabilized the situation temporarily, but by early 1852 Carvajal had attacked Camargo again, this time with a force that included four hundred Texans. The participation of so many foreigners in the rebellion prompted Mexicans to call Carvajal a traitor and a "sellout" to gringo/a gold. Carvajal's "army of liberation" subsequently occupied Mexican territory in 1852, 1853, and 1855, but the successes were always temporary, and the idea of setting up a new "republic" was soon forgotten.[18]

While Carvajal and his Texas allies sought to "free" portions of Mexico's northeast, Frenchmen and adventurers from throughout the United States used California as a base of operations to launch invasions of Sonora and Baja California. Thousands migrated from France into California in the late 1840s and early 1850s after revolution and economic depression devastated that country. Of course, the gold rush served as a magnet for many European as well as Latin American immigrants, who flooded California during the period. Before long the French learned of conditions south of the border, and their spirit of adventurism burst forth. Aware of Mexico's desperate need to populate its northern frontier, the French and other groups sought the approval of the Mexican government to establish colonies in the sparsely populated zones.[19] It soon became apparent, however, that the "colonizers" had other motives.

Gaston Raousset de Boulbon, a nobleman and soldier of fortune, is perhaps the best known of the French invaders of Mexico's northern frontier. In 1852 he organized 150 of his compatriots into a company whose purpose would be to establish a mining colony in Sonora. Underwritten by Swiss bankers and actually approved by Mexican officials, the French colonists set sail for Guaymas, but there local officials delayed their movement inland. After encountering continuing obstructions they proclaimed open rebellion and captured Hermosillo. Raousset unsuccessfully sought the support of the local people by posing as the champion of an independent Sonora. As Mexican hostility rose and as dysentery spread among the invaders, they decided to accept an offer to evacuate Hermosillo in exchange for unobstructed passage out of the country.

When Raousset reached California San Franciscans gave him a hero's welcome, and that encouraged him to plan an even bigger venture. At first the Mexican government became alarmed at Raousset's new preparations to retake Sonora. But the wily Antonio López de Santa Anna, who was then president, concluded that the French might be used as a buffer against the more dangerous European American expansionists, especially William Walker, the "king" of the filibusters who was then organizing his famous expedition into Baja California. With raised hopes, Raousset traveled to Mexico City, but he failed to get an official contract to establish his colony. Worse, he managed to anger Santa Anna and had to flee back to the United States, where he once again plotted a return to Mexico. His next scheme called for the establishment of a new country that would include Sonora, Chihuahua, Durango, and Sinaloa, but by then support was hard to come by because competitor Walker had become very popular in California. In 1854 Raousset received signals from Santa Anna's government that a colony under his leadership would now be welcome, and once again he made his way to Mexico, this time with 350 men. Not surprisingly, he succumbed to old imperialistic ambitions, seeking to convince Mexican military leaders in Sonora to join him in a rebellion against Santa Anna. Luck ran out as Raousset's forces tried to storm Guaymas; they were defeated and captured. Eventually, most of the Frenchmen were pardoned, but Raousset was shot by a firing squad. His demise brought an end to the era of French filibustering into Mexico.[20]

As mentioned, the most notorious of all the filibusters was William Walker, the lawyer from Tennessee who had gone to California in search of fortune. After Mexicans denied him permission to establish a U.S. colony in Sonora Walker used a brig that belonged to the U.S. consul at Guaymas to conquer Baja California in 1853. He landed at La Paz with fifty-three men, imprisoned the governor, allowed his mercenaries to loot the town, and established the "Republic of Lower California." The invaders then sailed up the coast to Ensenada, where Walker organized a government with himself as president. Local delegates reluctantly swore allegiance to Walker when they were summoned to a convention. Soon, however, the foreigners were driven from the area, whereupon they set out to conquer Sonora, which had previously been "annexed" to Walker's "republic." After a brief and fruitless stay in Sonora they returned to Ensenada, only to encounter fierce resistance from Mexican troops, civilian volunteers, and even bandits. Weakened and disrupted, the filibusters fled across the boundary, where they surrendered to the U.S. Army. U.S. authorities tried Walker for violating neutrality laws, but a sympathetic jury acquitted him. That ruling gave Walker the freedom to undertake a more successful conquest of Nicaragua in 1855. His brand of imperialism touched other parts of Central America, but, after running out of luck in Nicaragua, eventually he perished before a firing squad in Honduras.[21]

Another important filibuster of the period was Henry A. Crabb, who in 1857 led one hundred men into Sonora, intending to link up with local insurgents actively trying to overthrow the governor of that state. Crabb had understood that the eventual goal of the Mexican rebels was to seek annexation of any conquered territory to the United States and that his help would be welcome. Crabb's Arizona Colonization Company included influential Californians and former prominent U.S. politicians. By the time the Yankees arrived in Sonora the rebels had taken power, but instead of providing a welcome, the Sonorans repelled the foreigners. After a ten-day battle nearly seventy invaders surrendered; only a boy of fourteen survived the firing squad.[22]

As with previous generations of adventurers who preyed on Mexico, Crabb and the other golden age filibusters enjoyed considerable freedom to organize their expeditions on U.S. soil. Mexico repeatedly accused the U.S. government of failing to live up to its neutrality law, which provided that "if any person shall, within the territory or jurisdiction of the United States, begin or set on foot, or provide or prepare for, any military expedition or enterprise, to be carried on from thence against the territory or dominion of any foreign prince or state, colony, district, or people with whom the United States are at peace, every such person so offending shall be declared guilty of a high misdemeanor and shall be fined not exceeding three thousand dollars, and imprisoned not more than three years."[23]

U.S. officials did take measures, albeit weak ones, to prevent filibustering, including issuing warning statements, alerting military commanders, seizing boats, conducting arrests, and bringing alleged offenders to trial. These actions, however, proved insufficient and ineffective, allowing filibustering activity to flourish. Mexicans felt that Washington's lackadaisical attitude was due to tacit approval of the incursions, given the prospect that any territory taken from Mexico might eventually be annexed to the United States.[24] Historian J. Fred Rippy concludes, however, that Washington was *unable*, not *unwilling*, to restrain lawless adventurers. He argues that U.S. officials made sincere efforts to deal with the problem, but they faced obstacles that made it difficult to prosecute offenders. First, the language in the law was too imprecise; second, the law provided for apprehending suspects *after* commission of the crime, not before, thus making it difficult to arrest individuals only thought to be planning incursions; and third, the filibusters had the sympathy and support of the public. Federal prosecutors found convictions hard to come by in those areas where juries sided with the filibusters. For example, a jury in South Texas declared twelve members of the Carvajal expeditions innocent, and a California jury acquitted William Walker and dropped charges against his followers. It is true that three high-level accomplices of Walker were found guilty, but they were never punished for their crime.[25]

In 1853 the filibustering issue complicated the negotiations undertaken by James Gadsden to resolve the dispute over the southern boundary of New Mexico. The Mexicans would not accept a pact that did not obligate the United States to stop the unlawful incursions, and the document finally negotiated by Gadsden did provide for the U.S. Navy to pursue filibusters who eluded civil and land military forces. The U.S. Senate, however, eliminated the article from the treaty.[26]

By the late 1850s the filibustering spirit still remained strong in the United States, but actual incursions had declined. Some ambitious undertakings never got beyond the planning stage or they fizzled out as soon as they began. Sam Houston's bold plan of 1859 to use thousands of Texas Rangers and Indians to establish a protectorate in northern Mexico failed to materialize, apparently for lack of funds.[27] Former California Senator William McKendree Gwin's scheme in the early 1860s to become the "duke of Sonora" by leading a mining and commercial colony of disgruntled Southerners drew a mixed reaction from the French, who then ruled Mexico through Emperor Maximilian, and definite antagonism from the people of Sonora. Meetings in Paris with Napoleon and other high officials had raised Gwin's expectations, but his lobbying efforts in Mexico failed to get concrete results.[28] Many Confederates did succeed in getting French approval for setting up farming communities south of the border, and for a time their enterprises prospered. However, the ever-present native hostility toward foreign colonization, the disruptions caused by the fighting between Mexican patriots and the French imperialists, and the opposition of the U.S. State Department undermined the work of the southern exiles. When Benito Juárez deposed Emperor Maximilian in 1867, foreigners desirous of beginning colonies in Mexico no longer had the French connection available to further their plans, and the Confederate colonies dissolved.[29]

After the Civil War in the United States adherents to the ideology of Manifest Destiny continued to believe that further changes in the U.S.–Mexico boundary would surely take place. In the 1870s border raiding became such a troublesome issue that U.S.–Mexican diplomatic relations reached the boiling point, encouraging some to capitalize on the friction to annex Mexican territory. For example, Texas Ranger L. H. McNelly and army officer Dewitt C. Kells conspired in 1875 to precipitate a war by creating a border incident. Their plan called for the gunboat USS *Rio Bravo*, then scheduled to patrol the Rio Grande, to "return" fire from Mexico that would actually originate with Texas Rangers who would shoot from the Mexican bank after clandestinely crossing the river. The shooting would give the appearance of Mexican aggression, spark retaliation, and quickly escalate into a large-scale conflict. Mexico would lose, thus allowing Texas to extend its boundaries to the eastern Sierra Madre. However, U.S. officials discovered the plot before any planned exchange of fire took place and replaced Kells as commander of the *Rio Bravo*. That removed an important element in the provocation scheme, but trouble ensued when Captain McNelly's Rangers crossed into Mexico to "recover" stolen cattle, triggering a clash with Mexican ranchers and rural police at Las Cuevas. The subsequent arrival of U.S. troops on Mexican soil to aid McNelly's men threatened to escalate the hostilities, but the invaders soon withdrew to Texas. Fortunately, calm prevailed in Mexico City and in Washington during the altercation, defusing a potentially explosive situation begun by ambitious Texans who had the support of some U.S. military officers, albeit not the federal government.[30]

Two aborted filibustering schemes hatched in Southern California in the late nineteenth century illustrate the role of the U.S. press in exposing and stopping such activities. An important factor that precipitated international adventurism at this time was the termination of the Southern California land boom and the wishes of some European Americans to extend the bonanza beyond the border. Interest in Baja California among restless elements hoping to acquire land increased when the International Company, a U.S. concern with considerable holdings in Mexico, regularly advertised available tracts on the peninsula.[31] In 1888 Los Angeles resident Col. J. K. Mulkey organized the Order of the Golden Field, a secret society with branches in Texas and Arizona. The group intended to plant U.S. filibusters in Baja California posing as ordinary workers, farmers, and miners who in time would foment insurrection and proclaim the peninsula the "Republic of Northern Mexico." Mulkey unwisely talked about the plan with a reporter from the San Francisco Chronicle who pretended to be a potential member of the society. Armed with documents from U.S. and Mexican officials who purportedly favored the scheme, Mulkey asserted that twenty thousand troops would be available for service. "When the time comes," he boasted, "the order will be so powerful that there can be no successful opposition. It will simply be the story of Texas over again."[32] But Mulkey never got the opportunity to initiate another Texas-style movement, for the information he revealed doomed the enterprise. To protect himself the colonel later claimed he had purposely given a false account because he distrusted the reporter, but suspicions about the order's true intentions remained.

Two years after Mulkey's fiasco a more ambitious plan to detach Baja California from Mexico was organized by a group of U.S. businessmen and ex–military officers with backing by the Mexican Land and Colonization Company, an English syndicate. Anticipating a successful insurrection, the conspirators named a council of fifteen men to rule the peninsula following a declaration of independence. Most of the offices in the rebel government, which ranged from president to postmaster general, would go to European Americans, but two or three cooperative and "deserving" Mexicans would also be rewarded as a way of enlisting the support of the local population. Just before the uprisings were to take place at Tijuana and Alamo the San Diego Union broke the story, and the whole affair collapsed. Conspirator Capt. J. F. James saw that setback as temporary only, however, insisting that the desires of the people of Baja California for freedom made rebellion inevitable. Indeed, several Mexicans opposed to the Porfirio Díaz government had met with the European American plotters, presumably to join their efforts, but the feelings of the people of the peninsula at large are unknown. Frémont, the old "bear flag" filibuster of an earlier age, called the aborted scheme "a mad one and thoroughly improbable. It has its origin in the wish of certain people to see the peninsula of Baja California annexed to the United States. They believe that annexation would mean a rise in the value of land and personal emolument is at the bottom of the whole thing."[33] As usual, denials followed, with some people taking the matter lightly; others, including the publishers of the *San Diego Union* and the *San Diego Review*, felt enough evidence was available to sustain the theory that a real and elaborate plan to "liberate" Baja California had certainly existed.

The Last Filibusters

As the twentieth century began most of northern Mexico found itself in the midst of an economic boom. Porfirio Díaz's emphasis on political order and promotion of foreign investment accounted for much of the growth. Expansion of mining, agriculture, ranching, and trade was stimulated by closer external ties brought about by the establishment of a railroad network in the border region. The southwestern United States experienced even more prosperity, and great demand existed there for Mexican raw materials and cheap labor. A rapid rise in population accompanied the economic progress, as evidenced by the demographic increase that took place in northern Mexico between 1895 and 1910, which surpassed the growth achieved by other regions within Mexico. Important cities such as Chihuahua, Saltillo, Monterrey, and San Luis Potosí grew substantially faster than comparable urban centers in the interior. Along the border Nuevo Laredo, Piedras Negras, Paso del Norte (Ciudad Juárez), and Nogales also experienced significant growth once the railroads connected them to zones of major economic significance.[34]

But progress in northern Mexico was not uniform. While the states of Tamaulipas, Nuevo León, Coahuila, Chihuahua, and Sonora grew economically and demographically, Baja California remained isolated, sparsely populated, and underdeveloped. Distance and geographic barriers kept the peninsula effectively separated from the rest of the republic, and its inhospitable terrain acted as a deterrent to human settlement. Such conditions accounted for Mexico City's designation of the region as a territory rather than a state. Few Mexican investors found the remote northwest attractive, but Southern Californians, who had easy land and sea access to the peninsula, maintained a deep interest in exploiting its resources. People and products could easily cross back and forth at the Calexico-Mexicali and San Diego–Tijuana borders, and it was only natural that residents of Baja California had more contact with the United States than with their own country. Attracted by the favorable policies of the Díaz government toward foreign capital, European

Americans strengthened their economic foothold in the peninsula, acquiring more land and obtaining mining and other concessions. Foremost among U.S. investors in Baja California were Harrison Gray Otis and his son-in-law Harry Chandler, who controlled 832,000 acres of land through the California-Mexico Land and Cattle Company.[35] Hence the U.S. presence and Mexico's distant and perennially feeble rule of its northwest territory encouraged some expansionist-minded Southern Californians to keep alive the old idea of annexation of Baja California to the United States.

The opportunity to once again promote the independence of the peninsula arrived during the 1910s, when revolution engulfed Mexico. In early 1911, while Francisco Madero's forces attempted to capture northern Chihuahua as a prelude to deposing the dictator Díaz, Mexican Liberal Party leaders Ricardo and Enrique Flores Magón sought to launch a socialist-anarchist revolution in Baja California. The Flores Magón brothers had been trying to overthrow Díaz for a decade. When government repression forced them into exile in 1906, they continued plotting insurrection in St. Louis, El Paso, and finally Los Angeles, relying on sympathetic groups such as the Industrial Workers of the World to recruit adventurers and soldiers of fortune of various nationalities. The Flores Magón effort to attract foreigners to the cause worked well, and as preparations unfolded in January 1911 to launch an attack in the Mexicali area about 90 percent of the recruited revolutionists were non-Mexicans. As embarrassing as that situation was in an era of pronounced Mexican nationalism, the Liberal Party commenced its offensive, and within a few months the insurgent forces, which kept growing with each success, controlled the Mexican border between the Colorado River and the Pacific Ocean.[36]

Meanwhile, the Maderistas had captured Ciudad Juárez, where they forced the federals to sign a treaty providing for Díaz's resignation and new presidential elections. Díaz stepped down shortly thereafter, and Madero surged forward as the principal leader of the Revolution. But the Flores Magón brothers refused to follow the moderate soldier-politician, opting to continue their own radical struggle.

During the occupation of Tijuana the latent filibustering spirit among some of the foreigners in the Magonista army surfaced. Their adventurism was partly encouraged by the interest expressed by many Southern California newspapers in acquiring Mexican lands. "If Lower California should wake up some morning to find the stars and stripes floating over it," observed the *San Diego Sun* on May 12, "San Diego would suddenly become more than ever a City of Destiny."[37] In early June, amidst confusion and dissension then plaguing the Magonista forces, "Captain" Louis James proclaimed the "Republic of Lower California," complete with a provisional president (wealthy Southern Californian Richard Ferris), a flag, and a constitution. Ferris's "republic" died as quickly as it started, however, because Ricardo Flores Magón convinced Jack Mosby, one of his field commanders, to take charge of the operations and stick to the original plan. Nevertheless, the damage had been done, and things deteriorated rapidly for the Magonistas. On June 17 a group of Mexican railroad workers loyal to Madero forced them to evacuate Mexicali, and on June 22 Madero's soldiers routed Mosby's men in Tijuana, sending the foreign adventurers scampering to the United States, effectively ending the socialist revolution. The sensational publicity given these events at the time created the perception that a filibustering venture disguised as a revolution had been foiled by the Mexican federal army. "The Liberal army," commented the *San Diego Sun*, "has gone down in history with the band of William Walker that terrorized the peninsula 50 years ago."[38]

Subsequently, U.S. authorities tried the Flores Magón brothers and accomplices Richard Ferris, Jack Mosby, and Rhys Pryce for violation of the neutrality laws, but Ricardo Flores Magón was the only one convicted. He served time in prison for the neutrality offense and was then released, but within a few years he was put behind bars once again for violating the U.S. Espionage Act. He died at Leavenworth in 1922 under mysterious circumstances.[39]

The Flores Magón episode created considerable controversy both in Mexico and the United States. Mexican detractors of the Liberal Party, especially in Baja California, accused Ricardo Flores Magón of betrayal for participating in a conspiracy to wrest territory from Mexico. Support for his ideals in the Mexican labor sector and among intellectuals, however, assured that in time his countrymen would view with greater understanding how certain foreign opportunists manipulated the Liberal Party's movement for their own ends. Supporters of the Flores Magón brothers would emphasize instead the important contributions of the Magonistas to the Revolution of 1910. Indicative of the positive view of Ricardo Flores Magón that evolved in later years is the interment of his remains in 1945 in the Rotunda of Illustrious Men in Mexico City.[40] Closer examination of the evidence has likewise led historians critical of the Flores Magón movement to modify their views.[41] It is now recognized that the stillborn "Republic of Lower California" was the work of a small group of foreigners, some of whom were charlatans, and that the Liberal Party leadership did not approve of filibustering. The presence of recruits from various nationalities among the Magonistas is explained by Ricardo Flores Magón's adherence to an internationalist ideology that called for a Mexican workers revolution linked with external radical movements. Although Flores Magón obtained some financial help north of the border, neither U.S. capitalists nor the U.S. government influenced his struggle. Flores Magón's problems stemmed from letting too many soldiers of fortune join his army and later losing control over the actions of some of them.

Shortly after the Flores Magón episode a less dramatic but still intriguing event with a filibustering twist underscored again the vulnerability of Baja California. In 1915 the U.S. government indicted Harry Chandler, an owner of the *Los Angeles Times*, along with six other persons for conspiring to overthrow the established government of Baja California in violation of U.S. neutrality laws. The attorney for the southern district of California charged that Chandler intended to create an independent state, an interpretation shared by others as well.[42] The affair began when Baltazar Áviles, a supporter of Pancho Villa, recruited volunteers along the U.S. side of the border to help Áviles regain the Baja California governorship, an office the latter had lost to Esteban Cantú, a follower of Venustiano Carranza and the military commander at Mexicali, during a bloodless coup in 1914. Chandler allegedly participated in the plot because Áviles had promised to forgive unpaid taxes and to protect the family's vast holdings in the Mexicali Valley against land reforms recently announced by the Carranza government. At the trial prosecutors failed to present credible evidence establishing Chandler's complicity with Áviles, and the wealthy Southern Californian was acquitted. Defense attorneys destroyed the ill-prepared government's case by discrediting witnesses and implanting serious doubts about the conspiracy charges against Chandler. The Justice Department's bungling strengthened suspicions that the filibustering side of the story remained unexposed.[43]

The involvement of foreigners in the Flores Magón and Áviles incidents reinforced the view long held by Mexican government leaders that only Mexican colonization and economic control of Baja California would counteract dangerous external influences. As early as 1911 provisional president Francisco León de la Barra promised to study methods of Mexicanizing the distant province and of building a railroad across the Colorado River to facilitate its contact with the mainland. The Revolution delayed those plans, but in the late 1910s Governor Cantú introduced large numbers of mainland colonists into the Mexicali Valley and resettled Mexican workers returning from the United States on land near Tijuana. In 1921 the Álvaro Obregón government began a colonization project that included the development of local resources and the building of a railroad from Magdalena, Sonora, to Ensenada, Baja California. By 1930 25 miles of track had been completed, but the world depression forced a halt in the construction until 1938. With the slow progress on the railroad and the failure to speed up national land reform during the 1920s the colonization plan languished. Ironically, the stimulus for population growth during the period came not from Mexico but from the United States, where Prohibition triggered a boom in tourism in the Mexican border towns. Even so, many of the new residents who settled in Tijuana were European Americans, and foreign businessmen clearly dominated the entertainment establishments.[44]

In the early thirties two developments in the United States alarmed Mexican leaders. For a time rumors circulated in the U.S. Congress that the International Water Commission, an entity of the State Department, had recommended U.S. purchase of Baja California. Then U.S. Senator Harry F. Ashurst of Arizona introduced his fifth resolution since 1919 calling for the purchase of the peninsula along with Sonora. The State Department denied the rumor, and Ashurst's idea failed to garner significant support. Just the same, throughout the decade resolutions and propaganda about Baja California persisted in the United States, causing continued concern among Mexicans. Urging his government to immediately build roads in Baja California as a means of tying the area to the mainland, Secretary of Communications Juan Andreu Almazán warned in 1931 that "to oppose such works would show an utter disregard of the very real and immediate danger of a new mutilation of the Fatherland."[45]

Mexico's long-standing desire to remove foreign control of Baja California and thereby eliminate the threat of U.S. annexation finally materialized during the administration of President Lázaro Cárdenas in the 1930s. This nationalist leader expropriated lands belonging to the California-Mexico Land and Cattle Company, thus encouraging individual Mexican farmers to purchase plots and allowing villages to establish *ejidos* (communal holdings). By 1938 European Americans had given up ownership of 268,000 acres of land in Baja California. The Otis-Chandler monopoly had been broken, and Mexican colonists poured into the area. In addition to his bold land policies Cárdenas stimulated the Baja California economy by allowing free foreign trade and by continuing the building of the railroad to Sonora.[46] With the completion of the line in 1948 more Mexicans migrated to the region, causing the peninsula's population to rise to 286,000 by 1950. By virtue of the overwhelming concentration of the peninsula's population close to the border the northern district became a state in 1952, while the southern part remained a territory. A new age had arrived. At last Mexican control of a remote province long threatened by expansionist neighbors was secure.[47]

Summary and Conclusion

Filibustering constitutes a central part of U.S. expansionist aggression directed at Mexico. The periods of greatest intensity of unlawful invasions organized in the United States coincide with weakness and instability in Mexico, conditions that made that country's northern frontier exceedingly vulnerable to conquest.

In the 1810s Spain was consumed with wars of independence throughout Latin America, thus leaving remote areas like Texas short on military protection. Between 1821 and 1867 Mexico endured perennial political unrest, civil conflicts, depleted treasuries, separatist movements, war with the United States, and colonization by a European power. During the 1850s, when the most spectacular filibustering took place, Mexico's usual political problems were compounded by the recent trauma of the U.S.–Mexico War of 1846–48 and its devastating consequences. It was an opportune moment for adventurers to seek further despoliation of Mexico's relatively unprotected border areas. The late nineteenth century witnessed infrequent attempts at filibustering that did not get very far. A major factor in that lack of success is the order and progress that prevailed in Mexico during the period, but equally important is the fact that the Porfirio Díaz government granted many generous concessions to foreigners, thus lessening the impulse to take Mexican land and resources by force. During the Mexican Revolution of the 1910s cries for interventionism rose in the United States, and that, along with the confused state of affairs south of the Rio Grande and the continued isolation of perennially vulnerable Baja California, prompted some U.S. adventurers to use the domestic insurrection to foment separatism.

It is remarkable that Mexico managed to hold onto its northern frontier (such as it became after 1848) in light of the persistence of the filibustering syndrome in U.S. society even into the twentieth century. In retrospect, filibustering failed for a variety of reasons, including inadequate planning by the aggressors, insufficient human resources, poor judgment, lack of official support, and Mexican resistance. More than any other factor, firm opposition to the foreign invaders on the part of the Mexican people explains the collapse of countless invasions. Although separatist tendencies existed for generations along Mexico's northern frontier, the intervention of foreigners in such movements was hardly seen in a positive light, especially after the experience in Texas in the 1830s and the massive loss of territory in 1848.

Filibustering and pseudofilibustering added considerably to the legacy of distrust between Mexicans and European Americans first engendered by diplomatic and military conflicts that led to changes in the boundary. Suspicions surfaced with regularity in Mexico City that Washington encouraged private attempts to wrest more lands from Mexico. As long as the dark cloud of possible foreign conquest of Mexico hovered in the background, it was difficult to sustain amiable and productive international relations. Not until the late 1930s and early 1940s, when the entire northern frontier became more effectively integrated into the Mexican republic, did that fear begin to disappear south of the border. Along with other major changes in a traditionally conflict-ridden relationship, that development helped usher in a new climate of greater mutual respect and cooperation between the two neighbors.

3 Border Indians

When the Spaniards pushed northward from central Mexico in the 1600s they encountered Indians whose way of life contrasted sharply with that of highly urbanized groups like the Aztecs. Numerous nations and tribes with diverse linguistic and cultural characteristics lived in what today is northern Mexico and the southwestern United States. Anthropologist Edward H. Spicer has identified four types of Native groups in the region that he calls *ranchería*, village, band, and nonagricultural band.[1] Ranchería people practiced farming and had fixed but scattered settlements. In numbers they constituted the largest category and included such groups as the Tarahumaras, Yaquis, Mayos, and Pimas. Villagers adhered to the Pueblo style of living in compact villages sustained by either irrigation or dry farm agriculture. Band Indians such as the Apaches and Navajos mixed agriculture with hunting and gathering and lacked permanence in their settlement patterns. Numbering only a few thousand, nonagricultural people like the Seris formed roving bands that gathered wild foods, hunted, and fished for a living.

Extended contact with Spaniards, Mexicans, and European Americans not only altered the lifestyles of these heterogeneous groups but set the stage for considerable conflict, given that the Native Americans inhabited a region that came to be viewed by whites as a "borderland." For the indigenous inhabitants the only borders that ever mattered were the limits of tribal living spaces. Although conflict often erupted when other Natives trespassed on territory claimed by a tribe, the trouble tended to be localized. That tendency changed radically when the white man organized the region according to his political and economic concepts. Spain was the first to claim the borderlands, followed by Mexico, and finally Mexico and the United States divided the area between them by creating what seemed to the Indians a vague line called a "border." Native Americans were caught in that middle ground, sandwiched in by aggressors who kept dribbling in from the south and east. If the initial encounter with encroachers marked one major turning point in the history of the borderlands Indians, the creation of the U.S.–Mexico border marked another. The region's indigenous groups had to grapple with external controls imposed by non-Indians, including the restriction of physical movement beyond approved international limits. Those tribes that lived at or near the new border would find it especially difficult to adjust to the new way of life.

Indians as a Border Problem

The Natives of New Spain's northern frontier strongly resisted the Spanish effort to change their culture and religion and to incorporate them into a new

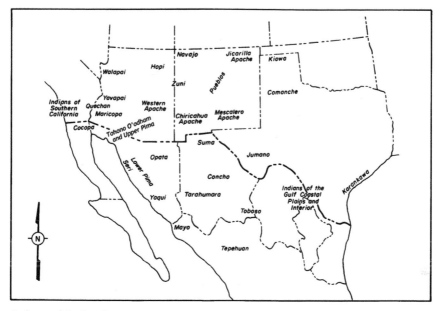

Indians of the border region.

economic system. Among the early revolts that broke out were the Tepehuan uprising in Durango in 1616, the Tarahumara insurrection in Chihuahua in the 1640s, and the Pueblo Revolt in New Mexico in 1680. The Spaniards responded with force and intensified their efforts to congregate the Indians into missions and pueblos. In some areas this approach worked well, but in the plains and in the deserts it failed to subdue fiercely independent and aggressive peoples such as the Apaches, Navajos, Utes, and Comanches. Not only did these groups refuse to submit to external control, but they took the offensive against the newcomers, raiding their settlements and taking captives. By the late eighteenth century perennial Indian attacks had heightened the concern of the Spaniards for the security of the borderlands, an area that was already threatened by the imperialistic designs of the French, English, and Russians.

Spain responded to the crisis by reorganizing its frontier defenses in the 1760s and 1770s.[2] Major changes included the creation of new presidios (garrisons) and the implementation of a cynical policy of "pacification by dependency" toward the indigenous peoples. Henceforth, the Spaniards would endeavor to make treaties with individual bands, persuade them to settle near military stations where they would receive food rations, give them low-quality weapons for hunting, encourage trade, increase their appetite for Spanish goods, "hook" them on liquor, and use divide-and-conquer tactics where appropriate. The Spaniards hoped these measures would result in the disorganization of Indian life and in the establishment of a dependency relationship. This is precisely what materialized, and for nearly twenty-five years peaceful relations came to exist between the two groups. In the early nineteenth century, however, that tendency was seriously disrupted when Spain's attention shifted to containing Mexico and other Latin American colonies then fighting for their independence. The political unrest led to a decline in Crown resources destined for the Mexican northern frontier and contributed to a general breakdown in the system established to deal with the Indians. The Sonora Apaches gradually drifted away from their settlements and resumed raiding, while Apaches from Arizona and New Mexico swept southward into Chihuahua, leaving behind destruction and desolation. With the rising Indian attacks going unchecked, many norteños/as, especially sonorenses, abandoned their homes in the ensuing years. Conditions continued to be much the same after Mexico achieved independence, for the young republic faced seemingly endless civil strife and seriously depleted economic resources. Repeated pleas from norteños/as for the authorities to contain the Indian assault went unheeded, bringing devastating results. According to Spicer, five thousand Mexicans along the northern frontier lost their lives, and four thousand others left the area between 1820 and 1835.[3]

Along the Texas-Mexico frontier population changes and political turmoil complicated the problem with the Indians. By 1830 Comanches and Kiowas were forced to raid throughout Texas and as deep into Mexico as Zacatecas due to loss of land and game brought about by the advance of the European Americans into their homeland.[4] In the middle and late 1830s, as the Texans accelerated their drive toward independence from Mexico, many Mexicans felt the rebels used the Indians as an auxiliary to their movement, encouraging them to attack Mexican settlements. Those victimized complained that Texans supplied arms to the Natives and that European American traders readily accepted spoils taken by the Indians in their raids. The U.S. government also came under criticism for driving some tribes from the southern states and placing them in areas adjacent to the Arkansas and Red rivers, which they then used as bases to carry out raids in nearby Mexico. In an official investigation conducted by a commission of the Mexican government many years later U.S. political leaders of the 1830s and 1840s were accused of tolerating, permitting, and even stimulating such depredations into Mexico.[5] Of course, raiding was not a one-way proposition. European Americans and Mexicans frequently invaded Indian territory, often killing people and taking captives. Usually the rationale for such attacks was "pacification" or retribution for Indian hostilities. One particularly deplorable practice found in New Mexico was the taking of Native hostages who were then relegated to a life of servitude and peonage.[6]

Mexican concern over the Indian problem became so pronounced that President James Polk sought to use it as justification for absorbing Mexican territory. As negotiations to end the U.S.–Mexico War of 1846–48 progressed in December 1847 Polk suggested that since Mexico was unable to protect its frontier, it might wish to transfer the region to the United States, allowing European Americans to prevent the Indians "from committing . . . outrages and compel them to release . . . Mexican captives and to restore them to their families and friends."[7] Mexico rejected the offer, but once the Mexicans resigned themselves to the reality that the northern provinces would have to be ceded, they argued forcefully for a U.S. commitment to restrain the troublesome Indians situated to the north of the proposed boundary. The Chihuahua state legislature insisted that the peace treaty then under discussion include guarantees that Indians incorporated into the United States by acquisition of Mexican territory would not be placed in a situation that would force them to raid in Mexico. Specifically, Chihuahua asked that Indians not be displaced from their territories, that they not be furnished arms for making war, and that no U.S. residents be permitted to buy stolen goods or animals from the Indians.[8] U.S. negotiator Nicholas Trist informed his government that in order to make the treaty acceptable to Mexico's northern states, it would be requisite for the United States to assume responsibility for the Indians. Despite opposition in the U.S. Senate, Article XI of the Treaty of Guadalupe Hidalgo incorporated most of the stipulations desired by Mexico. Henceforth, the 160,000–180,000 Indians who lived in the territory acquired by the United States would need to live by new rules, including restraining themselves from crossing a new political line that for them had little or no meaning.[9]

The United States faced the awesome task of establishing peaceful relations with the Indians, protecting its own citizens, and preventing plundering into Mexico. A vast expanse of barren terrain, extreme weather, remote mountain Indian enclaves, and the extent of the border complicated that challenge. Unable or unwilling to carry out the treaty commitments, the U.S. government failed to stop Indian forays across the border. Between 1848 and 1853 Indian raids, originating mostly in the United States, led to the death of over one thousand Mexicans in the states of Nuevo León, Coahuila, and Sonora. Hundreds more were wounded or taken into captivity, and residents of these states sustained losses from theft of horses, cattle, mules, and other property. The people of Chihuahua also suffered considerable personal and property damage, although statistics are not available for that state. One consequence of the deplorable conditions was the further depopulation of many zones within northern Mexico.[10]

Major responsibility for the transborder incursions rested with people north of the border who profited by buying goods and captives from the Indians. According to James S. Calhoun, a well-known Indian agent in New Mexico, attractive female captives brought $150 and males about half that price. By comparison, mules sold for $20 to $30. Indians used some of the money obtained from such transactions to purchase arms that were generally better than the ones used by Mexican soldiers, thus complicating the defense problem for Mexico.[11]

Mexican officials filed numerous complaints against the United States, but Washington responded that everything possible was being done and that Mexicans should not expect greater protection than that offered U.S. citizens. Indeed, the people who lived in the U.S. Southwest endured many of the same hardships as those who resided south of the border. Comanches frequently attacked Texans, and Apaches and Navajos regularly victimized New Mexicans and Arizonans. In 1850 a joint resolution of the Texas legislature asserted that "vast numbers" of citizens had been killed and that "a vast amount" of property had been stolen by Indians. In New Mexico fifty-two longtime residents declared in a petition that the Indian troubles had never been worse.[12]

To deal with the problem the U.S. government established many forts from the Gulf of Mexico to the Colorado River, scattering four thousand troops throughout the region by the early 1850s. Indian agents busily negotiated treaties with various tribes, but these were doomed to failure not only because of mutual distrust but also because they brought few benefits to the Indians. European Americans who lived in the Southwest expressed dissatisfaction with their government's policies and frequently complained about the lack of adequate protection. Texas, in particular, found it difficult to accept the government practice of signing peace treaties, preferring instead a no-nonsense, ruthless approach to subdue the Indians. For many Texans the only answer was extermination.[13]

U.S. agents who negotiated agreements with Indians routinely insisted that the latter cease their raids into Mexico, but this objective was difficult to accomplish. Indians resented any restriction on their movement and thought it unfair to be required to give up profitable enterprises that had been a way of life for generations. It also seemed incomprehensible to the indigenous peoples for European Americans to demand that they stop attacking Mexicans, a common enemy. Such reasoning, coupled with the inability of the U.S. government to back up its policies with sufficient military power, guaranteed that the transborder raids would continue. That is not to say that the United States made no significant effort to live up to its treaty obligations beyond the signing of largely meaningless treaties with the Indians. U.S. troops did engage the Indians in combat, and on occasion Indian agents and soldiers recovered Mexican captives and restored them to their families. For example, Calhoun handed over thirteen captives to Mexican officials in El Paso in June 1850, with five more being delivered at the same place a year later.[14]

These gestures failed to impress Mexico, however. Mexicans insisted that the U.S. effort fell far short of actual needs and that a clear lack of commitment existed in the United States to deal with the problem. Indeed, the U.S. Congress either failed to appreciate the gravity of the situation or chose to ignore it, repeatedly turning down presidential requests to increase appropriations for military defense along the border. Mexican historian Luis G. Zorrilla observes that the U.S. policy of placing Indians on reservations failed because of the absence of resources and supportive mechanisms to ease the transition from a nomadic to a sedentary life. The United States also lacked the equivalent of the Spanish mission, notes Zorrilla, an institution that had proved successful in many areas for congregating Indians and keeping them stationary. Another U.S. weakness was the shortage of military forces along the border. At the end of 1849, for example, Texas and New Mexico had only eighteen hundred soldiers. Later the number of troops increased, but they still fell short of the desired level, and the most effective force against the Indians—the cavalry—never numbered more than six hundred at any time between 1848 and 1853.[15]

As damages from Indian incursions into northern Mexico piled up Mexico began to submit claims to the U.S. State Department. To the Mexican government the enforcement of Article XI of the Treaty of Guadalupe Hidalgo constituted a small price for the United States to pay in the aftermath of the U.S.–Mexico War of 1846–48 in contrast to Mexico's huge loss of territory. In fact, the Mexican minister in Washington informed the U.S. secretary of state in 1850 that Mexico's only advantage from that treaty had been the expected fulfillment of Article XI. For a time the United States accepted the notion of being liable for damages caused by U.S. Indians who raided in Mexico, but as the Mexican claims escalated into the millions of dollars Washington took a hard line against compensation. Officials pointed out that the United States had no policy to indemnify its own citizens for losses resulting from Indian raids, so Mexicans should not be entitled to receive special treatment. Washington also accused Mexico of placing too much responsibility on the United States and doing too little to protect itself.[16]

In truth, Mexico invested considerable resources to secure its border area. Beginning in 1848 it established a chain of military colonies occupied by over one thousand soldier-settlers, including hundreds of cavalry personnel. In 1852 Mexico's northern states formed a defense coalition, organizing companies of troops that fought various campaigns against the Indians for several years. Data gathered by the Mexican commission sent to investigate border conditions in 1873 showed frequent battles between Mexican fighters and Indians, including thirty-three encounters in Nuevo León and forty in Coahuila between 1848 and 1853 and from thirty to forty in Sonora between 1848 and 1851. In 1849 the Chihuahua state legislature approved the controversial practice of paying for Indian scalps and captives, encouraging many Mexicans and foreigners to engage in this savage activity for many years. Hunters received $150 for each dead Indian and $250 for a prisoner of war or a woman over fourteen years of age. Tragically, peaceful Indians and even Mexicans were often victimized in the process.[17]

To free itself from what it saw as an onerous burden, the U.S. government proposed to Mexico abrogation of Article XI of the Treaty of Guadalupe Hidalgo in exchange for payment of up to $4 million and the assumption of U.S. claims against Mexico. But the Mexicans, who estimated actual losses at close to $40 million, would settle for no less than $12 million and the assumption of debts due the United States. While the two countries haggled over the amounts, the depredations increased, and so did the claims.[18] The issue eventually became part of the negotiating agenda taken to Mexico in 1853 by James Gadsden, whose main objective at the time was to resolve the dispute over the New Mexico–Chihuahua boundary. After prolonged negotiations Mexico agreed to make the abrogation of Article XI part of the Gadsden Treaty, but in turn Gadsden accepted continued U.S. responsibility for the Indians, although not in as comprehensive a fashion as under the Treaty of Guadalupe Hidalgo. When the Pierce administration sent the Gadsden Treaty to the Senate for ratification it advised modification of the statement agreed upon by Gadsden, urging new wording to reflect mutual obligation in the restraint of the Indians. The Senate, however, decided to absolve the United States altogether of the Indian responsibility by approving nothing beyond the abrogation of Article XI, and thus the Gadsden Treaty deprived Mexicans of a formal binding instrument for seeking relief from the United States.[19]

In the years that followed Mexico continued to press for compensation for its frontier citizens, arguing that the United States was still accountable for damages that had been inflicted since 1848. Washington countered with claims of its own citizens who had allegedly suffered even greater losses in Texas and in Mexico itself from a variety of causes. Not until the late 1860s did the two nations agree to set up a commission to settle the numerous claims that had accumulated over two decades, and in the 1870s awards were made to claimants from both countries.

Meanwhile, the Indians continued with their raids, darting across the line, striking at ranches or settlements, and then swiftly withdrawing to the other side, where pursuers were not supposed to follow. Mexico suffered most from this pattern, but the United States endured losses as well.[20] Tribes based in the mountains of Coahuila, Chihuahua, and Sonora frequently terrified residents of northwestern Texas, southeastern New Mexico, and Arizona. Of course, Indians were not the only ones involved in the plundering. Bandits of both U.S. and Mexican backgrounds took advantage of the lawless climate and general confusion to steal and kill on both sides of the border. Cattle theft along the Texas-Tamaulipas frontier became a particularly troublesome activity, eliciting desperate pleas from ranchers to their respective governments to provide added protection.

By the early 1870s the border situation had become so critical that it took center stage in U.S.–Mexican relations. Following a joint resolution of Congress, the United States appointed a three-member commission to investigate conditions at the Texas frontier. Shortly thereafter, Mexico appointed its own investigative commission. In its report, which focused on the Texas Lower Rio Grande Valley, the U.S. commission alleged that raiding activity that originated in Mexico had caused losses in Texas amounting to $28 million and that cattle holdings along the border had declined by 75 percent. Mexican frontier officials not only did little to help, declared the U.S. commission, but many of them participated in the illegal trade or simply chose to ignore it. The U.S. commissioners recommended an increase of cavalry troops to bring relief to the area.[21] The Mexican commission studied the border problems at greater length than did the U.S. panel, issuing a series of reports that sharply contradicted the U.S. commission's findings. Mexico's frontier had suffered far greater losses than the U.S. border area, asserted the Mexicans, and the United States was largely to blame because of its policies toward the Indians, particularly the practice of pushing Indians to the frontier, which encouraged them to prey on Mexico for a livelihood. Border Mexicans had repeatedly been victimized by horse and cattle thieves who used Texas as their base of operations. The Mexican commissioners strongly rejected the claims against Mexico presented by the Texans, arguing that the latter greatly exaggerated their losses. Most of the thieves who robbed the Texans were of European extraction, said the Mexican panel, and the few Mexicans who participated in this activity had been trained by Texans themselves. The Mexican commission further declared that the United States raised complaints against Mexico with the intent of finding excuses to annex more Mexican territory. In order to solve the problems extradition procedures would need to be simplified, each government would need to do more to police its own borders, and, above all, the United States would need to change its attitude from aggressive hostility to friendly cooperation.[22] To make sure that Mexico's viewpoint became known and understood in the United States the Mexican government had the commission's reports translated into English and published as a volume in 1875.[23]

The reports of both countries succeeded in documenting a host of border problems, but they contributed little toward providing solutions. Marauders continued their destructive activities. To make matters worse, Mexican internal politics deteriorated during the period, contributing to the lawless border climate and making it more difficult to carry on normal diplomatic negotiations. In 1876 Mexico's established government was overthrown by Porfirio Díaz. That event reinforced the perception long held in the United States that Mexico's political system was hopelessly chaotic and that U.S. interests could best be served by annexation of Mexican territory, or at least by establishing a U.S. protectorate along the border.[24] Díaz's inability to quiet the border delayed full U.S. recognition of his regime for a year and a half, heightening existing confusion and misunderstanding. By the late 1870s the border friction had ballooned into a full-scale crisis. Tensions rose particularly because the United States, unable to secure an agreement from Mexico for reciprocal crossings of the border to pursue marauders, unilaterally decided in 1877 to enter Mexican territory to punish offenders. Some ten to fifteen U.S. trans-

border expeditions followed during the next two years, eliciting loud protests from Mexico. Later, when the center of border disturbances shifted from
the Texas Rio Grande area to the New Mexico and Arizona borders, the two
countries finally entered into an agreement permitting troops of either country to cross the boundary in pursuit of hostile Indians. A new era of cooperation had begun. The reciprocal crossing pact remained in force from 1882 to
1886, when most of the Apaches were subjugated, but subsequent sporadic
incidents necessitated several renewals of the pact into the 1890s.[25]

Thereafter, conflict over Indian transboundary incursions faded as an issue in the relations between Mexico and the United States. The troublesome
indigenous groups had largely been eliminated or banished to reservations,
both governments had more effective administrative and military control of
the region, and modernization had penetrated sufficiently to reduce the isolation of the borderlands. Long-awaited peace had arrived, but the remaining
Native Americans would face other problems for generations to come.

The Continuing Indian Dilemma

Fundamentally, the trouble faced by the United States and Mexico with the
Indians of the border region stemmed from the impossible situation in which
the Indians were placed by their conquerors. The Indian territories became
the frontier area for outsiders who aggressively moved in to claim land and
resources. Spaniards, Mexicans, and European Americans fought wars, signed
treaties, created borders, and regulated life on the frontier with insufficient
concern for the effect these momentous events would have on the indigenous inhabitants. That approach guaranteed conflict, but, of course, the nature and degree of the friction varied depending on time, place, and actors.
Spaniards, who had a sense of religious mission toward the Indians, typically
encountered little resistance in their initial relations with Native peoples. But
as the newcomers commenced imposing regulations and restrictions, rebel-
lions broke out, followed by suppression and subsequent Indian submission
to external domination. Spaniards and Mexicans felt a duty to "civilize" the
Natives and to incorporate them into their societies, but invariably at the
bottom of the social order. European Americans, on the other hand, generally pushed the Indians aside, forcibly isolated them, and, when nothing else
worked, exterminated them.[26]

The Indian response to domination ranged from peaceful integration to
armed resistance. The California Indians, for example, accommodated themselves to the mission system, but the Tarahumaras of Chihuahua repeatedly
rejected that way of life. To a significant extent violence against the whites
stemmed from the dislodging of the Indians from hunting grounds or fertile
valleys that supported their way of life. In the first half of the nineteenth century European Americans evicted several eastern tribes into western lands,
and later they established ill-conceived reservations in the territories ceded
by Mexico. Often, tribes were moved from one reservation to another for the

convenience of the whites, causing bewilderment and resentment among the Indians. In many cases reservations lacked good agricultural land, water, or game, forcing the Indians to look elsewhere to meet basic needs. Not surprisingly, many chose stealing and plundering as the practical response to their difficult situation. Indians had been known to raid each other before they ever encountered whites, but the conditions imposed by the latter served to reinforce such practices.

An examination of those parts of the Treaty of Guadalupe Hidalgo that refer to the borderlands peoples incorporated by the United States illustrates the marginality of the Indians. Article XI, which focuses on the responsibility of the United States to restrain Indians from raiding in Mexico, took care of Mexico's main concern—protection from perennially unfriendly northern tribes and prevention of possible conflict with tribes that might be displaced within U.S. territory in the future. But what of the rights of the Indians as newly incorporated subjects of the United States? Articles VIII and IX, which specifically mention citizenship, property, and religious rights for Mexicans, say nothing about Indians. It has been argued, however, that the term "Mexican" implied inclusion of the Indians, for Mexico itself has long counted Indians among its citizens, and a lengthy tradition existed dating to the Spanish period of protecting Indian communities from encroachment by outsiders.[27] Under this interpretation Indians were entitled to all the rights guaranteed to the Mexicans of the Southwest, including protection from unlawful loss of land. But as students of the Southwest well know, the United States failed miserably to protect the rights of Mexicans, and the latter soon became second-class citizens in U.S. society. If the U.S. government neglected the Mexicans, who at least had the Mexican government to remind the United States of its obligations, how could it be expected to pay attention to the Indians, who lacked a strong institutional advocate?

Hence, despite the protection implied for Indians of the Southwest in the Treaty of Guadalupe Hidalgo, they fared no better than Indians from other parts of the United States. Lacking sorely needed assistance, the borderlands Indians suffered massive population decline, isolation, persecution, and economic dislocation. Early constitutions written by the southwestern states specifically disenfranchised the Indians, and the machinery set up to validate land claims bypassed most of them. For decades the federal government did little beyond embarking on pacification campaigns, signing meaningless treaties, and establishing ineffective reservations. Not until 1924 did Washington confer U.S. citizenship on the Indians. When confronted with the issue of Indian rights stemming from the Treaty of Guadalupe Hidalgo, the government maintained that no obligation had been incurred under that document. Of course, the Indians themselves knew little about the treaty; it was reformers of the late nineteenth century who first linked Indian rights to the treaty.[28]

When conditions became unbearable in the United States, several U.S.

tribes sought refuge south of the boundary. Mexico accepted these refugees on the condition that they stop raiding and that they help in pacifying other troublesome Indians. Driven by U.S. troops, a small group of Karankawas left Texas after 1848 and crossed into Mexico. In 1850 a group of Seminoles, Kickapoos, and Muscogees asked for and received colonies in Coahuila after declaring that their lands in the United States had been appropriated. Because of unsettled conditions along the border some of these Indians later moved deeper into Mexico. For example, the Seminoles and Kickapoos sent a delegation into Mexico City in 1852 to arrange for a reservation in the interior of Coahuila, which the Mexican government agreed to grant to them. The colony, located about 125 miles southwest of Piedras Negras, became known as Nacimiento and endures to this day. In 1854 U.S. troops reported that a tribe of Lipans and three bands of Mescaleros had settled in Tamaulipas and Chihuahua. Within a few years of their arrival in Mexico most of the refugees had abandoned their settlements, choosing to relocate elsewhere in Mexico or to return to the United States. Destitution and conflict with non-Indians forced them to pull stakes initially, and much the same condition prompted subsequent moves.[29]

During their stay in Mexico these Indians received blame for countless atrocities committed in Texas, and, on occasion, they were accused of perpetrating crimes in Mexico as well. The charges were often exaggerated, but there is an element of truth to them. European Americans became particularly incensed at the aid given runaway black slaves by the Indians who had settled in northeastern Mexico. Seminole leader Caacoochie, better known as Wild Cat, was one of the most successful liberators of the slaves. For years he cagily directed their flight through Texas and into Mexican territory, where many of them became part of the Seminole and Kickapoo tribes.[30]

Among the indigenous population of the U.S. Southwest the Indians of Texas were subjected to particularly harsh treatment, suffering extermination or banishment after they came into contact with the white man. Sedentary tribes who submitted to the Spanish Mexican systems lost much of their cultural identity, and thousands of Indians fell victim to diseases for which they had no immunity. By virtue of their nomadic and aggressive disposition, the Plains Indians made poor subjects for mission life; thus they successfully maintained their independence and lifestyle, at least until settlers from the eastern United States encroached on their homeland. From the very beginning of their contact with Texas Indians European American–Indian antagonisms abounded. For example, as some of Stephen F. Austin's colonists made it to shore in 1821 after being shipwrecked they were killed by Karankawas. Hostilities with this tribe continued until European Americans and Mexicans forced the Karankawas to sign a treaty in 1827 after literally driving them to the sea. Facing further pressures, the tribe split into subgroups that scattered along the coast, went inland, or left for Mexico. Later soldiers and ranchers almost annihilated some of these roving bands.[31]

As European Americans spread throughout Texas following secession from Mexico in 1836 frontier lands were taken or sold to settlers, with the result that Indians were constantly retreating to less desirable areas. Cherokees and allied tribes who had settled on fertile lands in eastern Texas faced brutal attacks in 1839 following white agitation against them. Survivors fled to other parts of the United States and Mexico. Along the way some of the displaced bands encountered white troops and hunters who shot at them. With eastern Texas free of Indians and with middle Texas occupied by more peaceful Wacos, Tawakonis, and Wichitas, the battle lines shifted to the northwestern plains, the land of the Comanches.[32]

In the 1830s Comanches and Kiowas experienced great hardships when the European American presence led to loss of land and diminishing game, forcing these Indians to increase raiding activity in Texas and Mexico, which engendered harsh attacks from revenge-seeking Texans. Demoralized Comanche groups sought peaceful relations with the whites, and signing of peace treaties followed, but these were routinely disregarded by both sides, and conflict continued. Annexation of Texas to the United States in 1845 put the Indians at a greater disadvantage, as Texas, unlike other western states, kept its land under state rather than federal domain, thus avoiding the responsibility of providing land for the Indians.[33] Texans expected the federal government to solve the Indian problem, but Washington could do little to bring about pacification without having land to give to the Indians. One thing federal agents did do was to advise the Indians that they must not raid in Mexico because that would violate an international treaty entered into by the United States. Of course, the Indians felt compelled to disregard that admonition, but in so doing they had to contend with U.S. troops who guarded the frontier. From the Indian perspective the situation had become impossible.

After prolonged indecision on assigning land to the Indians the Texas legislature resolved in 1854 to create reservations, but as these lands were situated in the path of white settlement, the continuation of conflict was assured. Five years later the Texans decided on a drastic measure: forceful removal of the Indians from the state to a reserve north of the Red River. Maj. Robert S. Neighbors, the agent in charge of escorting the Indians out of the state, compared the exodus to that of the Israelites many centuries earlier. Henceforth Indians could not reside legally in Texas. Defying Texas law, some continued to rampage through the state and along the Mexican border, bringing desolation to countless communities. For example, the state of Nuevo León blamed over one hundred deaths on Comanche raids carried out between 1857 and 1870.[34]

By the mid-1870s attention had shifted from Texas to the Indian troubles farther west along the boundary. Approximately fifty thousand Indians lived in Arizona and New Mexico at the time the United States took over the Southwest in 1848. Most had a seminomadic lifestyle and strongly resisted the U.S. effort to subdue them, with the notable exception of the peaceful and fully settled Pueblos of the Upper Rio Grande area. The Navajos, a branch of the Apaches, constituted the largest group. Jicarilla Apaches inhabited northeastern New Mexico, along with bands of Utes who roamed into the area from their home in Colorado. Along the border lived the Mescalero and Lipan Apaches of southeastern New Mexico, the Chiricahua Apaches of western New Mexico–eastern Arizona, and the Tohono O'odham (formerly Papago) and Yuma tribes of southeastern Arizona. These Indians created major problems for the United States by resisting white attempts to subdue them, by opposing efforts to relocate them, and by continuing the long-established practice of raiding. It took many years and hundreds of offensives conducted by U.S. troops before the Arizona–New Mexico Indians were finally subjugated. In 1863–64 alone 143 battles in New Mexico resulted in 600 dead Indians and almost 900 Indian prisoners.[35]

The case of the Navajos illustrates the desperate measures taken by the United States to suppress Indian resistance. Following a chaotic decade that witnessed countless hostile actions and atrocities on both sides, the U.S. government practically starved the Navajos into surrender in the early 1860s. Thousands were then forcibly driven on foot in 1864 through 300 miles of rugged terrain to a barren area in eastern New Mexico known as Bosque Redondo. Pathetic conditions at their new reservation led to two thousand deaths and forced the government to reverse its action, allowing the Navajos to return to their homeland in 1868. The experience became deeply etched in the memory of the tribe, whose members still bitterly refer to it as the Long Walk.[36]

But problems with Navajos were exceeded by conflict with Apaches. In parts of Arizona white-Apache relations deteriorated to the point where U.S. settlers faced the prospect of being driven from their homes. Reduction of U.S. troops in the region during the Civil War partially explains the troubles, but a concerted campaign to imprison Apache chiefs significantly increased the anger of the Indians. The Apaches not only attacked European Americans, they also raided Pimas and Tohono O'odham as well as Mexicans from Sonora. In 1865 the military commander of Arizona reported that Tubac had been deserted and that only two hundred souls remained in Tucson. To the north most white settlements faced annihilation or abandonment. Several years of living in that dangerous environment drove angry Arizonans to demand greater protection from the U.S. government, but the response from Washington, which called for a peace policy toward the Apaches, greatly disappointed many whites who saw extermination of the Indians as the only solution. Inevitably, the highly charged atmosphere produced calamities. One tragic incident occurred in 1871, when a large mob from Tucson killed more than one hundred Apaches, including men, women, and children, during a dawn attack at Camp Grant, where the Indians were temporarily camped. Indignation and outrage expressed by people from the eastern United States forced a trial, but a Tucson jury acquitted the 104 participants, who included

European Americans, Mexican Americans, Mexicans, and Tohono O'odham among their number. Some of the mob members were prominent settlers.[37]

As a way of keeping the Indians and whites apart while seeking a permanent and peaceful solution to the conflict, the federal government created temporary reservations and refuge stations between 1866 and 1872. That practice was then replaced with a policy of concentrating the Indians in a few permanent reservations, some of them of considerable size, where the Indians were to receive material aid and instruction in farming.[38] By 1887 all the Indians of New Mexico and Arizona had been officially settled in specified locations. New Mexico Apaches received two reservations, the 1,165-square-mile Jicarilla tract in the northwest and the 741-square-mile Mescalero reserve near the Mexican border. In Arizona the government brought together more than thirty-five hundred Indians from several tribes and placed them at the White Mountain reservation. Problems soon developed at White Mountain because of the traditional hostility that existed among many of the bands and because white settlers coveted the resources found in the region. Consequently, the government detached parts of the reservation over the next few years, and in 1896 what remained of White Mountain was split in two parts, the northern tract becoming the Apache reservation and the southern part the San Carlos reservation. Major reservations established in northern Arizona during the period included the Hopi reservation (1882) and the Hualapai reservation (1883).[39]

The case of the Chiricahua Apaches, whose homeland straddled Arizona and New Mexico at the Mexican border, is of special interest because of the magnitude of violence that touched their lives and because they figured so prominently in U.S.–Mexican relations for a number of years. Historically, the Chiricahuas had terrorized Spaniards and Mexicans on the Sonora-Arizona frontier, and when European American miners, ranchers, and farmers settled in the area they too felt the wrath of these Indians. The new colonists obtained some relief when the federal government established a reservation for the Chiricahuas in 1872, but raiding into Mexico went on as before. Problems on the Chiricahua reservation developed in 1876, when internal dissension among the Indians led to a fracas in which several whites died. As the situation deteriorated the Arizona governor called for the removal of the Indians, and the federal government, which already questioned the wisdom of having a reservation of troublesome Indians so close to Mexico, followed suit by abolishing the reservation and relocating over three hundred Chiricahuas to San Carlos. Chiricahua Chief Geronimo and his followers refused to go along and fled to Mexico. About the same time Victorio, another major Chiricahua leader who had been living in Warm Springs, New Mexico, also rejected the San Carlos option, choosing instead to lead a nomadic and predatory existence along the border.

In the ensuing decade Geronimo, Victorio, and other Apache chiefs led their warriors in protracted and devastating attacks against European Americans and Mexicans in Arizona, New Mexico, Sonora, and Chihuahua. During the reign of terror hundreds died and considerable property was lost. In 1880 Mexican troops killed Victorio along with seventy-eight of his followers in the mountains of Chihuahua. Some of the survivors settled in Mexico, and others returned to reservation life in Arizona. Four years later Geronimo and other renegade leaders returned to the Fort Apache region but stayed only a short time. In 1885, after U.S. troops harassed Indians at Fort Apache over the manufacture of homemade liquor, the famous chief left for Mexico once more, taking with him a large number of warriors. By then an agreement existed with the Mexican government that allowed U.S. troops to cross the border to chase Indians, and soldiers undertook a long pursuit of Geronimo in the Sonora mountains, finally forcing him to surrender in 1886. Geronimo's days as a guerrilla fighter along the border had come to an end. He and other Chiricahuas were sent by train to confinement centers in Florida. After a few years of prison life the proud Geronimo was reduced to a tourist attraction in major fairs and expositions around the United States; that too came to an end in 1909, when he died. Most of his people were sent to the Mescalero reservation in New Mexico in 1913.[40]

Apache troubles did not end with the elimination or capture of the famous Chiricahua chiefs. As late as the 1920s Apache warriors still used the rugged border mountains as a base from which to carry on marauding operations. One incident that received considerable press coverage occurred in 1926 in Sonora. A group of Apaches attacked a ranch, killed a woman, and kidnapped her child, prompting the husband and father, Francisco Fimbres, to begin a passionate and protracted campaign to punish the assailants. Fimbres sought his government's help in tracking down the Indians, but the authorities hesitated out of fear of arousing the recently pacified Yaquis. In 1929 Fimbres did receive some official assistance; however, his effort to rescue his son was unsuccessful. A proposed second, larger campaign involving the Mexican Army received widespread attention in the United States, where newspapers dubbed the operation the "West's last Indian roundup." Hundreds of people from the United States and Canada volunteered to join the chase, but the Mexican government, conscious of previous troubles with foreign adventurers on its northern frontier, approved the participation of only a few. The big "roundup" never materialized due to political unrest in Mexico at the time and to the continuing concern over the presence of foreigners on Mexican soil. That forced Fimbres and other Sonora ranchers to continue on their own. In 1930 they killed five Apaches, and in 1935 they hunted down the rest of the suspected band, but Fimbres never found his son.[41]

In California Indian-white relations involved considerably less violence owing to the presence of generally peaceful and sedentary indigenous groups. Many of these West Coast Indians were readily incorporated into the Spanish mission system but were later displaced by the process of secularization that occurred in early-nineteenth-century California. Further disruption ensued when European Americans encroached on their lands following the Mexican cession of 1848. Treaties signed by half the Indians in California with the U.S. government called for the creation of reservations, but in 1852 the U.S. Senate refused ratification, effectively stripping the Indians of their land altogether. They also had little success with the U.S. Land Claims Commission, which confirmed only a handful of land grant claims to the Indians. Deprived of their traditional means of livelihood, thousands fled to white settlements to enter a life of servitude and destitution, and eventually large numbers perished from malnutrition and disease. In 1848 the Indians of California numbered between 150,000 and 200,000; by 1885 they had declined to only 17,000.[42]

The deplorable conditions among the California Indians moved reformers to call for new government policies. Reports written during the 1880s and 1890s stressed Indian rights derived by historical presence as well as from the Treaty of Guadalupe Hidalgo. Best known among the works of the reformers is Helen Hunt Jackson's statement of outrage entitled *A Century of Dishonor: A Sketch of the United States' Dealings with Some of the Indian Tribes* (1891). In the San Diego area sympathizers were prompted by the revocation in 1871 of an executive order that had established four townships for the Indians. Opponents of the Indian townships bitterly complained that white settlers had occupied the land in question and made some improvements. Their pressure worked, and the president of the United States abolished the townships, although later the government did create many reservations in San Diego County. Even so, most were only between 1 and 3 square miles in size, and the greater part of the land was unsuited for cultivation.[43]

As awareness of the plight of the California Indians increased, additional lands were made available for their use. In 1928 Congress authorized the state's attorney general to bring suit against the federal government for its rejection of numerous treaties that had been signed in 1852. Sixteen years later the Indians involved in the case received $5 million in compensation from the court of claims.[44]

Use of the Boundary for Survival: Kickapoos and Yaquis

Two Indian groups in the border region, the Kickapoos and the Yaquis, stand out for their use of the boundary to escape persecution and to maintain their ways of life.[45] In the nineteenth century the Kickapoos, a U.S. tribe from the Great Lakes region of the United States, witnessed the migration of a portion of its population into Mexico, while the Yaquis, a Mexican tribe from northwestern Mexico, sent some of its people to the United States. Both groups experienced considerable conflict with authorities from their own countries and lost much in the process. Nevertheless, long after their exodus from their homelands the border Kickapoos and Yaquis retained their identities as indigenous peoples and kept their ties with the mother tribes. For both groups the boundary has been of fundamental importance.

Friction with other Indians and with succeeding waves of European American settlers caused the Kickapoos in the Great Lakes area to migrate westward, and by the 1820s splinter bands had moved into Texas. When Texas became an independent republic in the 1830s the Kickapoos, who had experienced violent clashes with the Texans, fled to Oklahoma and to Mexico. About eighty settled at Morelos, Coahuila, a town some 40 miles south of Eagle Pass, Texas. In 1850 they were joined by about five hundred Kickapoos from Missouri, who brought along a group of Seminoles and African Americans as well. Two years later, however, most of the Kickapoos left for Oklahoma, leaving only twenty in Mexico. In 1862 an estimated thirteen hundred Kickapoos left Oklahoma and Kansas to settle in Mexico, but part of the group disliked what they found and returned to the United States. Another major migration occurred in the early 1870s, when U.S. troops, seeking to eliminate Indian raiding along the Texas border, forced the removal of several hundred Kickapoos from Mexico. By 1875 only about 350 Kickapoos remained south of the border. Finally, in the late 1890s two groups returned to Mexico when the U.S. government instituted new land policies at the Oklahoma reservation that worked against the interests of many Kickapoos.[46]

Among the root causes of the recurring Kickapoo migration between the United States and Mexico in the nineteenth century was constant confrontation with whites. Often the Kickapoos found themselves caught in the middle of factional fighting in U.S. society. For example, during the Civil War one Kickapoo band chose to go to Mexico rather than join the forces of the South or the North. On their way, while in Texas some local Confederates attacked them, forcing them to hasten their trip across the border. That incident, which occurred in 1862, left the Kickapoos with strong anti-Texas feelings. Those bitter sentiments were reinforced in 1863, when another band of Kickapoos, who were also on their way to Mexico, had to fight an attack by Texas Rangers and Confederates at Dove Creek, Texas.[47]

These encounters led the Kickapoos to think of the Texans as among their worst enemies, and a prolonged era of raiding of Texas settlements followed. Trouble between the Texans and the Kickapoos from Mexico reached such serious proportions that the U.S. Congress launched an investigation in 1872. The investigative committee concluded that the Kickapoos were operating under the protection of Mexican officials, and the only solution was to induce the exiles to leave Mexico and migrate to Indian Territory in Oklahoma. Efforts followed to peacefully persuade the Kickapoos to abandon their settlement in Coahuila, but to no avail. U.S. agents sent to negotiate the proposed departure encountered opposition not only among the Kickapoos themselves but among Mexicans, who saw these Indians as protectors against marauding tribes such as the Comanches and Mescaleros. Indeed, the Kickapoos fought numerous campaigns alongside Mexicans against these traditional enemies of the non-Indian population of northern Mexico. Many Kickapoos served in the Mexican military, and in return for the service rendered to Mexico they received land concessions and sanctuary from their enemies in the United States.[48]

Upon seeing the futility of attempting the peaceful removal of the Kickapoos from Mexico, a force of four hundred European Americans led by Col. Ronald S. Mackenzie crossed the border without permission from the Mexican government and invaded the Kickapoo village near Remolino while the Indian men were away on a hunting expedition. The raiders took some forty frightened women and children to San Antonio, Texas, and later to Oklahoma. When the U.S. government refused to return the captives, several hundred Kickapoos bowed to the pressure and removed themselves from Mexico in order to join their kidnapped kin in Oklahoma. Other Kickapoos left Mexico in later years, but those who remained continued their raiding in Texas, perpetuating the instability that had long existed along the border.[49]

During the Mexican Revolution the Kickapoos once again found themselves in the middle of a conflict that did not concern them but that they could not escape. For some time they fought with the forces of Pancho Villa but later joined those of Victoriano Huerta. At one point a contingent of Carrancistas (followers of Venustiano Carranza) burned their village and forced them to flee into the mountains. For years the Kickapoos left their settlement only at night, fearing attacks from revolutionaries or federal troops. Peace finally arrived around 1920, and the Kickapoos once again resumed their traditional life of farming, ranching, and hunting.[50]

For a quarter century following the Mexican Revolution the Kickapoos enjoyed relative stability in their Nacimiento settlement, but by the mid-1940s troubles began to appear that once again disrupted their lives and forced them to resume their old migratory ways. Water shortages, mechanization, conflicts with neighboring ranchers, and plant diseases reduced their agricultural productivity, prompting many to seek employment elsewhere. By the 1960s almost all the Kickapoos had joined the stream of workers from Mexico who annually crossed the border to work in the United States. Their way of life assumed the character of international migrant farmworkers, complete with a way station at the Rio Grande. For years they left Nacimiento for part of the year to travel to the United States, stopping temporarily at the "Kickapoo Village" underneath the international bridge that connects Piedras Negras, Coahuila, with Eagle Pass, Texas. The Kickapoos retained rights to cross into U.S. territory based on possession of a letter signed by a military officer in Illinois in 1832 that guaranteed the tribe recognition and protection by the U.S. government. During the 1980s reportedly some still possessed a photocopy of that letter and used it to cross the border. Most simply identified themselves as Kickapoo to U.S. immigration inspectors familiar with their status and migration patterns. From Eagle Pass the Kickapoos followed the crops in Texas, Florida, the Midwest, and the Northwest. Only a few families remained in Nacimiento during the picking season.[51]

In the last three decades important government decisions came about that dramatically changed the migratory lifestyle that had locked the Kickapoos into a chronic cycle of poverty. In 1977 Texas, once enemy territory, recognized them as a tribe, paving the way for state assistance. Then in 1983 the U.S. government passed the Texas Band of Kickapoo Act, which extended them official recognition at the federal level. That recognition made the group eligible to obtain reservation land in Texas and to receive government services provided to U.S. Indians.[52] Using donated funds, in 1986 the Kickapoos purchased land for a 125-acre reservation and later built a small gambling hall known as the Lucky Eagle Casino. Money began to pour into the tribe's coffers. By the mid-1990s the tribe owned a 9,000-acre Texas ranch, which it used for hunting and religious ceremonies, and close to 800 acres adjacent to the reservation, which it targeted for a new and bigger casino. The new Lucky Eagle Casino, three times the size of the old one, opened with great fanfare in October 2004. Gambling revenues have completely transformed the lives of the 580 members of the border Kickapoo tribe; today they live in relative affluence. The newfound security, however, has spawned new problems and challenges, such as maintaining cohesion within the group and preserving tribal traditions and customs.[53]

Looking back, the border Kickapoos can take pride in their perseverance and triumph over potent forces that repeatedly threatened their survival as a group. Their legacy of disruptive migration actually began before they made contact with whites, for their original homeland could support human life only up to a certain level. Interaction with European Americans resulted in the breakup of the Kickapoos into various roaming bands. Those who settled in Mexico lived a precarious existence, for the U.S. enemy was uncomfortably close, and the possibility of eviction from their adopted homeland always concerned them.

The government of Mexico from the very beginning explicitly agreed to let the Kickapoos maintain their traditional language and culture, although it did require them to abide by the laws of Mexico and actively participate in frontier defense against "barbarous" tribes. In sum, the strong will of the Kickapoos, their adaptation to changing circumstances, and their use of the boundary to their own advantage helped them to overcome many crises. They will need to draw from those collective experiences to successfully adjust to yet another new situation as an officially recognized U.S. band with the privilege of sponsoring casino gambling.

Like the Kickapoos, the Yaquis of Mexico have survived as a distinct people despite forced fragmentation and dispersal. Moreover, a portion of the Yaqui population used the border as bands of Kickapoos had done before them, crossing it to escape persecution. Whereas the Kickapoos took refuge in Mexico, many Yaquis found asylum in the United States.

The emigration of the Yaquis from their homeland in Sonora to other parts of Mexico and to the United States began in the 1880s during a rebellion against the Mexican government led by Chief Cajeme. Following a long tradition of resistance against attempts by outsiders to dominate them, the Yaquis during this period sought to assert their autonomy as an independent nation. Cajeme kept them in a perpetual state of war, causing many to flee the fighting. Others took advantage of the new railroad that connected Sonora with the United States to move northward in search of employment. Eventually, in 1897 Cajeme was captured and executed, beginning a process of fragmentation for the Yaqui nation.[54]

Another major Yaqui revolt occurred in 1895, prompting Porfirio Díaz to initiate a policy of extermination for some and forced labor in the henequen plantations of far-off Yucatán for others. More Yaquis fled to safer areas of Sonora, and hundreds migrated to Arizona, settling among the Tohono O'odham and in Nogales and Phoenix. During the administration of Sonora Governor Rafael Izábal, who carried out the most determined campaign to deport Yaquis to Yucatán, approximately one thousand Yaquis entered Arizona. Some denied being Yaquis to elude the Mexican rural police and make it to the border.[55] Another exodus occurred in 1916–17, when the government renewed the campaign against the Yaquis.[56] Trouble erupted again in the 1920s with a last-ditch government attempt to flush the Yaquis from the mountains, prompting more Indians to flee to the United States. Slowly, peace returned to the Yaqui homeland, inducing some to leave Arizona and resettle in Mexico. In subsequent decades small numbers of Yaquis continued to trickle across the border, but the bulk of the migration had taken place by 1920.[57]

The Yaquis who settled in Arizona arrived both individually and in groups that had unified for mutual support and protection during the years of pronounced persecution. Some of the immigrants took jobs as farm laborers around Tucson, Phoenix, and Yuma, and others worked with the railroads, moving throughout the U.S. Southwest. They found it difficult to transplant traditional family and community institutions because of their fragmented situation and their precarious economic status in the United States. Yet they managed to retain a strong identification with the Yaqui nation, although their way of life came to differ somewhat from that of the main group in Sonora.[58]

In the 1930s President Lázaro Cárdenas initiated a new era for the Yaquis by establishing an "indigenous community" in their traditional tribal lands that included the right to run their own local government. Later, federal aid became available for agricultural development, and the Yaquis experienced some economic advances. However, lack of water for irrigation and other needed resources kept most at subsistence level, despite the availability of good land. By contrast, large commercial farmers south of the Yaqui River who had external capital, imported technology, and access to water provided by government-built dams prospered greatly. Indeed, the Yaqui Valley became one of the most productive zones in Mexico, but the benefits of this development bypassed the indigenous population.[59]

Despite three and a half centuries of calculated efforts by outsiders to destroy their cultural heritage, Yaquis in Sonora and in Arizona have refused to be absorbed into the mainstream of society on either side of the border, and they have maintained ties with each other. That they have endured as an identifiable indigenous group is a tribute to their strong will and sense of self-determination. In 1981 historian Evelyn Hu-DeHart wrote that the Yaquis "stand out for having waged the most . . . enduring and successful war against involuntary absorption."[60] Despite having been deeply influenced by the controls exercised by government officials and by increased interaction with groups outside their communities, "they have not yet surrendered the ethos of resistance."[61] At present there are about thirty thousand Yaquis; most live in the Yaqui River area, but there are several thousand scattered throughout Mexico and about six thousand residing in the United States.

Life has not been easy for the Yaquis in the United States, but for at least one tribe in Arizona, the Pascua Yaquis of Tucson, the last four decades have brought about favorable, life-altering changes. In 1964 the U.S. government gave the Pascua tribe 202 acres of land for its reservation in the Tucson area, and in 1978 Washington recognized the group formally as a created tribe. Four years later the Pascua Yaquis expanded their reservation with the acquisition of an additional 590 acres. Then, in 1989, having obtained permission to engage in gaming operations, the tribe opened the Casino of the Sun, a small facility that offered limited gambling. In 1994 the federal government changed the tribe's designation to a historical tribe, clearing the way for gaining total sovereignty and becoming eligible for the complete range of federal benefits. Full government recognition strengthened the group and allowed for expansion of its membership rolls. In 2001 the Pascua Yaquis opened the grand Casino del Sol, one of the largest gaming and entertainment complexes in Arizona, comparable in size and operations to its nearby competitor, the Tohono O'odham–owned Desert Diamond Casino. All these developments have radically affected the lives of the three thousand members of the Pascua Yaqui tribe. Like the once Mexico-based Kickapoos, the Pascua Yaquis transitioned into a full-fledged U.S. tribe and in the process transformed themselves from a condition of dependence to a state of economic self-determination.

Struggles, Triumphs, and Setbacks: Tohono O'odham and Tiguas

In the Arizona-Sonora region the presence of the international border continues to affect the lives of twenty-four thousand Tohono O'odham in significant ways, pitting this tribe against both the U.S. and Mexican governments. Recently, the O'odham, whose sizeable ancestral homeland overlapped the boundary created by the Gadsden Treaty in 1853, have tried, without success, to recover the right to cross the border without inspections or interrogations. In the 1980s, during a period of rising cross-border drug smuggling and illegal immigration, U.S. Customs and Border Patrol agents began demanding identification of O'odham entering into the United States through reservation land. Prior to that time O'odham from both countries could cross freely in both directions to work, shop, visit relatives, and participate in religious ceremonies within the territory comprising their historic homeland. The new restrictions upset the tribe and prompted its leaders to seek relief through federal legislation, but as of early 2005 the U.S. government had not yielded. The O'odham, however, have experienced success in getting both the United States and Mexico to recognize at least some of their members as dual citizens, thereby making it easier to cross the border. The O'odham have vowed to continue fighting until they are granted all the freedoms, rights, and privileges that they feel are theirs as a sovereign binational people.[62]

In the economic realm the O'odham have aggressively capitalized on opportunities offered by the post-1988 allowance by the U.S. and Arizona state governments of gaming operations on reservation land. The tribe opened the Desert Casino in 1993, the Golden Ha:añ Casino in 1995, and the fifty-two-million-dollar state-of-the-art Desert Diamond Casino in 2001. The latest casino is an imposing, glittery, and spacious facility strategically located adjacent to Interstate 19, the well-traveled artery that connects Tucson and Nogales. Since the opening of the Desert Diamond Casino, throngs of Tucsonans and out-of-town visitors have found their way to its gambling tables, slot machines, bingo hall, and entertainment complex that features first-rate concerts, comedian acts, and boxing matches. These entrepreneurial ventures by the Tohono O'odham have created needed jobs and brought varied improvements to tribal members. The casinos have also generated millions of dollars in federal taxes as well as revenues that are used by state and local governments for public services for the general population. Without question, the establishment of gaming operations has been a major turning point in the lives of the Tohono O'odham, and their relationship with non-Indians has been redefined.

Near El Paso, the Tigua tribe, also known as the Ysleta del Sur Pueblo, has experienced its share of travails in its effort to maintain its identity and find its way out of poverty.[63] The current 1,250 Tiguas of Texas are descended from refugees who left the Tiwa Pueblo in New Mexico during the Pueblo Revolt of 1680, an uprising that drove out the Spaniards and their indigenous allies southward along the Rio Grande. During their residence at Ysleta del Sur the biggest challenge faced by the Tiguas turned out to be retention of their land. Among the grants given to Indians in the El Paso–Ciudad Juárez area in 1751 the Tiguas received an award for nearly 18,000 acres. Subsequently, Spanish and Mexican decrees and laws during the late eighteenth century and first third of the nineteenth century not only reaffirmed the Tigua grant but also extended protection to the tribe as well as other Indian groups against loss of their patrimony to outsiders.

Problems pertaining to landownership by Indians in the area surfaced after the U.S.–Mexico War despite extant official recognition of grants. A census undertaken by the New Mexico territorial legislature in 1847 included the district where the Tiguas lived, implicitly accepting their right to the land they occupied. The federal superintendency of the Bureau of Indian Affairs in Santa Fe, which had jurisdiction over the Tiguas, explicitly sanctioned their grant, as did the U.S. General Land Office.

Unfortunately, the effort to have the Tigua land grant permanently recognized by the U.S. government became muddled when, under the terms of the Congressional Compromise of 1850, the El Paso area, which had historically been a part of New Mexico, officially became a part of Texas. Both as a republic (1836–45) and then after it joined the United States as a state (1845), Texas had claimed all territory east of the Rio Grande, including El Paso, as part of its domain. Because Texas retained ownership to all land in the state when it joined the Union, once the 1850 compact took effect the burden fell on the Tiguas to validate their claim with Texas authorities. Texas assumed jurisdiction over the Tiguas, despite previous U.S. Supreme Court rulings that designated the group as a domestic dependent nation under federal supervision.

The task of legitimizing the Tigua grant in Texas proved much more difficult than it appeared in the 1850s. The Texas Constitution, after all, had recognized extant Indian treaties and land grants. But Texas Indian agents had not established administrative relations with the Tiguas as they had with other tribes in east Texas. Until 1847 Mexico actually had jurisdiction over the El Paso area, and, once it became part of the United States, both New Mexico and Texas claimed the area between 1847 and 1850. These jurisdictional disputes confused the land issue. Furthermore, the protection in the Treaty of Guadalupe Hidalgo accorded to holders of land grants in the territories ceded by Mexico in 1848 did not extend to the Tiguas because that document did not pertain directly to Texas.

Texas further undermined the Tigua land grant in 1854 when a law passed by the legislature regarding the town of Ysleta referred to the Tiguas as "inhabitants" rather than "Indians." This seemingly minor change in terminology had significant repercussions because land belonging to Indians had legal protection, but land owned by non-Indians, commonly referred to as citizens, residents, or inhabitants, could be acquired by the state under the eminent domain doctrine. When the state identified land considered necessary to pursue the public good, owners of such property could be compelled to sell it. Legally, then, the Tiguas began losing their distinct identity as an indigenous tribe.

Other deleterious actions followed. In 1859, in an election in which Indians could not vote, the male residents incorporated Ysleta, including Indian lands, as a town. In 1871 Texas approved a second incorporation designed to divest Indian families, again referred to as inhabitants, of all remaining land titles. This incorporation made all lands within the original grant subject to taxation. Moreover, so-called surplus lands were given to petitioners in an attempt to perfect existing titles. That led to further land loss. In short, the state of Texas gained sovereign tribal lands by treating the Tiguas as non-Indians.

Forced to abandon their village, the Indians of old Ysleta relocated to the Barrio de los Indios, a dispersed settlement. During the ensuing years formerly self-sufficient Indian farmers and hunters became farm laborers and domestic servants. Some displaced Tiguas became paupers. Conditions worsened with the arrival of the railroads in the 1880s as imported industrial products and commodities replaced many Indian cottage industries. Private capitalists developed large irrigated tracts of cotton and alfalfa and truck gardens. Traditional processing techniques gave way to industrial methods used in establishments such as corn mills and cotton gins.

Despite being alienated from their land and having to adjust to a new social order, by the turn of the nineteenth century the Tiguas still remained a cohesive tribe. Many of them survived by working for others or by selling traditional products such as pottery. Some managed to save money and purchase small farms. Composed of approximately three dozen families, the tribe sought education for their children and exercised their civic duties by serving on juries and on the Ysleta town council. Unlike other Indians who had been less successful in maintaining separate identities and were slowly assimilating into the surrounding non-Indian society, the Tiguas kept their customs and traditions and acted as a unified ethnic population. By celebrating the feast day of Saint Anthony every June 13 with a mass, dancing, and other rituals, the Tiguas reminded themselves as well as the outside world of their continuing group identity.

In the mid-twentieth century efforts escalated among the Tiguas to gain official recognition as a tribe and to recover the lost land. Through the Texas Indian Commission, founded in 1954, Texas oversaw the welfare of the Tiguas and the Alabama-Coushatta, an east Texas tribe and, at the time, the only other remaining indigenous group in the state. A major breakthrough for the Tiguas occurred in 1967, when they received enough land from the state to establish an urban reservation. Using public funds, the tribe built an attractive complex that showcased the Tigua heritage and tapped into the tourist trade. Most important, the new reservation symbolized the sovereignty that the Tiguas had long sought.

In the ensuing years the Tiguas pressed hard for federal recognition. Wisely, they enlisted the assistance of national Native American organizations with experience in this area. The effort paid off. In 1983 the U.S. Congress designated the Tiguas as a federally protected indigenous group. That opened the door for legally pursuing the recovery of land lost in the previous century. Though urbanization made the restitution of the original land grant impossible, the courts eventually awarded the Tiguas several million dollars in compensation for their historic losses. The Tiguas also won full federal recognition as a tribe in 1987.

Following approval of some forms of gambling by Texas voters, in 1991 the Tiguas opened the Speaking Rock Casino, a facility that offered poker, blackjack, slot machines, and keno to its patrons. Inevitably, the presence of the casino and the flow of large amounts of money caused controversies. Texas officials declared the casino an illegal operation, pointing out that state law prohibited casino gambling and claiming that the federal Indian Gaming Regulatory Act of 1988 required the Tiguas to comply with Texas law. The Tiguas contested that opinion just as they rejected the claim of state and local officials that casino earnings should be subjected to taxation. Texas officials then initiated legal proceedings to close the casino, leading to court decisions against the Tiguas. In 2002, following a refusal by the U.S. Supreme Court to intervene, the casino finally shut down. About 2,200 jobs disappeared, along with $60 million in payroll. The Tiguas then sought to get the U.S. Congress to pass a law allowing them to reopen the casino. Tragically, the main outcome of that initiative was to get cheated out of $4.2 million by Jack Abramoff and other unscrupulous lobbyists who, while professing to promote the Tigua casino cause, actually worked against it by secretly joining forces with antigambling conservatives who sought to keep the Speaking Rock Casino closed. The lobbyists manifested their contempt for the Tiguas by calling them "monkeys" and "morons" in emails obtained by the press. The behavior of the crooked lobbyists generated a grand jury inquiry, a congressional hearing, and indictments in 2004–2005.[64]

Border Indians Today

After four and a half centuries of contact with non-Indians some twenty-five indigenous peoples in the borderlands remain as distinct groups within U.S. and Mexican societies. Their numbers have been substantially reduced from the time of initial contact, but most have achieved a degree of stability that has allowed for group continuity. One third of the approximately 2 million Indians in the United States reside in Texas, New Mexico, Arizona, and California, with about seventy-two thousand Indians living in the U.S. counties adjacent to the boundary (table 3.1). Included in that figure are Kickapoos, Tiguas, Mescaleros, Tohono O'odham, Yaquis, Pimas, Maricopas, Yumas, and various California tribes. On the Mexican side some eighty thousand indigenous peoples, including several Baja California groups, Kickapoos, Tohono O'odham, Ópatas, Seris, Yaquis, and Tarahumaras, live in the states of Baja California, Sonora, Chihuahua, and Coahuila. The Tarahumaras of Chihuahua, numbering some fifty thousand, constitute the largest Indian group in the Mexican border area.

Over the years many studies of borderlands Indians have revealed widespread isolation, economic deprivation, and political powerlessness. For example, a report by the U.S. Commission on Civil Rights published in 1973 characterized the living standards of New Mexico and Arizona Indians as "grim," noting "few hopeful signs or positive action" for future improvement.[65] The commission found deplorable economic problems, with unemployment rates at just under 40 percent in New Mexico and between 50 and 60 percent in Arizona. Educational data revealed achievement levels of Indian children at

Table 3.1 Indian Population in the U.S. Border Region in 2000

	Number	Percentage of U.S. Indian Population	Percentage of State Indian Population
United States	1,959,243	100.00	
Border states			
Texas	65,877		100.0
New Mexico	134,356		100.0
Arizona	203,527		100.0
California	242,164		100.0
Total	645,924	33.0	
Border counties			
Texas	11,721		17.8
New Mexico	2,904		2.2
Arizona	30,053		14.8
California	27,003		11.2
Total	71,681	3.7	

Source: U.S. Bureau of the Census, *Census of Population,* 2000.

two to three years below and dropout rates far above those of the general population. Lacking adequate health care, Indians had a high infant mortality rate and a short life expectancy. The application of justice toward the Indians was found to be unfair. For example, Indians had a much higher arrest rate on drunk charges than non-Indians. In Phoenix Indians accounted for about one fourth of all the male and half of all the female arrests on alcohol-related offenses, although the Indians comprised less than 1 percent of the city's population. In their testimony before the Civil Rights Commission Indians charged that law enforcement was harsher in rural areas and in border towns than in the cities.[66] For a large percentage of the Indian population in the Southwest conditions have not changed much since the publication of that report.

As severe as the situation is among U.S. Indians, conditions are far worse south of the border. In Mexico there are no reservations, and economic opportunities generated by such enterprises as tourism and gaming casinos are nonexistent. Serious difficulties continue to plague Mexican Indian groups from one end of the border to the other, including unemployment, poor housing, substandard education, bad health, and exploitation at the hands of outsiders.

Anyone who has visited urban centers like Ciudad Juárez and Chihuahua City in recent years has seen the effects of economic displacement on Indians such as the Tarahumaras. Increasing numbers from this tribe have migrated from their mountain homelands to the cities, seeking to eke out an existence by selling candy, cigarettes, and the like on the streets. Barefoot women wearing their traditional tribal dress routinely stake out sidewalk spaces, where they tend their children while attempting to sell their goods to passersby. Some try to carry on such activities or to beg near the international bridge between Ciudad Juárez and El Paso, but the police frequently drive them off to remove them from the sight of foreign tourists.

Since the 1980s the Tarahumaras have faced one of the most difficult periods in their history. Commercial exploitation of their mountain homeland, bad harvests, a prolonged and crippling drought, extreme violence generated by drug traffickers, and government neglect have caused chronic crises. Logging activity in the Sierra Madre has particularly hurt the Tarahumaras, driving away game traditionally hunted for food. In 1983 a document distributed by the Catholic Church indicated that infant mortality had risen 60 percent and that nearly four fifths of the Tarahumaras were afflicted with tuberculosis. Church leaders called for donations totaling 4.5 million pesos to buy 300 tons of corn for emergency distribution to several mountain communities.[67] In September and October 1994 at least thirty-four babies died from malnutrition during a drought that severely cut food production. That prompted the governor of Chihuahua to declare the Tarahumara region a disaster area, but the federal government dragged its feet on providing relief. The greatest recent tragedy to descend upon the Tarahumaras is violence and social devastation caused by the influx of drug traffickers in search of secluded lands on which to grow marijuana and opium. Killings have become commonplace, and fear has overtaken many Tarahumara communities. In 1995 a *New York Times* reporter related a conversation with a local farmer who, as he described what the drug trade had done to the town of Coloradas, identified the spots where seven men had been executed: "[The farmer] could also show the place . . . where his father, an Indian leader, was shot through the stomach and killed, the school from which frightened teachers fled and never returned, the construction site of the new clinic where no mason has dared come back to lay a brick, [and] the graveyard filled with young Tarahumara Indians who died violently in this dying place."[68]

Summary and Conclusion

The historical experience of the Indians of the U.S.–Mexico border region has varied significantly since the arrival of non-Indians. Because of their cultural heterogeneity, some groups accommodated peacefully to the lifestyles introduced by Spaniards, Mexicans, and European Americans, but others violently resisted external dominance. What distinguishes the indigenous peoples of the borderlands from other non-border Indians is their misfortune of having been conquered in cycles and their having to abide by restrictions imposed by the creation of an international boundary meant to separate two nation-states. Groups whose homelands straddled that border or whose traffic lanes cut across it had to contend thereafter with a major disrupter of their ways of life. Dispossessed of lands they had occupied for centuries and forced into reservations that frequently had inadequate resources to support them, many tribes had no choice but to prey on non-Indians; if the border could be used to their advantage, so much the better.

The difficult situation of the Indians led to prolonged violence, and, predictably, tragedy befell both Indians and non-Indians. Transborder raiding by Indians generated so much friction between the United States and Mexico that war seemed a real possibility in the 1870s. Reciprocal agreements to cross the boundary in pursuit of raiders finally eliminated the problem for both countries, but that policy took a heavy toll on the Indians. They emerged from those troubled years decimated in numbers, segregated from the mainstream society, and destined to live marginal lives in a modern industrial world. Yet many groups managed to survive as culturally identifiable groups, and to this day they fiercely resist absorption into U.S. or Mexican society. That determination to endure despite continuous assaults on their way of life constitutes one of the major stories in the heritage of the borderlands.

Viewed in historical perspective, the situation of the Indians of the U.S. Southwest resembles in some important ways that of Chicanos/as. As a result of a war of conquest Indians and Chicanos/as were involuntarily incorporated into the United States. It mattered little that the rights of Chicanos/as were explicitly and those of Indians implicitly protected by the Treaty of Guadalupe Hidalgo; both groups became second-class citizens in U.S. society, with Indians occupying an even lower position than Chicanos/as. Countless separate treaties signed by the U.S. government with individual tribes proved largely meaningless because they were seldom observed. Only after several generations did the United States recognize the injustices suffered by the Indians. Official acceptance of tribal status, granting of reservations, permission to operate gaming casinos, and other positive initiatives in recent decades meant to redress past wrongs have helped, but most Indians in the U.S. Southwest still find themselves at the bottom of the social order. The same is even more true of Indians in the Mexican border zone and throughout Mexico, where marginalization is far greater and where government assistance is extremely scarce.

Thus, for both Mexico and the United States the dilemma of the past continues. In the nineteenth century the overriding concern of non-Indians was how to establish peaceful relations with the indigenous peoples. Today's challenges center around how to integrate Indians into mainstream society without further disrupting their way of life, how to lessen exploitation, and how to improve their standard of living in an era of continuing economic crises. For Indian tribes such as the Tohono O'odham, Yaquis, Kickapoos, and Tiguas, all of whom have eagerly embraced casino gaming as an economic development strategy, life has taken a radical turn. Newfound prosperity has placed them in uncharted waters. It remains to be seen how affluence will affect tribal cohesion and identity in the long term.

4 Mexican Americans, Ethnic Conflict, and Identity Issues

Since the Texas insurrection of 1836 and the U.S.–Mexico War of 1846–48 the experiences of borderlands Mexican Americans, or Chicanos/as, have been profoundly affected by the political boundary that separates the two countries. With the detachment of Mexico's northern frontier approximately one hundred thousand Mexicans residing in Texas, New Mexico (including Arizona), and California became subjects of the United States, forcing permanent severance of political ties with the motherland. The choice of the Rio Grande as the dividing line had the immediate effect of partitioning various population clusters that had formed along that stream since Spanish settlement in the eighteenth century. Later, shifts in the course of the river produced further disruptions in community life and physical displacements of local populations, affecting the interests of Mexican Americans in numerous ways.

Throughout the late nineteenth century immigrants from Mexico expanded the Mexican-origin population in the southwestern United States, and with the outbreak of the Mexican Revolution in 1910 that initial migration flow evolved into a major movement that continues to the present day. Consequently, Mexican Americans became a major component in the population of the U.S. borderlands.

An unfortunate element in the history of Mexican Americans in the U.S. border region has been their strained relations with the dominant society. The record reveals an enduring pattern of racial, ethnic, and cultural confrontation, much of which is directly traceable to border tensions. Armed clashes, raids, thefts, rapes, lynchings, murders, and other outrages became commonplace in border areas from Texas to California. In time the violence subsided, but Mexican Americans in the borderlands remained a second-class population in the United States, even until recent years.

This chapter examines the unique circumstances of border Mexican Americans by discussing key aspects of their lives since they came in contact with European Americans. Attention is directed in particular to the effect on the group living in the boundary zone, physically close to Mexico but decidedly distant in many ways from their roots. To give a sense of what border Chicanos/as have thought and felt about their peculiar condition, I have drawn from selected historical events, characters, and situations that seem to me to personify the border experience. My aim, then, is to interpret the condition of border Chicanos/as rather than to narrate the historical record.

Table 4.1 European American–Mexican American Conflict in the Border Region, 1830–1916

Time period	Place	Incidents
Protracted "microviolence"		
Entire period	U.S. Southwest, including the border area	This period witnessed hundreds, perhaps thousands, of small-scale encounters between European Americans and Mexicans, with the latter, because of their subordinated status, predominantly the victims. Incidents include discrimination, harassment, miscarriages of justice, land invasions, swindles, thefts, rapes, murders, and lynchings.
Violence on a larger scale		
1830s–1840s	Texas	Instability stemming from Texas rebellion against Mexican government leads to widespread persecution of tejanos/as.
1848	Border towns	Forty-niners harass Mexican settlements and steal from local residents; U.S. slave chasers cross into Mexican territory.
Early 1850s	New Mexico	About two thousand native New Mexicans leave their homes and cross the border into Mexico when European Americans encroach upon their lands.
1856–57	Los Angeles area	"Juan Flores Revolution." San Quentin escapee Juan Flores leads a gang that kills a sheriff, triggering harassment of Mexican suspects, arrests, and at least nine hangings. The gang is captured, and Flores is executed.
1857	South Texas	"The Cart War." European American cartmen attack Mexican competitors, killing seventy-five.
1859–60	Brownsville, Texas	"Cheno Cortina Raids." Juan Nepomucena Cortina and sixty followers engage Texas lawmen in a series of skirmishes motivated by racial tensions. Fifteen Texans and eight Mexicans die in the raids.

Table **4.1** cont.

Time period	Place	Incidents
1870	Arizona-Sonora border	"Mission Camp Affair." A theft allegedly committed by a Mexican leads to reprisals and shootouts, resulting in the death of four European Americans and two Mexicans.
1870s	all along the border	The old problem of transborder Indians raids and bandit depredations flares up into a crisis in U.S.–Mexican relations. Countless clashes in the 1850s, 1860s, and 1870s result in hundreds of deaths, widespread destruction of property, and repeated violations of national sovereignty.
1871	Mesilla, N.M.	"Mesilla Riots." Nine men, most of them Spanish-speaking supporters of politician Col. J. Francisco Chávez, are killed in a political dispute. Additionally, forty to fifty are wounded.
1873	Lincoln County, N.M.	"Lincoln County War." Range war between rival Anglo cattlemen traps Mexican vaqueros in the middle. Thirteen Mexicans die along with many European Americans.
1875	Corpus Christi	Bandit activity precipitates attacks on Mexican settlers. Many die.
1877	El Paso	"The Salt War." Mexicans from San Elizario rebel against European American entrepreneurs who take over the community's salt deposits. Texas Rangers are brought in to reestablish peace but are repelled. Several European Americans and several Mexicans die in a series of violent clashes and summary executions.
1880s	Texas Panhandle –New Mexico border	Retaliating for the murder of a sheepman, Texas cowboys rampage in Tascosa, killing several innocent Mexicans and lynching others suspected of complicity in the murder. Gunman and folk hero Sostenes l'Archeveque, of French Mexican descent, is identified as the killer and is executed in a trap.

Table 4.1 cont.

Time period	Place	Incidents
1889–90	northern New Mexico	"Las Gorras Blancas Raids." In an attempt to preserve the old Hispano/a way of life, Las Gorras Blancas raid European American settlements, destroying considerable property and precipitating injuries from shootings.
1915–16	Texas-Tamaulipas border	"Plan de San Diego raids." Raids associated with the "Plan de San Diego" keep the Texas Lower Rio Grande Valley in continuous turmoil. Raiders include Mexican revolutionaries, Mexican American guerrillas, and bandits of various backgrounds. U.S. troops, Texas Rangers, local lawmen, and vigilantes retaliate against the attackers, sometimes crossing into Mexico to avenge losses. Hundreds die in the raids.
1916	Texas–New Mexico–Chihuahua border	"Santa Ysabel Massacre." In January Villistas kill sixteen European Americans at Santa Ysabel, Chihuahua. Racial riot erupts in El Paso.
		"El Paso Jail Fire" (March 6). About twenty Mexican and seven non-Mexican inmates die in a fire caused by the lighting of a match close to a gasoline solution used to soak the clothing of the prisoners while they are in the process of being deloused with a kerosene solution. Many people, including Mexican revolutionaries, believe this horrible act is in response to the killing of the U.S. engineers in Santa Ysabel.
		"Columbus Raid" (March 9). Villistas attack a New Mexican border town, killing about twenty European Americans. Some one hundred raiders are killed by the U.S. military, and thousands of U.S. troops invade Mexico in a futile pursuit of Villa. International and ethnic tensions remain extremely high for about a year.

Border Confrontation and Violence

Relations between *norteamericanos/as* and *mexicanos/as* in the borderlands have evolved significantly since initial contact in the early nineteenth century. When European Americans began dribbling into New Spain's northern frontier, the local people welcomed them. Immigration, regardless of its source, meant greater protection against hostile Indians, and expanded population implied increased economic activity in an area ripe for development. European American traders, merchants, and trappers brought much-needed goods that the mother country would not or could not supply. Small in number and dependent on the frontier Mexicans for their livelihood, the first wave of European American immigrants integrated themselves into the local society. Peaceful ethnic relations prevailed, although the European Americans often had problems with government authorities who sought to enforce, albeit unsuccessfully, the strict trade and immigration policies of the Spanish Crown.

The character of European American–Mexican relations on the frontier began to change in the 1820s, when norteamericanos/as arrived in greater numbers following Mexico's independence from Spain. The newcomers became more assertive in promoting their personal interests and in seeking greater autonomy from Mexico City; underlying those efforts was a desire, which became more pronounced as time passed, to annex Mexico's northern provinces to the United States. In Texas, where European Americans outnumbered tejanos/as by six to one by the end of the decade, assertiveness gave way to aggressiveness as the European Americans constantly expressed resentment toward Mexican rule and contempt for the Mexican way of life. As frontiersmen who had long advocated greater autonomy for their province, many tejanos/as joined the European Americans in opposing the centralist policies of the Mexican government, but, given prevailing European American attitudes toward Mexicans, the union was far from an ideal coalition. A historic European American–led movement for Texas independence followed in the 1830s, ushering in a decade of conflict with Mexico and pronounced ethnic hostility on the Texas-Mexico border that lasted several generations. Confrontations generated by ethnic friction and economic competition also broke out in New Mexico, Arizona, and California after the acquisition of these provinces by the United States as a result of the U.S.–Mexico War of 1846–48. The European Americans who moved into the region soon imposed a political, social, and economic system that promoted their interests and relegated those of conquered Mexicans and Indians to secondary consideration.

The period from 1848 to 1920 was particularly difficult for the frontier Mexicans who had become part of the United States through annexation and for their compatriots who later emigrated from Mexico. These people became politically powerless, economically impotent, socially marginalized, racially stigmatized, and culturally maligned. Ethnic tension and class friction frequently gave way to violent encounters, as shown in table 4.1. Clashes were particularly pronounced along the border, where uneasy international relations added fuel to the explosive ethnic climate. The frequent military engagements triggered by the secession of Texas from Mexico had left bitter memories, and, more than any other event, the U.S.–Mexico War left a legacy of enmity among the people of the borderlands. Mexicans in the annexed territories were free from the neglectful and often oppressive control of Mexico City, but in the new U.S. social order they had become at best inconsequential bystanders and at worst colonial subjects in their own land. European Americans assumed the role of conquerors, demanding subservience from the Mexican population in the annexed territory while contemplating extension of the border deeper into Mexico.

Of the many violent encounters that took place along the border during the nineteenth century, the El Paso "Salt War" of 1877 perhaps best illustrates how the imposition of the boundary gave rise to conditions that the local Mexican population found hard to accept, thus setting the stage for transborder conflicts that carried ethnic overtones. The Salt War was essentially a rebellion at San Elizario, Texas, a town located about 20 miles east of El Paso–Paso del Norte, that involved the participation of up to four hundred Mexicans from both sides of the Rio Grande. Three European Americans and three Mexicans died in the disturbances, and many others suffered personal injury or loss of property. For a time San Elizario and the adjoining communities of Socorro and Ysleta were practically evacuated, with Mexicans finding refuge south of the Rio Grande and European Americans retreating to El Paso, Texas.[1]

The uprising stemmed from the efforts of a European American entrepreneur to stake a claim near San Elizario on salt deposits that the people of the region had long considered community property on the basis of old grants made by the Spanish government.[2] In the 1850s a similar dispute had arisen at the Salina de Andres, a salt deposit in New Mexico some 70 miles from El Paso, when Texas resident James Magoffin confiscated salt, carts, and oxen belonging to residents of Dona Ana County on their return home from the site. In both the San Andres and the San Elizario cases Mexicans from the El Paso–Paso del Norte area and other towns in Chihuahua had helped to build roads to the deposits, mined the sites, and ignored what they considered outrageous attempts on the part of outsiders to appropriate the deposits and charge for the salt. The intrusion of the European American entrepreneurs seriously affected the welfare of the border community and intensified racial animosities that had existed since the U.S. invasion of the area in 1846.[3]

Just as the local people from both sides of the border had worked jointly to mine the salt deposits, so they stuck together during San Elizario's uprising of 1877. "The inhabitants of the adjacent towns on both sides of the river . . . are intimately connected by the bonds of a common faith, like sympathies and tastes, and are related in numerous instances by marriage," reported the board appointed by the president of the United States to investigate the rebellion. "Hence each would naturally support and defend the other, if occasions . . . demanded their aid, to any sacrifice." The strength of the bonds across the border is evidenced by the participation of some 150–200 Mexicans from south of the river in the disturbance. The importance of the latter's role is illustrated by the fact that the members of the squad who executed three European Americans identified by the rebels as the principal culprits in the controversy were all from Mexico. Further, the people from the Mexican side not only gave sanctuary to scores of tejanos branded as "rioters" but ignored repeated pleas from U.S. authorities to extradite seventeen self-exiled Mexican Americans accused of various "crimes" during the uprising.[4]

Various witnesses testified before the investigating board that the uprising was motivated not only by the salt issue but also by resentment of European American authority in the area. One letter signed by six European Americans and three Mexicans from San Elizario stated that local sheriff Charles Kerber had "been treated with cool contempt" when he had tried to collect state and county taxes and that "the mob" had cried that "they had been fooled long enough, that . . . they had no use for . . . the American government." Another letter signed by the same six European Americans reported that "armed men promenaded the town, shooting and crying 'Death to the Gringos.'" One deputy sheriff wrote that among the threatening cries uttered by the insurgents was the following: "Death to all white men [who] . . . try to uphold the laws of the State of Texas or of the United States." Other witnesses repeatedly emphasized that if U.S. troops were not sent to the area, the lives of all European Americans would be in danger. "It seems that we have no claims on our government and we have to give up all our property for the sake of a lot of greasers [sic]," wrote Sheriff Kerber in a moment of despair over what he considered to be too slow a response by the U.S. government to the local crisis.[5]

An important lesson taught by the San Elizario incident was that the border had little meaning for Mexicans of the Rio Grande region. "The people on the left bank of the river were supposed to be American citizens and their cousins a hundred feet away on the other side of a sometimes nonexistent stream were supposed to be Mexicans," writes C. L. Sonnichsen. "Most of them paid no attention. They and their ancestors had passed and repassed the river at their pleasure for ten generations, and the idea of a 'boundary' set up by a handful of gringos who had moved in only twenty-five years before was a little comic."[6] Fundamentally, it was that prevailing sentiment among the border Mexicans that kept authorities from ever punishing the "rioters" or the European Americans who lost property from recovering their losses. Without the cooperation of the people from the Mexican side, who not only sympathized with the insurgents but harbored them, U.S. officials could do nothing except establish Fort Bliss as a permanent military installation at El Paso to guard against recurrence of similar incidents in the future.

Ethnic confrontations, which declined somewhat at the turn of the century, resurfaced with great force during the 1910s, when the Mexican Revolution created extremely unsettled conditions along the 2,000-mile border separating the two nations. Not only did Mexico's civil unrest bring injury and property loss to European Americans who lived south of the boundary, but the ferment also spilled over into Texas, New Mexico, Arizona, and California, spawning a strong reaction among the European American border population. The unstable climate set the stage for repeated incursions of Mexican revolutionaries and bandits into U.S. territory and punitive or "defensive" movements by U.S. troops into Mexico. Such events produced repeated violent incidents along the entire border and added to the existing anti-Mexican hysteria in the United States. The most tragic clashes occurred in 1915–16 in the Lower Rio Grande Valley when adherents to the "Plan de San Diego," a document that called for Mexican insurgency in the Southwest, repeatedly raided Texas settlements.[7]

With the end of the Mexican Revolution in 1920 the nature of ethnic relations changed. Deep-seated differences continued to exist, and racial confrontations surfaced from time to time, but large-scale violent encounters, the pattern during preceding generations, became less common. Perhaps the single most important factor that accounts for this transformation was that threats to national sovereignty ceased to be a major issue between Mexico and the United States, causing the border area to shed its traditional role as a staging ground for imperialistic invasions, unlawful incursions, Indian depredations, bandit raids, and other confrontational activity. The disappearance of armed movements in the binational frontier zone diminished significantly the intense nationalistic feelings aroused in previous years that frequently carried over into the sphere of ethnic relations. Population growth and the onset of modernization in the border region also helped to ease tensions by reducing the ill effects of geographic isolation. Overt frontier lawlessness gave way to more subtle and "acceptable" forms of conflict, bringing forth a significant decrease of incidents that could flare up into serious disorderliness.

Psychological Dimensions of the Mexican American Border Experience: The Nineteenth Century

The Mexicans who became part of the United States through annexation had considerable problems adjusting to a European American–imposed social and cultural system fundamentally different from their own way of life. The new political order offered the freedom, personal security, and economic prosperity they had not known under Spanish or Mexican rule, but those lofty promises failed to materialize. Instead, the status of Mexicans in U.S. society became one of conquered subjects and foreigners in their own homeland. They found themselves pressed on one side by the European American conquerors and restricted on the other by a border that legally and symbolically disjoined them from their Mexican roots.

The dilemma of these people is poignantly illustrated by the experience of tejanos/as, those Mexicans who found themselves within the jurisdiction of what became the Republic of Texas. When the Texas independence movement broke out, tejanos/as had to choose between the rebellion and loyalty to Mexico. Another alternative for them was neutrality, and it is apparent that the overwhelming majority of tejanos/as chose this course, hoping that non-alignment would spare them from the ravages of war. Yet neither neutrality nor alliance with one side or the other shielded them from the unfortunate fate that befalls frontier ethnic or racial minorities trapped in conflict-ridden zones created by altered borders.

European Americans deeply distrusted the loyalty of the tejanos/as, despite the presence of men like Lorenzo de Zavala and Juan Seguín in prominent positions in the rebel army and government. Some European American leaders, fearing that tejanos/as, Indians, and black slaves would form an alliance against them, called for the occupation of tejano/a settlements suspected of Mexican sympathies, and others urged the segregation of tejanos from "white men" in the military ranks. Neutral Mexicans were often seen as enemies, as exemplified by an order given by the European American mayor of Nacogdoches to all able-bodied tejanos to join the rebel army or leave Texas.[8]

European American ambivalence toward tejanos/as was reflected in official documents of the Texas Republic. On the one hand, the Texas Constitution of 1836 guaranteed tejanos/as equal rights along with the rest of the population, but the Texas Declaration of Independence had concluded that Mexicans in general were "unfit to be free, and incapable of self-government." The contradiction in the two documents could only be resolved by viewing tejanos/as completely apart from Mexicans who lived south of the Rio Grande, where political instability prevailed, but few European Americans could or would consciously draw that distinction. To them, Mexicans were Mexicans, adversaries of the European American population and likely enemies of the Texas Republic.[9]

Such attitudes bred intense persecution, particularly during periods of heightened conflict between Texas and Mexico. For example, following the battle of San Jacinto, tejanos/as in large numbers were driven from the towns of Victoria and Goliad. In the early 1840s many tejano/a families left San Antonio to avoid continued harassment by European American mobs and also to escape expected battles between Mexican troops and Texan forces. During a period of relative calm they returned to their homes but had to face an unfriendly European American reception. Many refugees from towns such as Victoria, San Patricio, Nacogdoches, and Goliad found their lands occupied by European American squatters, who felt these migrants had forfeited their right to the land by failing to fight for the insurrection.[10] Under these circumstances the tejanos/as had little hope of recovering their lands.

Tejanos/as had little room to maneuver within the dilemma that afflicted them during those difficult years. The European Americans demanded that they support the movement for independence, yet even those tejanos/as who did precisely that could not be free from problems with the arrogant and suspicious Texans. On the other hand, Mexico also expected the tejanos/as' loyalty, but the frequently insolent and abusive conduct of the Mexican soldiers seriously undermined sympathies for the motherland. Several incidents illustrate the tejanos/as' difficult position of being subjected to this dual jeopardy. In 1835 Mexican troops disarmed and mistreated residents of Goliad; the following year European Americans plundered the town, forcing many to flee. The people of Nacogdoches endured repeated thefts from both sides. On one occasion Juan Seguín's ranch in San Antonio was robbed by Mexican troops, only to be burned the next year by European Americans. Victoria resident Fernando de León, a supporter of the republic, suffered arrests from both sides in 1835 and 1836, each time for allegedly "conspiring" with the enemy.[11] At least one Texas newspaper understood the predicament faced by the tejanos/as, observing that although these people lived on the frontier, ever exposed to attacks by Mexican troops, they received "no protection from our government," thereby being "compelled to temporize with both parties, or be subjected to the insults and depredations of each."[12]

It is unfortunate that few tejano/a documents are available that elucidate the feelings of this group regarding their dilemma. Juan Seguín, one of the few whose writings survive, left us a brief but revealing memoir. As someone made to feel "a foreigner in my native land," his story vividly illustrates the painful ambivalence felt by those who fought alongside the European Americans against Mexico, only to discover later that the new masters of Texas had nothing but contempt for the tejano/a way of life. Reflecting on the intolerable conditions that had forced him to seek exile in Mexico after his distinguished service in the Texas rebellion, Seguín wrote in 1858: "I embraced the cause of Texas[,] . . . filled an honorable situation in the ranks of the conquerors of San Jacinto, and was a member of the legislative body of the Republic. I now find myself, in the very land, which in other times bestowed on me such bright and repeated evidences of trust and esteem, exposed to the attack of . . . enemies . . . who . . . engender strife [and] falsify historical facts." Seguín lamented the treatment received by his fellow tejanos/as at the hands of European American ruffians and the enmity thrust upon him for coming to their defense.

> At every hour of the day and night, my countrymen ran to me for protection. . . . Sometimes . . . force had to be resorted to. How could I have done otherwise? Were not the victims my own countrymen, friends and associates? Could I leave them defenseless, exposed to the assaults of foreigners, who, on the pretext that they were Mexicans, treated them worse than brutes?
>
> Could I be expected to stoically endure their outrages and insults? Crushed by sorrow, convinced that my death alone would satisfy my enemies, I

sought shelter amongst those against whom I had fought [Mexicans]. I separated from my country, parents, family, relatives and friends, and what was more, from the institutions, on behalf of which I had drawn my sword, with an earnest wish to see Texans free and happy.

I had to leave Texas, abandon all, for which I fought and spent my fortune. . . . Unable any longer to suffer the persecutions of some ungrateful Americans, who strove to murder me, I had determined to free my family and friends from their continual misery on my account, and go live peaceably in Mexico. For these reasons I resigned my office [as mayor of San Antonio], with all my privileges and honors as a Texan.[13]

Seguín's treatment by European Americans is in sharp contrast with that accorded José Antonio Navarro, another prominent tejano who, unlike Seguín, never deviated from his staunch support for Texas and militant opposition to Mexico. Coincidentally, both men left Texas in the early 1840s, but for very different reasons. Seguín sought asylum in Mexico when he could no longer function in a European American–dominated environment. Once in Mexican territory he was arrested and given the choice of staying behind bars or fighting on the side of Mexico. Caught between a sword and a rock wall, Seguín decided to join the Mexican forces, a choice that intensified the wrath against him among European Americans. Navarro also became a prisoner of the Mexicans, but his arrest resulted from participation in the attempted Texan invasion of New Mexico in 1841, commonly known as the Santa Fe Expedition. Unlike the other prisoners of that expeditionary force, Navarro was given an extended prison term and singled out for cruel treatment. That was the price paid by those tejanos/as who chose to collaborate actively with the European American insurgents against the mother country. Navarro's sufferings and staunch support for Texas independence brought sympathy and admiration from European Americans, and when he returned to his homeland in 1845 following an escape while on parole in Veracruz he received a hero's welcome. Meanwhile, Seguín led other tejano/a exiles like himself against the Texan rebels. Later he served as a scout and guerrilla fighter on Mexico's side during the U.S.–Mexico War of 1846–48, after which he left military service and decided to take his chances by returning to his native Texas. Although scorned by those who considered him a traitor, Seguín was nonetheless permitted to live out his life quietly in the land of his birth.[14]

The racial strife engendered by the Texas rebellion was greatly exacerbated by the U.S.–Mexico War. Victory by the United States opened the way for European American immigration into southern Texas, but tejanos/as managed to maintain numerical superiority in the Lower Rio Grande Valley, an area that remained isolated for several decades. Greater numbers in the valley, however, did not prevent the subordination of tejanos/as to the newcomers, although numerical majority did allow greater opportunities to maintain

Mexican culture and traditional community institutions than in the interior of the state. The close proximity to Mexico also permitted the valley tejanos/as to retain intimate economic and social ties with fellow Mexicans south of the river, many of whom had relatives on the U.S. side. Since initial colonization of the area by the Spaniards in the eighteenth century, the settlements on both sides of the Rio Grande had developed as closely interdependent units within a relatively self-sufficient and independent-minded regional society. The establishment of the new boundary brought some disruption to that traditional integration, but the fundamental links uniting the two peoples remained fairly intact.

That is not to say that valley tejanos/as identified with Mexico politically. It seems apparent that they had little desire to be part of Mexico, and it is fairly certain that they had great ambivalence about being a part of the Texas Republic. As frontiersmen long isolated by distance, geography, and governmental neglect, the people of the valley on both sides identified primarily with their immediate surroundings. Residents on the Texas side of the river had no choice, however, but to recognize the political reality that resulted from the events of the 1830s and 1840s. The river that had been their lifeline for nearly a century had been imposed as a line of demarcation between the two nations, and that fact necessitated a new political orientation for those settlers who lived on the north bank. Yet culturally and socially, the new border made little difference for most valley tejanos/as, for they held on to their traditional lifestyle. If, politically, valley tejanos/as had to think of themselves as part of the United States, in many other ways they continued to identify with Mexico. Nationality, customs, kinship, and traditions bound them to the motherland, and it was only natural that they saw themselves as an extension of the population that lived in the Tamaulipas border frontier.[15]

One of the strongest bonds linking the Mexicans of the transborder Lower Rio Grande Valley was the need to defend themselves against the oppression of the European Americans. That harsh reality created a feeling of solidarity that transcended the boundary, bringing a measure of security and assertiveness to valley tejanos/as not found among their outnumbered compatriots to the north. The presence of the border itself placed valley tejanos/as in a better position to resist with greater intensity and determination the abuses of the newcomers, for moral and material support was readily available nearby, *al otro lado* (on the other side). In the worst cases, sanctuary from European American persecution could always be found in Mexico.

The spirit of valley resistance to external domination is well illustrated by the struggle led by Juan Nepomucena Cortina in 1859–60 in the Brownsville-Matamoros area. Assisted by hundreds of tejanos/as and volunteers from Tamaulipas, Cortina fought a "war" against Texas Rangers and U.S. troops that resulted in some 250 deaths and damages in the thousands of dollars. The mistreatment of a former family servant and the hanging of a friend served as Cortina's immediate motive for striking against the European Americans, but that personal grievance made up only a part of the set of outrages he had seen committed against tejanos/as. As a young man he had been a member of a local irregular force that helped the Mexican military attempt to repel the U.S. invasion of the valley in 1846. Important battles were fought near his home, and atrocities were committed in nearby settlements. The memory of the war and the continuous despoliation of tejanos/as thus contributed to his animosity toward European Americans. One especially troublesome point of contention in the valley, as elsewhere, was the aggressiveness and duplicity of newly arrived settlers in seeking to obtain land that had belonged to the local people for generations, some even dating to Spanish colonial days. Cortina's own family encountered problems holding on to their land in the Brownsville area.[16]

Cortina did not seek to drive the newcomers from the region or to overthrow their governmental authority. Thus he was not a revolutionary or a separatist, although as a young man he had been exposed to the sentiment for regional separatism that developed in his native Tamaulipas against Mexico's central government. Possessed of an adventurous spirit, Cortina took part in José María Carvajal's movement to establish the "Republic of Sierra Madre" in the early 1850s.[17]

At the height of his quarrel with European American authorities Cortina issued a series of proclamations that revealed his disillusionment with Texas, a land that had betrayed those who, like his family, had chosen to remain on the U.S. side with the hope of enjoying peace, freedom, and equality. Cortina's mother became a U.S. citizen in 1849, but whether her famous son followed suit is not entirely clear. Several pieces of evidence support the view that he did indeed take on U.S. citizenship. Because Cortina lived in Texas for several years before and after the signing of the Treaty of Guadalupe Hidalgo, a document that had bestowed U.S. citizenship within a year to Mexicans who chose to remain north of the boundary, it seems logical that he was one of those people so affected. Most of Brownsville's residents seem to have considered him a U.S. citizen, judging from references to him in the legal case that followed the raid of 1859. The Mexican Claims Commission that investigated conditions along the border in the 1870s denied Mexico's responsibility for Cortina's actions based on the premise that he was a U.S. citizen. Finally, Cortina's own comments regarding democratic ideals and equality of opportunity that supposedly flowed from the U.S. Constitution imply that he viewed himself as a U.S. citizen at the time of the raid, although in later life he opted for Mexican citizenship.[18]

Despite his problems with European Americans, Cortina had faith in the U.S. government and expressed a desire to make it work for all the people, particularly tejanos/as. He blamed a few evil and abusive men for the plight of his countrymen and, at one point, expressed hope that the newly elected governor, Sam Houston, would restore justice in Texas.[19] Cortina's sense of betrayal in the land that had promised freedom for Mexicans and his anguish toward Mexico are revealed in one of his proclamations to his fellow tejanos/as:

> The ills that weigh upon the unfortunate Republic of Mexico have obliged us for many heart touching causes to abandon it [Mexico] and our possession. . . . Ever diligent and industrious, and desirous of enjoying the longed for boon of liberty . . . we induced to naturalize ourselves in [the United States,] . . . flattered by the bright and peaceful prospect of living therein and inculcating in the bosoms of our children a feeling of gratitude towards a country beneath whose aegis we would have wrought their felicity and contributed with our conduct to give evidence to the whole world that all the aspirations of the Mexicans are confined to one only, *that of being freemen.*

> Having secured this ourselves, those of the old country, not withstanding their misfortunes, might have nothing to regret save the loss of a section of territory [the lands ceded to the United States in 1848], but with the sweet satisfaction that their old fellow citizens lived therein, enjoying tranquility. . . . All has been but the baseless fabric of a dream, and our hopes having been defrauded in the most cruel manner in which disappointment can strike, there can be found no other solution to our problem than to make one effort, and at one blow destroy the obstacles to our prosperity.[20]

Certain behavioral patterns in the life of Cortina exemplify the ambivalence and contradictions that many tejanos/as and other Mexican Americans had to confront in the United States. Cortina and other members of the upper classes who normally distanced themselves from those socially beneath them sometimes found themselves defending the interests of the poor in the face of European American oppression. As in other nations, in Mexican society it was rare for a person of means to side with the downtrodden. Along the border, however, strong nationalistic sentiments at times prompted the affluent to champion the cause of their humble countrymen who suffered mistreatment and exploitation at the hands of the hated gringos/as. Injury inflicted by a foreigner to any Mexican, regardless of his or her class standing, stirred strong feelings of ethnic solidarity. Group honor demanded counteraction, at the very least expressing indignation or filing formal protests against the perpetrators of the offenses. Cortina was one of those affluent fronterizos/as so outraged by the actions of oppressive European Americans that he chose violence as the way to strike back. Little evidence exists that Cortina had an ideological affinity with the class interests of the dispossessed; rather, he seems to have been motivated by ethnic unity, regional loyalty, a sense of social justice, youthful restlessness, and frontier adventurism.

Cortina's ability to function in various spheres of border society constitutes one of the most fascinating aspects of his life. His family background allowed him to move freely in upper-class circles, whereas his struggle against the gringos/as, coupled with his Robin Hood reputation, endeared him to the working class. Throughout much of his adult life he operated outside the law on both sides of the border; yet in the eyes of Mexican authorities the tension-filled frontier environment in which he lived mitigated his errant behavior, thus permitting Cortina to hold impressive positions in Mexico such as lawman, government official, and military leader.

Cortina was a man of remarkable leadership abilities whose natural constituency was the Mexican border population. However, he could not represent their interests in the assertive style that he preferred without placing himself in a state of limbo vis-à-vis the Texas power structure as well as the Mexican government. Thus his future as a leader lay not in Texas, where he was needed but where he could not function, but in Mexico, where his talents and passions for leadership could find full expression. Tejanos who had occupied privileged positions during earlier eras, when Spain and Mexico had governed Texas, found it especially difficult to accept their subordinated status under the European American system. Some, including Cortina, recognized the futility of attempting to rise to positions of leadership in Texas. Mexico was a troubled land, but it placed no racial or cultural barriers for strong-willed, capable men from the elite sector who wanted to rise to positions of power.

Cortina's decision to leave Texas gave him an opportunity to function outside of the troubled border area and helped him make the notable transition into the world of politicians and high-ranking soldiers in the state of Tamaulipas. Yet long after he had assumed a "respectable" life, suspicions remained that he continued in his old ways, engaging in unlawful activities such as cattle rustling. Eventually, those accusations bore fruit for his enemies. In 1875 Mexican officials jailed him for suspected theft and later exiled him to Mexico City, effectively removing him from the border region. In 1890 he returned to the border for a visit and was given a hero's welcome by the people who remembered him as a defender of Mexican rights.[21]

Identity and Language

Cortina and Seguín are examples of border Mexican Americans who took extreme measures to deal with the disruption in their lives brought on by the imposition of the international boundary. Variations of the same ambivalence that troubled these two leaders have disturbed most U.S. Mexicans since the mid-nineteenth century. Chicanos/as long have struggled for acceptance in the United States, often at the price of denying their heritage. This behavior is well illustrated by the rejection of the term "Mexican" by many within the group. Such repudiation stems from the decidedly negative connotation "Mexican" has had in the United States. Some early-nineteenth-century European Americans and especially Texans in the border region labeled Mexicans as "half-breeds," "intellectually inferior," "indolent," "dishonest," "immoral," "treacherous," and "backward." Such unflattering descriptors were routinely used in early newspapers, magazines, and books. Later, movies and television continued the tradition of using popular stereotypes and racist caricatures to portray Mexicans and Mexican Americans. These characterizations became firmly etched in the European American mind, continuing even to the present day.[22]

Under such circumstances many Mexican Americans along the border and elsewhere sought to establish some distance between themselves and their Mexican roots, particularly when interacting with European Americans. By blurring, minimizing, or obliterating their Mexican genetic and cultural inheritance Mexican Americans discovered that they received better treatment from members of the dominant society. Thus began the practice of passing as "Spanish" rather than "Mexican." By calling themselves "Spanish," defensive Mexican Americans "purified" their blood, "whitened" their appearance, and "Europeanized" their heritage. Later, other terms such as "Latin" and, more recently, "Hispanic" were also used as substitutes for "Mexican."[23] (By contrast, young activists in the 1960s demonstrated their pride in being Mexican by adopting "Chicano/a," a derivative of mexicano/a, as their preferred self-referent term.)

The tendency to avoid association with the term "Mexican" is evident in the names chosen for community organizations. For example, the largest Mexican American organization in the country chose to call itself the League of United Latin American Citizens (LULAC). LULAC emerged in 1929 from a unity meeting involving several Mexican American groups that did not use the term "Mexican" to identify their organizations: the League of Latin American Citizens, the Knights of America, and the Order of the Sons of America. It is also significant that LULAC was born in Corpus Christi, not far from the border, in an area known for its extreme anti-Mexican sentiment. Other visible organizations established during the World War II period such as the Community Service Organization, the American GI Forum, and the Political Association of Spanish-Speaking Organizations carried on the tradition of avoiding the label "Mexican."

It was only in the late 1950s and 1960s that "Mexican American" began to appear in names given to community and political organizations. By then racial discrimination in the United States had softened, and Mexican Americans had become a less oppressed group. Awareness that the true heritage of the group came from Mexico rather than from Spain had increased, easing the acceptance of a self-identifier like Mexican American. Better educated and more experienced leaders did not hesitate to assert themselves before the European American establishment. Thus a political group in California formed the Mexican American Political Association in 1959, students established the United Mexican American Students in the late 1960s, and tejano/a activists created the Mexican American Democrats in the 1970s. Nonetheless, the rejection of "Mexican" was still widespread among Mexican Americans.

Regardless of the milder racial climate, negative images, distorted perceptions, and destructive stereotypes toward Mexicans and Mexican Americans remained very strong in the U.S. mainstream culture, causing large numbers of people of Mexican background to jump at the opportunity to adopt "less offensive" labels. By the 1980s the term "Hispanic" had become widely accepted throughout the United States, and it quickly caught on in the Mexican American community as well.

The ambivalence mirrored in the use of varied self-referent terminology is also reflected in uncertainty over language. Historically, Chicanos/as have struggled to have the dominant culture recognize Spanish as a functional language in the Southwest and especially along the border, where the interaction with Mexico is intense. The view of the dominant society—that to be Mexican is to be inferior—has extended to language as well: speakers of Spanish have been perceived as inferior to speakers of English.

Until the 1960s it was common for children to be punished in schools for speaking Spanish. School officials pointed to the need to learn English as the reason for inflicting sanctions, but to Spanish-speaking students the message was a devastating one: using Spanish and practicing or exhibiting Mexican cultural traits were negative forms of behavior that should be eliminated. Outside of the schools that message was reinforced with negative characterizations of Mexicans in U.S. popular culture. Consequently, generations of Mexican American children grew up confused about and ashamed of their heritage, causing serious damage to their self-esteem and personal pride.

The advent of bilingual education in the 1970s introduced a more enlightened approach to the education of Spanish-speaking children. The program, however, has suffered from many problems, including insufficient resources, teacher shortages, inadequate training of teachers, improper use of teaching techniques, and hostility on the part of the European American majority. Bilingual education quickly became one of the most controversial issues in the borderlands, deeply dividing the Mexican American and European American communities. As public debate escalated, opponents of bilingual education in California and Arizona took the issue directly to the ballot box. By a 62 percent majority Californians voted in 1998 to end bilingual education in their state by passing Proposition 227, and 63 percent of Arizonans did likewise in 2000 by approving Proposition 203. Supporters of bilingual education have challenged these decisions in the courts, and, in the case of California, many students have continued to receive instruction in bilingual classrooms. But there is no question that Propositions 227 and 203 have seriously damaged bilingual education not only in California and Arizona but throughout the country.

Opposition to bilingual education goes hand in hand with efforts to make English the "official" language of the United States. Groups such as U.S. English and English First have campaigned hard to convince the U.S. public that the use of languages other than English fosters fragmentation in the country and threatens future political stability. By the mid-1980s twelve states, led by California, had declared English as their official language, sending a message to Hispanics and other language minority groups that they should rid themselves of their native tongues as quickly as possible. By 2002 twenty-three states had adopted Official English laws. In Arizona, following unsuccessful attempts to enact a law through the legislature, in 1988 the voters passed a constitutional amendment that declared English as the official language. However, in 1999 the U.S. Supreme Court ruled the Arizona initiative unconstitutional. Proposals to pass Official English laws in the legislatures of Texas and New Mexico have failed.

For border Mexican Americans the official end of bilingual education and the increasing militancy of Official English proponents is unsettling because Spanish (not to mention Indian languages) is the native language in the region. It has been spoken for centuries, and, because of the continuing symbiosis with the Mexican side of the border, it will remain a very functional and even necessary language, probably forever. Many opposed to the "English only" initiatives feel they are deliberate campaigns to undermine the development and advancement of Hispanics in the United States. There is, however, divided opinion among Mexican Americans on this issue. A significant percentage in the U.S. border states actually favors the declaration of English as the official language of the country. But it is far from certain whether the Mexican American community at large fully understands the negative educational and legal implications of such an action.

Other Border-Related Dilemmas

During their long struggle to become full participants in U.S. society, Chicanos/as have often questioned whether there is a place for them in the United States other than at the bottom of the social order. There have been times when European American hostility and rejection have actually driven large numbers of Mexicans back to Mexico, as evidenced by the migrations southward across the border of approximately three thousand New Mexicans and tejanos/as between 1848 and 1850; about ten thousand Sonorans during the California gold rush period; and, in the best-known movement of all, between 500,000 and a million Mexicans from throughout the United States during the Great Depression. In addition, countless individuals seeking refuge for a variety of reasons have made the trek southward before and since those larger movements.

Yet it is highly significant that for most of those displaced people the stay south of the border has been a short one. Few have made Mexico their permanent home, opting for an eventual return to the United States. What is more, they have been joined in their northward journey by millions of other Mexican nationals with aspirations to greater opportunity than they have enjoyed in their own country. The inescapable conclusion is that whatever the degree of antagonism, rejection, and marginalization found north of the border, life has been better in the United States than in Mexico.

The forces that have driven masses of Mexicans across the border have also conditioned and shaped their attitudes toward their homeland, their adoptive society, and the border itself. Above all, Mexicans have come to see the boundary as an escape valve for poverty and lack of economic opportunity in Mexico. Therein lies one of the most acute dilemmas that has confronted the Chicano/a community.

Mexican Americans have long been deeply troubled over the issues of migration from Mexico to the United States. As products of the process themselves, they naturally feel deep sympathy toward poor Mexicans who cross the border in search of economic opportunity. Chicanos/as directly extend the immigrants a helping hand, following a universal tradition of compassion toward foreigners who find themselves in a strange land. On the other hand, many Chicanos/as, just like other sectors of U.S. society, have questioned whether the United States has reached the saturation point with regard to immigration. At the border that concern has existed for many years, along with the related objection to the U.S. policy that permits green card commuters (Mexicans who have U.S. residency status) to live in Mexico and work in U.S. border cities. Labor unions, made up and led predominantly by Mexican Americans, have been particularly vocal in their demands to have the green card system eliminated and to close the border to the undocumented traffic.

Border labor leaders have long argued that both legal and illegal commuters depress U.S. wage scales, increase unemployment, serve as strikebreakers, and make union organizing and maintenance difficult. The struggle of the unions to force "green carders" to move to the United States led to hearings by the U.S. Select Commission on Western Hemisphere Immigration in 1968, to unsuccessful restrictive legislation introduced by Senator Edward Kennedy, and finally to a U.S. Supreme Court decision in 1974 that legalized the alien commuter program.[24] After the Supreme Court ruling the unions focused their attention on restricting the flow of undocumented workers. In 1974 Mexican American labor leaders in El Paso applauded a periodic U.S. Immigration Service crackdown on Mexican nationals who worked illegally in the United States. "It is about time something was done to keep illegal aliens from taking our jobs," stated Vice President Martin Reyes of the El Paso Building Trades Association. "For too long we have been at a disadvantage. Only eight percent of the jobs in El Paso are done with union labor."[25] A decade later border union leaders sought passage of legislation that would impose penalties on employers who hired undocumented workers. In part because of union lobbying efforts, the long-debated Simpson-Rodino Bill finally became law in 1986, ushering in a new era of immigration control in the United States. The landmark legislation, known as the Immigration Reform and Control Act, combined employer sanctions with other strong measures designed to curb the migrant flow and at the same time granted amnesty to undocumented immigrants who had lived in the United States continuously since January 1, 1982. In the 1990s the U.S. Border Patrol initiated blockades in urban areas along the border, and the U.S. Congress passed legislation that curtailed benefits for legal immigrants and exposed them to deportation if they ran afoul of the law. At the state level, California voters passed an anti-immigrant initiative in 1994, and Arizona followed suit in 2004.

The chronic debate over the immigration issue clearly reveals the divisions in the Mexican American community. Across the nation Hispanic politicians and middle-class organizations like LULAC, the National Council of La Raza, and the Mexican American Legal Educational Defense Fund strongly raised their voices in opposition to restrictive legislation in the U.S. Congress, border blockades, and anti-immigrant voter initiatives. At the grass-roots level, however, restrictionists have found considerable Hispanic support for tough immigration legislation to include sanctions against employers who hire undocumented workers. The discrepancy between the views of Hispanic leaders and the Hispanic population at large is to some extent explained by economics: the political leadership and the activist organizations are made up largely of businesspersons and professionals who face no direct threat from the presence of undocumented persons. On the other hand, working-class persons, who predominate in the Hispanic population, must compete to a certain degree with the immigrants; consequently, many feel more inclined toward restrictive policies.

The divided views of Chicanos/as toward Mexican immigrants is very much related to their ambivalence toward Mexico itself. Even in the frontier days of the early nineteenth century the people of Mexico's far north held mixed perceptions about the motherland. Culturally, they very much identified with their Mexican heritage, but their political allegiance was weak, and their criticism of policies formulated in Mexico City was strong. The waves of immigrants who have come from Mexico into the United States since the mid-nineteenth century have adopted similar outlooks. For them the border has come to represent a line that separates progress from backwardness, order from chaos, lawfulness from lawlessness, honesty from corruption, and democracy from domination by a privileged few.

Recurring economic and political crises in Mexico during the last century have caused Mexicans on both sides of the border to question the ability of Mexican leaders to solve that nation's problems. Cynicism toward the governmental apparatus grew to alarming proportions in the 1980s and 1990s because of Mexico's deep financial meltdowns and blatant fraud in the electoral process.

Mexican currency, reflecting the condition of the country's economy, has often been seen as the symbol of failure, especially along the border. Immigrants have close familiarity with changes in the value of the peso in relation to the dollar, for countless devaluations have occurred since the peso equaled the dollar in worth back in the 1880s. It is those devaluations that prompted many workers to leave Mexico in search of the life that accompanies the earning of U.S. dollars. Along the border Mexican Americans have laughed right along with European Americans when jokes are made about "no pesos accepted here."[26] Denigration of Mexican currency is often accompanied by expressions that imply contempt and pity for Mexico, a country said to be so riddled with inefficiency, incompetence, and corruption that it has failed to take advantage of unique opportunities to profit greatly from its vast oil resources. Instead, in the last quarter century on two occasions it created for itself disastrous economic collapses and allowed a disturbing rise in the nation's poverty rate.[27]

Consistent with prevailing views on both sides of the border, Mexican Americans relate Mexico's economic failures to atrocious government, particularly at the federal level. The political system imposed by the Partido Revolucionario Institucional (PRI), Mexico's ruling party between 1929 and 2000, was seen as undemocratic and corrupt. The heavy-handed manner in which the PRI maintained itself in power disgusted many Chicanos/as, and some publicly criticized the ruling party.[28] This departure from the traditional practice of not saying negative things about Mexico openly in the United States derived from the massive fraud observed in a number of elections, especially the Chihuahua election of 1986 and the national election of 1988. Interestingly, attitudes toward Mexico's political system have moderated since the opposition Partido Acción Nacional (PAN) rose to national power in the 2000 historic transparent election. But prevailing views remain exceedingly negative.

The important point for this discussion is that the unfavorable image of the Mexican political system is one more burden Mexican Americans must carry as they struggle to find acceptance in the United States, a society that has traditionally denigrated their heritage. Of course, people at large in the United States, including Mexican Americans, have always had a very superficial and simplistic understanding of Mexico. While criticisms of the PRI's thwarting of the democratic process have been justified, other unfavorable characterizations of the government and, indeed, of Mexican society in general have been largely based on biases and stereotypes. There is truth to perceptions of Mexican government inefficiency, mismanagement, and corruption, but what government, including that of the United States, is not guilty of such aberrations? In fact, voter irregularities, if not outright fraud, were clearly evident during the 2000 and 2004 U.S. elections, and unabashed duplicity, corruption, incompetence, and fiscal irresponsibility have been in full display during the two George W. Bush administrations. What is not appreciated about Mexico is that historically its political and economic systems have developed within a climate of disadvantageous geographic, demographic, and global forces. The opposite is true of the United States. The United States became superprosperous and superpowerful on the world stage fundamentally because of its great natural advantages. It is unfair to judge Mexico or any other nation by the achievement standards of the United States. Yet norteamericanos/as continue to do precisely that.

Another burden endured by Mexican Americans is the often cool and even hostile treatment encountered when they visit Mexico. Many Mexicans seem to feel that Chicanos/as are in some ways traitors to Mexico, having abandoned the motherland in preference to life in the land of the gringos/as. Mexicans from the middle and upper classes especially see Mexican Americans as people from *campesino/a* (peasant) and working-class backgrounds who, through their assumption of a *pocho/a* (culturally corrupted) style of life, embarrass all Mexicans. Chicanos/as who speak no Spanish are criticized for failing to learn the language of their parents, and those who speak "Spanglish" (a mixture of Spanish and English) draw contemptuous comments for their "mongrelized" mode of expression and "lack of culture." Those who "show off" U.S. clothes, personal articles, or flashy cars while in Mexico are deeply resented for their imitative European American materialism and alleged feelings of superiority toward Mexican nationals.

Despite the rejection from Mexicans and their own ambivalence vis-à-vis Mexico, Mexican Americans have always looked south of the border in their search for identity and cultural pride. During the height of the Chicano/a movement in the 1960s and 1970s it became very popular to study Mexican history, culture, and art. Many young Mexican Americans proudly proclaimed themselves descendants of the Aztecs, followers of Emiliano Zapata and Pancho Villa, and admirers of the great painters Diego Rivera, José Clemente Orozco, and David Alfaro Siqueiros. Pilgrimages to the pyramids and to Mexico City were organized by college groups, and summer study at Mexican universities became fashionable. In a very real sense the outward embracing of Mexico represented a repudiation of U.S. society. After decades of experiencing rejection in the United States, Chicanos/as felt a strong need to identify with their Indian Mexican roots and to show how their heritage was as good as if not superior to that of white Anglo-Saxon Protestants (WASPs).

Although the discovery of Mexican history and culture did much to enhance pride and self-esteem among Chicanos/as, there were certain realities in contemporary Mexican society that deeply disturbed them. They quickly learned that Mexicans generally looked down on Chicanos/as, that the poor in Mexico were even more oppressed than the poor in the United States, and that the pre-2000 Mexican political system left much to be desired. Mexican Americans found it difficult to reconcile the contradictions they observed in Mexico with their negative feelings toward U.S. society. Confusion, disillusionment, and resignation to their condition in the United States were natural consequences of the "back to our roots" experience for many who had romanticized the land of their forebears.[29]

One sector of the Mexican American population with a better understanding of the realities of Mexico consists of leaders of several community organizations, national associations, labor unions, and academia as well as a few elected officials. These spokespeople have sought to establish informal relations with Mexico in recent years. Whatever apprehensions they had about the Mexican government, they recognized an opportunity to derive some benefits from direct contact with Mexican officials. Frustrated by their lack of political power in the United States, this loosely tied group established links with Mexico City both to legitimize their leadership status in the United States and to gain Mexico's support for Chicano/a issues. The contact began in 1971, when the Luis Echeverría administration, sensing the growing political force of Mexican Americans in the United States, initiated a series of meetings to discuss issues of common concern. The Chicano/a leaders responded enthusiastically to that initiative, believing that the U.S. government would have to take notice of their "recognition" by a foreign state and consequently take them more seriously in U.S. domestic politics. Access to the international media in Mexico City provided a means to make Chicano/a problems widely known and to embarrass Washington for its unresponsiveness to the group's needs. Of course, Mexico stood to gain from the Mexican American connection as well. By befriending Chicanos/as, Mexican officials hoped that a sizable pro-Mexican lobby would emerge in the United States, making it much easier for Mexico to negotiate with Washington on issues ranging from immigration and trade to sales of petroleum.[30]

The Mexican American–Mexico relationship, however, involved complications for both parties. Close identification with Mexico risked a severe anti-Chicano/a backlash in the United States, where historically many European Americans have viewed Mexican Americans as less than "true" Americans. Political, social, and economic gains made by Chicanos/as since the 1960s could be jeopardized by possible retaliatory actions against the group by the U.S. government. Mexico risked alienating Washington by appearing to be manipulating a U.S. minority group to promote its interests, some of which appeared to clash sharply with U.S. policies. These considerations, along with serious economic downturns and heated political controversies within Mexico during the 1980s and 1990s, slowed the Mexican American–Mexico relationship. A drastic shift in priorities in Mexico City temporarily relegated the Chicano/a "connection" to low-priority status during the early part of the Miguel de la Madrid administration. Scholarship programs for Chicanos/as to attend Mexican universities, for instance, suffered cutbacks as a direct result of austerity in government spending.

Compared to the 1970s, in recent years the relationship between Mexican Americans and the Mexican government has become rather low key, steering away from any activities that might place Mexico on a collision course with Washington. Mexican presidents have stated explicitly that Mexico will follow its long tradition of avoiding actions that could be interpreted as interfering with U.S. domestic politics. As of 2005, contact with Chicanos/as continued to be maintained through the Instituto de los Mexicanos en el Exterior, an agency of the Secretaría de Relaciones Exteriores. Apart from its interest in promoting educational and cultural ties with Mexican Americans, the institute has increasingly reached out to Mexican nationals in the United States, seeking to assist them with basic problems and protecting their rights.

The underlying reasons behind the efforts of Chicano/a leaders to maintain links with Mexican officials and the often passionate concern of Mexican American youth for cultural identification with Mexico provide further evidence of the enduring ambivalence of the Chicano/a population as an ethnic minority in the United States. In short, because of unique historical, social, and cultural circumstances Mexican Americans have found it very difficult to fit into U.S. society, and because of their physical separation from Mexico they ceased long ago to be a part of Mexican society. Thus Chicanos/as have been a group that fit on neither side of the border, destined to live a defensive lifestyle vis-à-vis both their adoptive society and their country of origin.

Summary and Conclusion
The creation of the U.S.–Mexico border in the mid-nineteenth century separated those Mexicans who lived north of the Rio Grande from the motherland, converting them into an ethnic minority in the United States. Henceforth they would live an "in-between" life, removed from their natural Mexican *ambiente* and unable to function as full participants in U.S. society. Those who lived close to the boundary maintained many social and cultural ties with Mexico, and that provided a measure of security in a hostile environment. Yet by keeping old customs, traditions, and language, border Mexican Americans enlarged the distance that separated them from the European American mainstream.

Another effect of the border for Chicanos/as has been its role in precipitating friction and violence. Conflicts between the United States and Mexico over myriad issues in the region placed the Mexican American border population in an uncomfortable middle ground. Territorial disputes, banditry, irredentism, and revolutionary activity engendered intense nationalism and anti-Mexicanism among the U.S. public, continuously placing people of Mexican origin on the defensive. As border violence subsided, the character of Mexican American–European American relations changed, and the conflict between them became less intense. Nevertheless, generally speaking the two groups have continued to live in separate worlds.

Changing conditions in the borderlands in recent decades have resulted in improvements in the status of Mexican Americans. The region is fast becoming more similar to the U.S. heartland as a result of large-scale migration of capital and people to Sun Belt areas. That has increased economic opportunities for southwestern Hispanics and has sped up the process of integration into the dominant culture. An indication of that trend is the impressive growth of Hispanic political power in the Southwest. Yet the basic pattern of Mexican American ambivalence in regard to the U.S. mainstream remains. Controversial border-related issues like migration, bilingual education, and "English only" movements assure that Chicanos/as will face unsettling dilemmas in their lives for years to come. For border Mexican Americans the psychological consequences of continued separation from the U.S. mainstream and of mixed emotions toward Mexico will remain deep and acute.

5 Norteños/as, Fronterizos/as, and Foreign Dependence

The recession of Mexico's frontier to the Rio Grande in the nineteenth century had far-reaching consequences for the provinces immediately to the south of the new boundary. After the transfer of Texas, New Mexico, and California to the United States the states of Tamaulipas, Nuevo León, Coahuila, Chihuahua, Sonora, and Baja California assumed the role of guardians of Mexico's territorial limits, with the settlements on the Rio Grande constituting the first line of defense against the U.S. menace. Mexicans in the border area faced new challenges emanating from the imposed proximity to the powerful and aggressive nation next door. Economic pressures and unwelcome cultural influences compounded long-standing frontier problems such as isolation and danger from Indian attacks. Enduring remoteness and the ensuing economic orientation toward the United States would place the border region in a unique position with respect to the rest of the republic.

This chapter focuses on the special characteristics of norteños/as and fronterizos/as that serve to distinguish them from their compatriots in other parts of Mexico. Since pronounced regionalism is a basic hallmark of the north, attention is given to tensions between norteños/as and the central government. The trend toward increased external relationships is also examined, with particular attention given to new forms of economic dependence brought on by the emergence of foreign-controlled assembly industries and the enactment of the North American Free Trade Agreement (NAFTA). Finally, U.S. influences on norteño/a lifestyles are assessed in relation to national desires to reduce the process of "de-Mexicanization" perceived to prevail in the border region.

El Norte de México

To understand the heritage of the Mexican borderlands it is important to consider some of the unique features of northern Mexico.[1] Physically, the area is characterized by vast open spaces, rugged mountain terrain, desert lands, and few rivers and lakes. The harsh natural conditions acted as a deterrent to effective colonization from the south for many years, and the border states remained sparsely populated well into the twentieth century. Until the advent of modern transportation the north was practically cut off from the Mexican interior, and population centers in the region itself were isolated from each other.

Different ethnic patterns are also noticeable among norteños/as. Because of the limited Indian population and its strong resistance to assimilation into the Mexican way of life, little *mestizaje* (Spanish-Indian miscegenation) took place in the region. Consequently, norteños/as as a group are more white than their compatriots to the south. The large number of mestizos now found throughout the north are largely a product of recent migrations from the interior. Norteño/a elites are descended to a significant degree from pioneer Spanish and Mexican families who arrived centuries ago.

In contrast to economic tendencies in the interior, ranching and mining dominated the economy of El Norte for many generations, leading to the development of certain occupational patterns that promoted individual and group self-sufficiency, mobility, and independence. Peonage thrived to a lesser degree in the north because of the absence of *encomiendas* (the Spanish system of exacting tribute from Indians) and the less exploitative character of local haciendas (large estates). Agricultural workers also had the option of becoming sharecroppers, thus increasing their independence from hacendados. Vaqueros (cowboys) enjoyed the freedom to move about, seeking the best rancho on which to practice their trade. As in the rural areas, urban norteño/a workers also enjoyed better conditions and higher wages than in the south. In short, traditional patterns of paternalism and rigid control of workers were ameliorated in the north by different environmental and economic circumstances.

Mexicans recognize a norteño/a culture distinct from that of other parts of Mexico. Norteños/as are said to be different in their manner of thinking, speaking, acting, and dressing. A strong spirit of struggle, determination, adaptability, and hard work is attributed to norteños/as because of the harsh conditions traditionally encountered in the region. Additionally, the people of the north have been affected by the modernizing influences of the United States; thus more democratic ideas and institutions are said to have developed in El Norte. Remoteness from the central government in Mexico City has bred regionalism and independence, and norteños/as have demonstrated in a strong way their dissatisfaction with national policies at various points in Mexican history.

In the mid-nineteenth century separatist movements erupted in various northern provinces. The attempts to establish a "Republic of the Rio Grande" in 1839–40 and a "Republic of Sierra Madre" in the early 1850s serve as indicators of the level of dissatisfaction among norteños/as with central authorities. To a degree, the separation of Texas and subsequent loss of New Mexico and California to the United States is explained by chronic local insurgency that weakened Mexico City's control in those provinces. Norteños/as had plenty of reasons to rebel against the federal government, and that made the conquest of the territory in the mid-nineteenth century easier for the United States.

Northern rebelliousness exploded again in the 1910s, when Mexico endured one of the world's great revolutions. Significant events that preceded

the unrest occurred in the northern provinces, and major battles were subsequently fought in countless northern cities. It is fitting that the first important encounter between *federales* and *revolucionarios* took place in the
border town of Ciudad Juárez in May 1911. That battle resulted in the deposing of the dictator Porfirio Díaz and the ascension of Francisco Madero, "the
Apostle of Democracy." Most important, norteños produced the majority
of major leaders who fought in the revolution, and subsequently several of
them became presidents. Apart from Madero, who hailed from Coahuila, other northerners who assumed the highest office in the postrevolutionary years
were Venustiano Carranza (Coahuila), Eulalio Gutiérrez (Coahuila), Roque
González Garza (Coahuila), Adolfo de la Huerta (Sonora), Álvaro Obregón
(Sonora), Plutarco Elías Calles (Sonora), Emilio Portes Gil (Tamaulipas), and
Abelardo Luis Rodríguez (Sonora). The most famous personality of the period, Pancho Villa, was also a norteño (Durango and Chihuahua).

In the early 1980s the north once again sent shock waves throughout
Mexico by rebelling against the Partido Revolucionario Institucional (PRI),
the party in power between 1929 and 2000, in countless local and state elections. Significant losses for the ruling party took place in 1983 in Durango
City, Chihuahua City, and Ciudad Juárez, where the conservative Partido
Acción National (PAN) won the mayorships and city councils of all three
cities. Then in 1985 voters in Ciudad Juárez elected three PAN members to
the federal congress. By the end of that year the PAN had achieved unprecedented power in Chihuahua, the largest Mexican state: it controlled the seven
most important cities and had six state representatives (out of fourteen) and
ten seats in the federal congress. The PAN had also given the PRI a tough
fight in the governor races in Nuevo León and Sonora, but massive electoral
fraud in those states derailed the opposition candidates.[2]

The losses of 1983 and 1985 in the north severely shook the ruling party,
and a decision was made not only to prevent the PAN from winning further
elections but to recover the offices the PRI had lost. This was to be accomplished using whatever means necessary. The opportunity to implement the
hard-line policy came in July 1986 in Chihuahua, where the PRI used ballot
stuffing and other blatantly fraudulent tactics to smother the opposition.[3]
According to the official results announced by the PRI-controlled Chihuahua
electoral college, the PRI overwhelmingly won the governorship, all fourteen
seats in the state legislature, and sixty-five of the sixty-seven mayorships.
The only PAN victory officially recognized was the mayorship of Nuevo
Casas Grandes; the other mayorship (of Valentín Gómez Farías) was awarded
to the leftist Partido Popular Socialista.[4] The people of Chihuahua were expected to believe that the ruling party had suddenly recaptured the support
of the voters after their lopsided repudiation of it throughout the state during
the previous two years.

The PAN and its supporters reacted angrily to the official results, holding
a series of demonstrations, marches, blockades of streets and highways, and

hunger strikes and even picketing President Miguel de la Madrid when he met with President Ronald Reagan in August 1986 at the White House. The depth of the discontent was evident in the size of the demonstrations and the bold takeover of international bridges in Ciudad Juárez–El Paso. One gathering in front of the Ciudad Juárez city hall drew an estimated thirty thousand people, while thousands of protesters occupied the bridges for days at a time on several occasions. For six weeks following the elections the political climate in Ciudad Juárez and Chihuahua City remained extremely tense.[5] In Parral violence erupted in mid-August, including shootings and damage to property, prompting state authorities to issue arrest warrants for the PAN mayor and five other party activists. Feeling that their lives were in danger, they fled to El Paso and asked for political asylum in the United States.[6] Election-related violence also broke out in Piedras Negras, Agua Prieta, Mexicali, and Durango City.

These events triggered unprecedented massive activism among the citizenry, forcing the government to permit the revamping of the electoral system. That ushered in more opposition victories. In 1989 the PAN finally won the governorship of Baja California, and in the 1990s that party not only retained that important post but added the governorships of Chihuahua and Nuevo León. Most dramatic of all, in 2000 PAN candidate Vicente Fox won the presidency, ushering in a new political era in the country. The PRI, forced to relinquish the grip on Mexico that it had held since 1929, also became a minority party in the congress, where the PAN and the leftist Partido Revolucionario Democrático (PRD) together captured a majority of the seats. In regional terms the north, the stronghold of the PAN, achieved unprecedented power in Mexico's new political configuration. Nevertheless, by 2004 the PRI had begun to recover lost ground, winning some important elections at the state and local levels.[7] Clearly, the Mexican political landscape had changed in a fundamental way, with elections becoming transparent and highly competitive. Norteños/as could rightfully take much credit for making that happen.

Why did norteños/as rebel against central authority? The most compelling explanation is the harm caused to the economy of northern Mexico by the national economic collapses of 1982 and 1994. Though norteños/as and other Mexicans realized that recurring declines in oil prices, recessions in the United States, the unexpected withdrawal of investment funds by foreigners, and other unfavorable developments in the international economy had much to do with Mexico's misfortunes, they nonetheless felt that internal political tensions, government mismanagement, and corruption had played significant roles in precipitating and prolonging the crises. The antigovernment reaction was strongest in the north because the area, with its close economic ties to the United States, was the hardest hit by several devastating devaluations of the Mexican currency.

The drop in the value of the peso resulted in a drastic reduction in the purchasing power of norteños/as. Their pesos could no longer buy U.S. products, on which they had long been dependent. To add insult to injury, the central government in 1983 instituted a currency exchange controls program that made it very difficult for norteños/as to transact business with the U.S. side. With the nationalization of the banks in the early 1980s (a decision reversed within a few years), businessmen found it increasingly difficult to carry on normal financial dealings, and, worst of all, capital for investments became very scarce. Consequently, the economy of the north almost came to a standstill, and many people, particularly along the border, found themselves in a near state of panic.

Norteños/as thus expressed their discontent with the central government by voting for the PAN in many towns, cities, and states. It became easier for voters to support the PAN when it moderated its traditional conservative ideology, and the PAN's emphasis on the need for more honest, responsible, and efficient government struck a powerful chord with voters. After holding real power at the state and local levels throughout the north since the 1980s and at the national level since 2000, the PAN had built a record for the voters to judge. In 2004 independent-minded voters in Chihuahua expressed their frustration and dissatisfaction again, this time against the PAN. They reversed years of support for that party by voting for a PRI governor and a PRI mayor in Ciudad Juárez. The turn of events in Chihuahua as well as PRI victories elsewhere in 2004 set the stage for a hotly contested national election in 2006.

The Evolution of Foreign Dependence
While norteños/as have achieved relative self-determination within Mexico's political system, they have not been successful in freeing themselves from pronounced U.S. economic control over their region. The Mexican border states became dependencies of the United States in the late nineteenth century, in particular during the years when Porfirio Díaz held the presidency of Mexico. Díaz encouraged foreign capitalists to look to Mexico for big profits by offering them numerous concessions. European Americans readily answered the call, investing heavily in transportation and mining, two industries that changed the economic character of the north. It was primarily U.S. capital that financed the construction of major railroad lines from the interior to the northern border, making it possible to substantially increase the exportation of Mexican raw materials and labor to the United States and to expand the importation of U.S. manufactured goods into Mexico.

The revitalization of the mining industry during the period is evident in the rise of gold and silver production. In 1877 the value of gold production stood at 1.5 million pesos and that of silver at 24.8 million pesos; by 1908 the figure for gold was 40 million pesos and for silver 85 million pesos. U.S. companies operated large mines in Coahuila, Chihuahua, and Baja California. Most prominent among the foreign concerns were the Guggenheims, who owned mines and smelters throughout the northern states. In Cananea,

Sonora, entrepreneur William Greene ran one of the world's premier copper operations, employing thousands of Mexican workers.[8]

Apart from railroads and mining European Americans also invested in agriculture, ranching, commerce, and urban industries. Numerous U.S.–dominated company towns and colonies sprang up in Baja California, Sonora, and Chihuahua, stimulating economic activity and providing employment for local people. Thus large numbers of Mexicans in the north became directly dependent on foreign capital for their livelihood, and as the years went by many of them determined that their dreams could best be fulfilled working for U.S. companies rather than for Mexican employers.

The reality of pronounced economic dependence on the United States among the people of northern Mexico is best illustrated by the skewed relationship that developed between the Mexican border towns and their counterpart communities across the Rio Grande. Before the conversion of that stream into a boundary, towns such as Matamoros, Reynosa, Mier, Guerrero, and Paso del Norte (now Ciudad Juárez) supported themselves by engaging in agriculture, ranching, and limited regional trade. Isolation had, by necessity, given rise to economic self-sufficiency. After the U.S.–Mexico War of 1846–48 European American entrepreneurs penetrated the border markets with vigor, engendering a dependence on foreign products that would grow steadily as the population of the area increased. Before 1848 local residents could conduct trade northward with only minor impediments, but after the establishment of the new border Mexico applied its tariff laws to goods brought in from across the Rio Grande, an unwanted development that substantially increased the cost of living on the Mexican side. Consequently, many families migrated to nearby U.S. communities. Those who remained on the south bank asked Mexican authorities to allow the duty-free importation of foreign products to prevent further out-migration and to stimulate local commerce. Mexico City responded in the affirmative, but the concessions granted to the border were insufficient to meet local needs, prompting the states of Tamaulipas and Chihuahua in 1858 to establish a *zona libre*, or free trade zone, along their border frontiers. At the time the central government exercised reduced control over its provinces, allowing these states to make these decisions on their own.[9]

Free trade helped fronterizos/as cope with foreign economic competition, but the zona libre was a hotly contested political issue in the interior of Mexico because it was regarded as a regional privilege that created unfair competition for national products. Many Mexican officials also objected to the loss of tariff revenues. In addition, the zona libre aroused the ire of Texas merchants and the U.S. government when commercial activity favored the Mexican side and when smuggling into the United States proved difficult to control. Along the Chihuahua frontier the zona libre was an on-again, off-again proposition for several decades because of frequent changes in government in the state capital. Yet with or without the free trade zone foreign goods penetrated the

Mexican side, for even at times when duties had to be paid these could easily be avoided through the payment of *mordidas* (literally, "bites," or bribes) to customs inspectors. Internal and external pressures induced Mexico to finally abolish the free trade zone in 1905, but the continuing need for tariff exemptions would prompt fronterizos/as to petition repeatedly for its return. Free trade reemerged in Baja California and portions of Sonora in the 1930s as a stimulant to regional economic growth and to entice more Mexicans from the interior to settle on the northern frontier.

In the late 1950s Mexico City conducted studies of spending patterns of border Mexicans and confirmed a growing commercial integration with the U.S. side. A decision was made to promote the consumption of greater quantities of national goods by the border citizenry, and in 1961 the government began a comprehensive program to accomplish that objective. Manufacturers from the interior received tax and transportation incentives to send more of their products to the north. Additionally, modern shopping centers were constructed in the border cities. The results of these initiatives have been mixed. Business activity in the border area increased markedly in the 1960s and 1970s, with a corresponding slowdown of the Mexican "parade" to U.S. stores. Much of the consumption on the Mexican side, however, still involved products imported (legally or illegally) from the United States. Only peso devaluations that drastically cut the purchasing power of the national currency could stop fronterizos/as from patronizing U.S. stores or purchasing foreign goods in Mexican stores.[10]

The foreign-oriented consumption patterns on the border, along with acute job reliance on foreign companies and tourists, underscored the reality of firmly established external economic dependence in the region. Acceptance of that reality led Mexico City to allow more foreign products to enter the border communities without having to pay the usual duties. Then in the 1980s extraordinary pressures wrought by economic crises prompted the Mexican government to adopt a neoliberal strategy for achieving growth on a national level that included lowering tariffs on imported goods and, by the early 1990s, embracing free trade with other countries. Negotiations by Mexico, Canada, and the United States produced in 1993 the watershed pact known as NAFTA, which provided for the elimination of tariffs, some under a short-term schedule and others over the long term. NAFTA also removed traditional obstacles to cross-border trade and business, such as extant barriers to foreign investment. Responding to concerns by labor unions and environmentalists, NAFTA established two commissions and a development bank to deal with worker displacement and pollution problems. However, much to the disappointment of advocates of workers' rights, the agreement did not allow the free flow of labor across the international boundaries of North America.

While NAFTA supporters have proudly emphasized that since the agreement took effect in 1994 a boom in international trade has stimulated growth and created many new jobs in the three countries, critics have focused on various perceived serious negative consequences. U.S. labor unions and their supporters have charged that NAFTA has encouraged more plant closures in the United States and the shift of assembly operations to Mexico. Indeed, a decade after the enactment of NAFTA the U.S. government certified that over five hundred thousand U.S. workers had lost their jobs because of that agreement, while the Economic Policy Institute estimated that number to be closer to eight hundred thousand. El Paso assumed the dubious distinction of being the city in the United States most affected by NAFTA, losing about twenty thousand jobs. In defense, supporters of NAFTA claimed that job gains far surpassed job losses as a result of dynamic growth in the export sector along the border and elsewhere, citing as evidence declining unemployment rates in El Paso and other U.S. border cities. The debate over job statistics mattered little to the thousands of Mexican and Mexican American women in El Paso who experienced profound shock when the garment factories where they worked shifted their operations to Mexico. Closure of textile plants in the U.S. borderlands had, of course, occurred before NAFTA, but the trade agreement gave new impetus to that trend because of the new tariff reductions for finished garments imported from abroad.[11]

Environmentalists have contended that the safeguards created by NAFTA have been insufficient to deal with the serious ecological problems that have plagued the overcrowded border cities. In Mexico critics have bitterly complained that the increased influx of foreign capital and consumer products has harmed key national industries such as agriculture and has displaced large numbers of domestic workers. With NAFTA in place the project to "liberate" the Mexican border cities from foreign commercial domination became moot, as U.S. products flooded the region. These differing perspectives confirm what knowledgeable observers predicted in 1994, namely, that in the period of adjustment to the new system of economic exchange some sectors would derive great benefits from free trade while others would be gravely injured by it.

Clearly, free trade in all its forms has benefited Mexican fronterizos/as, albeit to the detriment of important sectors of the national economy and at the cost of economically tying the border region and, now with NAFTA, Mexico as a whole closer to the United States. In reality, had the free trade zone never existed at the border and NAFTA never been enacted, U.S. merchants would still have maintained hegemony over Mexican border consumers. Over time the U.S. economy has simply been too powerful and has overwhelmed Mexico's economy under any arrangement, including the one based largely on illegal trade that functioned for generations. The reality of the ever-growing foreign orientation has caused Mexicans in the interior to view fronterizos/as as a different breed within the nation's society, a group whose lifestyle has been conditioned by their "addiction" to foreign tastes and products.

The economic dependence of Mexico's fronterizos/as on the United States has also long been evident in the reliance of the border communities on tourist industries. Tourism is a beneficial addition to any economy, but certain activities that emerged locally have seriously marred the image of the border zone. Historically, cities like Ciudad Juárez and Tijuana have been seen by many on both sides of the boundary as wide-open recreation centers for foreign visitors, appealing particularly to U.S. military personnel eager for thrills from sex, liquor, drugs, and other vices. This aspect of border life has been popularized in books and the media, much to the detriment of local residents, who have been subjected to unkind criticism from both sides of the border. Given the powerful image formed by many of the Mexican border communities as "sin cities," it is important to place the development of border nightlife in proper perspective and to underscore the ties to U.S. investors and clientele that have existed over time. In the broadest sense this facet of the border economy started because of frontier economic necessity and has thrived because of a continuing consumer demand and a favorable operating climate. Moreover, it needs to be understood that vice is usually found in large doses in border areas and ports throughout the world, especially in regions visited by affluent tourists.

The "culture of sin" took root in the Mexican frontier during the last few years of the nineteenth century, when a depression, triggered by external forces, devastated the local border economies. Foremost among the causes of the disruption of that period were restrictions imposed on border trade by the Mexican government, a series of peso devaluations, and, in the case of the Chihuahua frontier, severe shortages of Rio Grande water for agricultural use precipitated by excessive appropriation by farmers in New Mexico and Colorado. Fronterizos/as desperately needed new sources of income. Coincidentally, many European American "merchants of sin" at about the same time needed safe pastures in which to relocate their operations when they were driven out of countless communities throughout the United States during a period of moral reform. It is in that context that operators of brothels, gambling joints, and bars in El Paso moved to Ciudad Juárez at the turn of the century. The construction of such prominent tourist facilities as the bullring in 1903 and the racetrack in 1905 reflects the transformation of the Ciudad Juárez economy as the twentieth century began. Steadily, foreign capital played a crucial role in the building and maintaining of the border tourist industry.[12]

During the U.S. Prohibition era (1918–33) foreign investors poured substantial amounts of money into the Mexican frontier, capitalizing on the demand for liquor and entertainment not legally or readily available north of the border. Results of a Chamber of Commerce study in 1926 in Ciudad Juárez indicated that persons with English surnames controlled about 40 percent of the value of forty-one structures in the city. Two prominent companies, the D & H and D & W distilleries, moved their plants from Kentucky to Ciudad Juárez, while, according to a U.S. newspaper, "nearly all of the bars formerly in El Paso and many other parts of the United States relocated in Juárez."[13] Although the spending of dollars stimulated economic activity on the Mexican side, a great portion of these funds found their way back to the United States because of the heavy dependence of fronterizos/as on U.S. stores for their daily necessities.

The boom in tourism created in the 1920s began to dissipate once the effect of the Great Depression began to be felt along the border in 1930 and 1931. Greater declines in the tourist trade followed when Prohibition came to an end in the United States in 1933 and when the Mexican federal government closed gambling casinos and related establishments during a wave of moral reform.

World War II brought another major upswing in tourism in the Mexican border towns. Millions of U.S. servicemen and civilians patronized Mexican shopping centers, bars, and brothels, thus providing new revenues for the struggling border communities. The new earnings allowed fronterizos/as to make civic improvements and stimulated nontourist activities that aided in the diversification of the economy. Yet the heavy reliance on the entertainment sector, especially its seedy component, strongly reinforced the image of the border cities as "centers of vice," "Sodoms," "Gomorrah cities," and other such epithets.

Today liquor, drugs, and prostitution no longer provide the magnetism they once did for visitors from north of the Rio Grande. The emergence in the United States of sexual permissiveness, topless and bottomless bars, X-rated movies in theaters, X-rated videotapes, and pornography on the Internet as well as the availability of drugs diminished the attraction of the Mexican border nightlife. Even so, foreigners continue to frequent diversion centers on the Mexican side, and in the process many needy Mexicans dependent on tourism, particularly women who work as prostitutes, must endure humiliations and indignities in their struggle to make a living.

Although foreign-based tourism has been a prominent industry at the Mexican border for generations, an even more important and longer-standing source of income has been jobs available north of the boundary. During the late nineteenth century, when northern Mexico and the U.S. Southwest experienced rapid economic growth, Mexicans in significant numbers began working for U.S. companies on both sides of the border. The towns adjacent to the boundary became strategic recruiting points for Mexican labor, and soon a system developed by which large numbers of fronterizos/as, both documented and undocumented, used the area as a jumping-off point to cross into the United States to work. Over time that labor system became institutionalized and continues to function to the present day. Transborder workers include commuters who cross the boundary on a daily basis and migrants who penetrate deeper into U.S. territory, working on a seasonal basis and making periodic return trips to their border home bases.[14]

Historically, Mexican worker commuters have consisted of persons who

Table 5.1 Mexican Border Worker Commuters, 1970 and 1980

Port	1970	1980
Nuevo Laredo–Laredo	3,456	10,553
Piedras Negras–Eagle Pass	2,089	11,211
Ciudad Juárez–El Paso	13,493	50,454
San Luis–Yuma	3,616	12,340
Mexicali-Calexico	8,979	27,968
Tijuana–San Ysidro	11,697	28,351
All other ports	1,159	18,206
Totals	42,209	159,083

Source: Based on Aramburo, *Encuesta sobre transmigración*, from data in Herzog, "Border Commuter Workers," 7.

hold U.S. residency cards, persons who illegally use local crossing permits (issued to shoppers, students, business-people, tourists, and others) to work, and persons who cross the border without any documents. Data are hard to come by, but a survey conducted in 1970 counted 42,209 Mexican commuters from one end of the border to the other, and a follow-up study in 1980 recorded a significant increase in this number, up to 159,083 (table 5.1). There is little doubt that these figures underestimated the actual Mexican commuter worker traffic, those for 1970 in particular, simply because over time many crossers interviewed by researchers have refused to identify themselves as workers, especially those who have lacked the proper documentation to hold jobs in the United States.

Before the imposition of U.S. "blockades" in border urban centers in 1993 large numbers of undocumented or improperly documented Mexican border commuters crossed into the United States on a regular basis, including many who made the trip every day. But as it became tougher to evade the authorities increasing numbers of commuters began to spend extended periods north of the boundary, staying in touch with their families by phone and going back to the Mexican side only periodically. This new arrangement as well as other new patterns of cross-border migration throughout the borderlands is reflected in the data in table 6.2 in the next chapter.

One more category of commuter workers needs to be considered: U.S. citizens who live on the Mexican side and who, just like the others, cross the border daily to work in U.S. border cities. Although data are not extant, it is known that tens of thousands of U.S.–born and U.S.–naturalized individuals reside in Tijuana, Mexicali, Nogales, Ciudad Juárez, Laredo, and other Mexican border communities. It is a given that most depend on jobs on the U.S. side for their livelihood.

Table 5.2 Maquiladoras in Mexico, 1970, 1984, and 2004

	Number of Plants			Number of Employees		
	1970	1984	2004	1970	1984	2004
Entire republic	120ᵃ	680	2,805ᵇ	—	211,200	1,100,000ᶜ
Matamoros	23	38	128	2,565	20,300	52,602
Reynosa	—	20	139	--	13,867	73,701
Nuevo Laredo	17	13	43	3,472	3,700	19,234
Piedras Negras	5	18	31	1,240	3,900	12,402
Ciudad Acuña	—	—	47	—	—	34,240
Ciudad Juárez	22	159	278	3,165	75,200	196,500
Nogales	5	46	81	1,202	17,300	27,170
Mexicali	22	71	123	5,002	10,900	49,464
Tijuana	16	143	566	2,190	24,400	143,837

Source: Martinez, *Border Boom Town*, 133; American Industrial Parks, Inc., El Paso, *Twin Plant News* 19, no. 10 (May 2004).
ᵃEstimate.
ᵇDown from 3,735 in 2001.
ᶜDown from 1.3 million in 2001.

Another very important sector of the Mexican border labor force that relies on the U.S. economy are the people who work in predominantly U.S.–owned assembly plants known as maquiladoras. The products manufactured in these factories are made almost exclusively from imported raw materials, components, and parts, and their final destination is largely markets outside of Mexico. Thus maquiladoras are not integrated with other domestic industries in Mexico; they operate largely as foreign enclaves in the national economic system. The maquiladora program began operations in the Mexican border cities in 1965 at a time of heavy unemployment in the region. In subsequent years foreign-owned factories mushroomed and spread to other parts of Mexico. By 2001 the number of maquiladoras had reached a staggering 3,735, employing 3.1 million workers. But an economic downturn brought those figures down to 2,805 and 1.1 million by 2004 (table 5.2). Historically, most of the plants have been heavily concentrated in Ciudad Juárez and Tijuana, while Matamoros, Reynosa, and Mexicali have emerged as second-tier centers of maquiladoras and Nuevo Laredo, Piedras Negras, Ciudad Acuña, and Nogales as third-tier centers.

The maquiladoras demonstrate in a dramatic way the external dependence of the Mexican border. In Ciudad Juárez, the "assembly capital" of the world, an estimated three fourths of the economically active population is tied in directly or indirectly to the maquiladoras.[15] The overwhelming foreign orientation of the Ciudad Juárez economy becomes evident if maquiladora workers are combined with border commuters and employees of tourist-related activities. In 1982 one source reported that those three sectors accounted for at least two thirds of the total earnings of the local labor force.[16]

The acute vulnerability of the maquiladora industry to international wage competition and periodic global recessions has been demonstrated repeatedly in the past several decades, but never so dramatically as during the crisis of 2001–2. As a result of sluggishness in U.S., European, and Asian markets and the devastating impact of the terrorist attacks of 2001, droves of maquiladoras shut down operations or moved to China, Thailand, and Vietnam, lured there by production costs much lower than those found in Mexico. Wages topped the list of push factors that drove maquiladoras to relocate. In 2002 entry-level workers could be hired for as low as $.25 (U.S.) an hour in Asia, compared to $1.50–$2.00 in Tijuana and Ciudad Juárez. The stability of the Mexican peso kept wages from dropping in Mexico, disappointing multinationals accustomed to periodic declines in their payroll as a result of devaluations. New taxes imposed by the Mexican government and the prospect of more regulation constituted two additional push factors influencing maquiladoras to leave the Mexican border region.

Maquiladoras have increased the economic dependence not only of the border region but of Mexico in general. These industries have become one of the top earners of foreign exchange in the nation. If for some reason the maquiladoras should significantly reduce their operations (e.g., as a result of maquiladora migration to countries with cheaper labor), Mexico and the border zone in particular would experience a crisis of immense proportions.

Mexicans have denounced maquiladoras for other reasons as well. In the 1960s and 1970s critics pointed out that the original purpose of the program—to alleviate the pronounced male unemployment at the border—had not been accomplished. Indeed, at the time, women who had only recently joined the workforce and who could be paid lower wages dominated the maquiladora employee ranks. In recent years, however, the representation of men has increased significantly. All along, detractors of the program have noted that with rapid industrial expansion on the border have come attendant social ills such as inadequate housing, an alarming shortage of social services, increased crime, and family disintegration. Many have also felt that maquiladoras have encouraged more migrants from Mexico's interior to head toward the border, thus contributing to a persisting overpopulation problem. For example, with an unofficial current population of about 2 million each, Ciudad Juárez and Tijuana are among the most overcrowded cities in Mexico. Finally, environmentalists have accused the maquiladora program of aggravating pollution problems on the border.

From the standpoint of the United States the availability of large numbers of Mexican workers close by has been an important factor in the growth and development experienced by the U.S. borderlands. This reserve army of labor has been built up over the decades by a combination of push-pull tendencies that have characterized the economies of Mexico and the United States. One significant factor has been the efforts of those who benefit from cheap labor to induce large-scale migration to the border. For years U.S. corporations sent labor recruiters deep into Mexico and to the border cities, seeking workers for U.S. railroads, mines, and agriculture. The U.S. government, often with the cooperation of Mexico City, aided U.S. employers in securing labor by overlooking violations of labor laws, ignoring or bending immigration legislation, and instituting contract labor operations such as the Bracero Program during World War II. These various currents have fed on each other to bring about a steady migration stream involving millions of human beings caught in an irreversible social process.[17] This situation has been especially favorable to employers, who derive large profits from the rock-bottom wages they pay undocumented workers. Middle- and upper-class people in the U.S. borderlands also benefit from low-cost maids, gardeners, and other service workers, not to mention the availability of comparatively low prices for certain consumer goods, such as food products, that involve the participation of undocumented labor at some stage. These benefits to U.S. society are usually forgotten during hard times north of the boundary, and pressures build up to seal the border to north-bound migrants. Such a pattern has been in evidence for many years, continuing to the present.

U.S. Cultural Influences on the Mexican Border

From the Mexican point of view the overwhelming reliance of the border economy on the U.S. side has not only subjected the region to disruptive economic cycles that originate abroad but also tended to pull border residents within the cultural orbit of the United States. That condition has kept fronterizos/as on the defensive in relation to the rest of Mexico. It has long been traditional for Mexicans from the interior to criticize fronterizos/as for their alleged complacency concerning the illegal practices that permeate the border dollar economy, their eagerness to learn the English language, and their tendency to adopt norteamericano/a consumption habits, customs, and dress styles. As early as 1828 one Mexican observer commented on the negative effects of the proximity to the United States for residents of the frontier town of Nacogdoches: "Accustomed to the continued trade with the North Americans, they have adopted their customs and habits, and speak Spanish with marked incorrectness."[18] Similar comments regarding the border have been repeated by interior Mexicans time and again in subsequent eras. The Prohibition, World War II, and Korean War years produced particularly strong verbal attacks from Mexicans, who expressed outrage at what they considered to be excessive levels of immorality and "de-Mexicanization" at the northern frontier, prompting angry rebuttals from leading border residents. For example, one writer wrote in 1948:

> Some stupid reporters from faraway regions say Ciudad Juárez is the headquarters for gangsters, gamblers, smugglers, thieves, or drug pushers,

marijuana and morphine users, and alcoholics. But if we read their writings carefully, we find that none of their arguments are good, that they cite no concrete facts, that those cited are not verifiable, and if an event is true it is exaggerated; that they lie, are badly informed or badly mistaken in their impressions, and that in most cases these writers are imprudent or ignorant, and many of them do not even know the city.[19]

Other writers have reacted with less emotion but with equal resolve to reassure their compatriots in the interior that they remain culturally loyal to the motherland. "We hope that the whole Republic comprehends us and understands our mexicanidad, for through our service clubs and scientific organizations . . . we defend our language, art, customs, religion, songs, and everything else that distinguishes our people and makes us feel proud of living on the border to carry out our role of first defenders of our native soil," stated an editorial written by the Unión de Profesionales e Intelectuales de Ciudad Juárez in 1954.[20] "In Juárez we breathe and live in an environment of profound mexicanidad," wrote an essayist in 1957. "People known as *pochos* do exist, but it can be said with absolute certainty that they number but a few in the city and that they more than likely are offsprings of Mexicans born on the other side, who have tried to adopt the forms and styles of life in the neighboring nation."[21]

The continuing concern over de-Mexicanization at the border is exemplified by attempts from Mexico City to increase awareness in the frontier cities of Mexico's history and culture. As part of the Programa Nacional Fronterizo of the 1960s the government constructed museums, arts and crafts centers, and auditoriums to exhibit native artifacts and art and to hold musical, dance, and educational events that reflected traditional and contemporary life throughout Mexico. To complement that effort the Secretaría de Educación Pública targeted the border region for greater dissemination of books on Mexico and for the development of programs through the schools to strengthen national identity.[22]

The government's preoccupation with de-Mexicanization is most dramatically illustrated by the creation of the Comisión Nacional para la Defensa del Idioma Español, whose "main goal was the protection of Spanish from the onslaught of English, insofar as this language had presumably derogated and deformed the national standard. By emphasizing language in the enhancement of patriotic values, the central authority of Mexico intended to reactivate a dormant national consciousness and infirm ethnic identity."[23] The commission directed its efforts primarily to three areas designated as "disaster" zones: (1) the three largest Mexican cities, that is, Mexico City, Guadalajara, and Monterrey; (2) centers of tourism; and (3) northern border cities. In Ciudad Juárez from 1979 to 1982 the commission disseminated films and books, held theatrical presentations, and assisted in the building of a new public library.[24]

The government initiatives to reinforce Mexican culture are commendable, but, because of the limited resources invested, in reality they have done little to change existing conditions at the border. As long as the U.S. economy dominates the Mexican frontier, foreign cultural and linguistic influences will be forcefully felt. It is to the advantage of fronterizos/as to link themselves with the dollar economy, to learn English, and to become familiar with U.S. lifestyles. That tendency has never been as enticing and perhaps as necessary as it is at present, given the reality of greater ties to the United States brought about by NAFTA. Regardless of what interior Mexicans think concerning the perceived de-Mexicanization at the border, many fronterizos/as will continue to look northward in their quest for material improvement. Such has been their destiny since the border's creation, and the future promises no alteration in that long-established pattern.

However, if fronterizos/as link their economic interests and consumption patterns with the United States, it does not follow that they reject their "Mexicanness." A study conducted by Mexico's Colegio de la Frontera Norte (formerly CEFNOMEX) during the 1980s revealed that feelings of national identity were actually stronger among residents of Ciudad Juárez and Matamoros, where foreign linguistic influences are most pronounced, than in interior centers like Acapulco, Uruapan, Zacatecas, and Mexico City. It is significant that among the seven cities surveyed national identity sentiments were the weakest in Mexico City.[25] Assuming the validity of these findings, Mexico should find comfort in the degree of allegiance to the motherland among fronterizos/as. The traditional attacks on fronterizos/as for alleged "disloyalty" and "lack of cultural integration" appear to be based on stereotypes and misconceptions.

Summary and Conclusion

The people of northern Mexico have long been seen as a special breed by other Mexicans because of their isolation from the rest of the republic, their different cultural strains, and their close association with the United States. Residents of border cities in particular have been subjected to considerable criticism for their adoption of U.S. customs and heavy consumption of U.S. products. Though the charge that the process of de-Mexicanization is rampant in the north is exaggerated, by necessity and circumstances norteños/as have had intense interaction with the United States. Large segments of the population of cities like Nuevo Laredo, Ciudad Juárez, and Tijuana function directly in the U.S. economy by working in maquiladoras, in tourism, or in a variety of jobs in the U.S. border cities. Over generations tens of thousands of fronterizos/as have actually used the Mexican border cities as jumping-off points for eventual emigration to the United States. It is not far-fetched to characterize many fronterizos/as as "Mexican Americans in the making," for their experience at the border prepares them well for life in the United States should they decide to emigrate.

Long concerned over the close ties of norteños/as and fronterizos/as with the United States, Mexico City determined in the 1960s that the time had arrived to integrate the border economy with the rest of the country. Border cities assumed high priority within the grand scheme of decentralized national development, which led to the creation of economic and cultural programs intended to improve the fronterizo/a standard of life and to reinforce Mexican culture and customs. The strategy achieved some significant results. Border urban centers expanded their economic base and improved their appearance. The old "sin city" images of Ciudad Juárez and Tijuana changed dramatically as prostitution and related illicit activities diminished or shifted to the U.S. side. NAFTA brought about greater commercial development, including the appearance of major U.S. retail outlets and restaurants. These developments have instilled a sense of pride among fronterizos/as that was absent in previous eras.

Yet despite the efforts from Mexico City to pull the border region into the national fold, norteños/as and fronterizos/as remain a society apart from the rest of Mexico. Economic crises during the 1980s and 1990s actually deepened the foreign orientation because of the declining economic opportunities within Mexico. For the first time since the years of the Mexican Revolution significant numbers of middle- and upper-middle-class Mexicans from the north and elsewhere emigrated to the United States, creating a minor "brain drain" in their homeland. Further, many wealthy Mexicans took substantial amounts of money out of the country, leaving the economy starved for capital. Billions of dollars were deposited in banks in the U.S. borderlands.[26] Finally, since the 1980s the Mexican border region has suffered a devastating blow from a new wave of lawlessness and violence brought about by the unprecedented concentration of drug traffickers in Ciudad Juárez, Tijuana, and other communities (see chapter 6).

In the political arena the norteños/as made their weight felt by vigorously protesting the absence of honest elections in Mexico. The democratic movement, begun in Chihuahua in 1986 with the participation of conservative and leftist parties, had a significant effect on Mexican politics. Subsequently, other parts of the nation joined the norteños/as in pressuring the central government to democratize the system. The efforts paid off in 2000, when the opposition party, the PAN, captured the presidency and ended the seventy-one-year reign of the ruling party, the PRI. Once again the north lived up to its reputation of forcefully expressing its independence and challenging central authority on issues of fundamental importance to all Mexicans.

6 Growth, the Environment, and the Border Flow

Recent population growth, urbanization, industrialization, booming trade, and other modernizing forces have transformed the once isolated and sparsely inhabited borderlands into one of the most rapidly developing regions of the United States and Mexico. Near the border and directly adjacent to it are many major urban centers supported by a vibrant economy that is fueled by increasing amounts of capital and an ever-rising stream of national and international migration. Many borderlands cities now function as prominent sites for the international transit of goods and services, manufacture and processing, and labor exchange. Without the economic symbiosis of the border it is inconceivable that the region would have become so attractive to the recent waves of entrepreneurs and immigrants.

These profound changes have produced new challenges. U.S. and Mexican borderlanders, keenly aware of problems of overutilization of scarce resources, overpopulation, poverty, undocumented migration, and delicate economic interdependence, continue to struggle to prevent serious deterioration of cross-border relations. Even if a friendly atmosphere cannot always prevail at the frontier, its residents recognize the compelling reasons to preserve a spirit of neighborly coexistence.

Growth in the Borderlands

Table 6.1 details the accelerated population growth experienced by the U.S. and Mexican border states since the World War II period. In 1950 the combined population of Texas, New Mexico, Arizona, and California was 19.7 million; half a century later that figure had risen to over 65 million. On the Mexican side the combined populations of Tamaulipas, Nuevo León, Coahuila, Chihuahua, Sonora, and Baja California grew from 3.8 million to 16.6 million during the same period. Taken together, at the beginning of the twenty-first century the U.S. and Mexican states had a population of over 81 million, with more than half of that number living within a 2,000-mile-long, 600-mile-wide belt bisected by the boundary.

U.S. cities in the interior borderlands with particularly high growth rates for the period include Houston, Albuquerque, Phoenix, and Tucson (table 6.2). At the border, El Paso and San Diego continued to be the largest U.S. cities, recording populations of 574,013 and 1,239,697, respectively, in 2000 (table 6.3). While interior Mexican borderlands cities such as Saltillo, Chihuahua City, and Hermosillo have also seen their populations rise dramatically, border cities like Ciudad Juárez and Tijuana have witnessed phenomenal growth.

Table 6.1 Population of Mexican and U.S. Border States, 1950, 1970, and 2000/2003[a]

Border State	1950	1970	2000/2003[b]
Mexico			
Tamaulipas	718,167	1,456,858	2,753,222
Nuevo León	740,191	1,694,689	3,834,141
Coahuila	720,619	1,114,956	2,298,070
Chihuahua	846,414	1,612,525	3,052,907
Sonora	510,607	1,098,731	2,216,969
Baja California	226,965	870,421	2,487,367
Total	3,762,963	7,848,180	16,642,676
United States			
Texas	7,711,194	11,198,655	22,118,509
New Mexico	749,587	1,775,399	1,874,614
Arizona	681,187	1,017,055	5,580,811
California	10,586,223	19,971,069	35,484,453
Total	19,728,191	33,962,178	65,058,387

Source: Censos generales de población, 1950–2000; U.S. Bureau of the Census, Census of Population, 1950–2003.
[a]Mexican figures are at best conservative estimates of the actual population in the border states. The Mexican census is well known for undercounting people, especially in rural areas. U.S. census data suffer from the same problem but to a much lesser extent.
[b]Mexican figures are for 2000; U.S. figures are for 2003.

According to official statistics, Ciudad Juárez grew from 122,566 to 1,218,817 and Tijuana from 59,950 to 1,210,820 between 1950 and 2000; some unofficial figures, however, place the current population at over 2 million for each city.

A number of factors, such as public sector spending, global economic competition, NAFTA, labor costs, climate, and geography, have combined to produce the recent dramatic expansion of the borderlands' urban population. During the World War II era a trend began in the United States to disperse defense installations to make their destruction more difficult in the event of attack by the former Soviet Union or other unfriendly Communist nations. That policy, coupled with the need for open spaces for ground training and good weather for airplane and missile testing, led to the growth of existing bases and the creation of new ones throughout the Southwest. In addition, new defense-related industries proliferated, bringing prosperity to cities like San Antonio, Albuquerque, and Phoenix. The public spending spree evident in the defense industry also made itself felt in other areas. Washington assisted states and localities in building superhighways and other infrastructure, making possible the urban sprawl so characteristic of countless modern cities in the southwestern United States. Other regions of the nation also benefited from the expansion of government spending for these activities, but not to the extent seen in the Southwest.[1]

Table 6.2 Population of Selected Cites in the Interior Borderlands, 1950, 1970, and 2000/2003

City	1950	1970	2000/2003[a]
Mexico			
Monterrey	339,292	830,336	1,110,997
Saltillo	98,603	191,879	578,046
Torreón	147,233	257,045	529,512
Chihuahua	122,468	363,850	671,790
Hermosillo	54,503	206,663	609,829
United States			
San Antonio	408,442	654,153	1,214,725
Houston	596,163	1,233,535	2,009,690
Albuquerque	98,815	244,501	471,856
Phoenix	106,818	584,303	1,388,416
Tucson	45,454	262,933	507,658
Los Angeles	1,970,358	2,811,801	3,819,951

Source: Censos generales de población, 1950–80; U.S. Bureau of the Census, Census of Population, 1950–90.
[a]Data for Mexican cities are for municipios, based on 2000 count. Data for U.S. cities are based on 2003 estimates.

Growing international economic competition in key industries such as electronics and textile manufacturing has also played an important role in stimulating growth in the U.S. Southwest. As Japan and other nations captured larger shares of world markets, U.S. industries sought more favorable settings within the country to produce goods at cheaper rates in order to remain competitive. Thus a trend began to shift operations from the labor-expensive and "stifling" business environment of the U.S. Midwest and Northeast to the more inviting climate of the Southwest. At the same time, many multinationals moved labor-intensive operations abroad, including the Mexican side of the border, where abundant labor at rock-bottom rates could be found. State and local governments throughout the Southwest took full advantage of these developments, offering numerous incentives to businesses and industries seeking new homes or looking for expansion possibilities. Cheaper and "more disciplined" labor, tax concessions, less regulation, and a "friendly" business climate served as the principal enticements. Good weather in the Southwest has also been promoted as an important advantage to companies weary of lost time during the often brutal winters in the U.S. "Frost Belt." Executives in particular have found the outdoor lifestyle of the mild Southwest especially appealing. In short, the Southwest, along with the other regions of the Sun Belt, has devised a successful formula to generate substantial economic activity south of the thirty-seventh parallel.[2]

Several of the same factors that have brought prosperity to the U.S. border area have been operative on the Mexican side as well. World War II, the

Table 6.3 Population of Major Twin Cities along the Border, 1950, 1970, and 2000[a]

	1950	1970	2000
Matamoros	45,737	186,146	418,141
Brownsville	36,066	52,522	143,783
Reynosa	34,076	150,786	420,463
McAllen	20,067	37,636	106,414
Nuevo Laredo	57,669	151,253	310,915
Laredo	51,510	69,024	181,255
Piedras Negras	27,578	46,698	128,130
Eagle Pass	7,267	15,364	22,413
Ciudad Juárez	122,566	424,135	1,218,817
El Paso	130,485	322,261	574,013
Nogales, Sonora	24,480	53,494	159,787
Nogales, Arizona	6,153	8,946	21,423
Mexicali	64,658	396,324	764,602
Calexico	6,433	10,625	28,086
Tijuana	59,950	340,583	1,210,820
San Diego[b]	334,387	697,471	1,239,697

Source: Censos generales de población, 1950–2000; U.S. Bureau of the Census, Census of Population, 1950–2000.
[a]Mexican figures are at best conservative estimates of the actual population in the border cities. The Mexican census is well known for undercounting people, especially in rural areas. U.S. census data suffer from the same problem but to a much lesser extent.
[b]San Diego is not a true border "twin city," but its city limits do extend to the border.

Korean conflict, and the Vietnam War triggered an extraordinary demand for Mexican raw materials and cheap labor found in the Mexican borderlands. Because of its proximity to the United States northern Mexico was the principal beneficiary in the growing movement of goods and people across the boundary. Border cities in particular benefited from a substantial increase in tourism, stimulated chiefly by a great expansion of U.S. military personnel in bases very close to the international line.

Keenly aware of trends in migration of U.S. capital to centers of low-cost labor, Mexican entrepreneurs, in cooperation with the federal government in Mexico City, enticed multinationals to establish assembly plants, or maquiladoras, in most of the border cities. Thus, starting in the mid-1960s, a Who's Who of global corporate giants opened operations in these cities, yielding huge profits because of the probusiness environment and availability of cheap labor. With Mexican manufacturing wages set at about 10 percent of U.S. manufacturing wages, companies achieved tremendous cost savings. Not surprisingly, border maquiladoras rapidly increased in number, from 120 in 1970 to over 3,700 by 2001. The number of employees in the maquiladoras grew from 20,327 to almost 1.3 million during those three decades (see table 5.2).

As on the U.S. side, government spending is also an important cause of recent growth in the Mexican borderlands. The impact of public expenditures is particularly evident in the projects developed under the Programa Nacional Fronterizo, a program carried out in the 1960s whose purpose was to beautify the border cities, to stimulate tourism, and to promote the consumption of Mexican products among the border citizenry. Mexico City has also invested heavily in public works, ranging from highways to public service buildings, thus expanding employment opportunities for the vast border labor force. In short, public capital outlays have contributed greatly to transforming Ciudad Juárez, Tijuana, and other cities adjacent to the boundary into important economic centers within the Mexican Republic.

Growth and the Fragile Borderlands Ecology

Apart from economic considerations, the emergence of large cities in the arid borderlands has been made possible by the utilization of modern technology to overcome environmental disadvantages inherent in the region.[3] Scarcity of water in particular has been a long-standing problem, but modern technology has made it possible to claim large amounts of water from underground sources as well as divert it from rivers and lakes situated both nearby and far away. Energy-producing resources and raw materials for construction have been extracted from the landscape in appreciable quantities. Without a doubt, the ability of cities to grow and prosper despite considerable environmental handicaps has been one of the most remarkable developments in the history of the borderlands. The region, however, has paid a high ecological price, raising serious questions about environmental practices and policies.

In the first half of the twentieth century both Mexico and the United States developed massive projects in the borderlands to provide water for agriculture. The zones of intensive cultivation under irrigation that arose between World Wars I and II often became the most-favored locations for the development of large cities. It is striking that the growth of these cities has had little relationship to the earlier agricultural economy; instead, millions of people have moved to these places for reasons quite unrelated to irrigated agriculture. They have thereby created large desert cities surrounded by older farmlands but with almost no subsistence connections to the natural environment. Many tracts of land once devoted to field crops have been converted to suburban residential developments, permanently removing farmland from productivity.

Both horizontal and vertical extensions of urban zones into hinterlands and into life zones with different habitats and resources have accompanied the success of many borderlands cities. Los Angeles has been one of the most effective cities for bringing outlying regions into its dominance. In order to exist it has had to overcome its aridity by gaining control of water resources hundreds of miles away and has even established rights to water falling in Colorado on the western slope of the Continental Divide. The dramatic effects upon the ecology of the Owens Valley arising from the diversion of water to Southern California are well known.

Phoenix and its satellites provide another example of urban extensions; here developers have built numerous subdivisions around artificial lakes, canals, fountains, and other aqueous artifacts in seeming defiance of the desert's ecological realities.[4] Like Los Angeles, Phoenix has had to establish its hegemony over water resources far from its city limits. Phoenix has withdrawn so much groundwater from the Santa Cruz and Gila river valleys that the topography of the region has actually subsided. The Central Arizona Project canal, begun in 1973 and completed in 1993, is the latest addition to the large-scale appropriation of water from the overutilized Colorado River. Mexico's efforts to build and sustain urban economies in the arid north is reflected in the construction of numerous dams and reservoirs since the 1930s. Torreón and its satellite cities in Coahuila and Durango are examples of areas whose growth resulted from large water projects. This zone boasts over 1 million people in one of the most barren locations of North America. Irrigation projects financed by the government have also affected large areas of Chihuahua, Sonora, and Sinaloa.

The ever-increasing need for water in the arid borderlands has generated considerable binational conflict as the two countries have struggled to fairly distribute the waters of the Rio Grande, the Colorado River, and the Tijuana River.[5] Controversy began in the 1870s, when irrigation reached the U.S. borderlands and European American farmers appropriated increasing amounts of Rio Grande water. Decades of negotiation resulted in two treaties that established terms for the division of waters, one in 1906 and another in 1944. Yet both documents contained serious flaws. The 1906 pact divided the water of the Upper Rio Grande (from its source to Fort Quitman) but left the apportionment of the waters of the Lower Rio Grande, the Colorado, and the Tijuana unresolved. These omissions triggered a generation of agitation. Matters calmed down somewhat in 1944 with the ratification of the second treaty, but the new pact (covering the waters of the Rio Grande below Fort Quitman and the Colorado and Tijuana rivers) not only overestimated stream flow but contained ambiguous provisions regarding drought and water quality, thus leaving both Mexican and U.S. farmers dissatisfied over the amount and type of water available for their irrigation projects. These and other problems severely restricted the treaty's effectiveness and revived international friction. The excessive salt content of the Colorado River water flow-ing into Mexico, which after 1961 began causing serious damage to thousands of acres of Mexican land, became a particularly troublesome issue. The two countries did not seriously address this problem until 1973, when a new binational pact provided for the reduction of salinity through the construction of a desalination plant by the United States, the cooperative rehabilitation and improvement of the damaged land, and the waiver of previous Mexican claims. While desalination has lessened the problem, saline water has not been totally eliminated. Further, the reduced flow resulting from upstream damming and diversion has practically ruined the once-thriving ecosystem of the Colorado River delta.[6]

Scarce rainfall has often sharpened the competition for the limited water resources in the arid borderlands. Most recently, a prolonged drought from 1992 to 2002 led to severe water shortages and sparked a bitter quarrel between Texas farmers and the Mexican government. The controversy stemmed from Mexico's inability to deliver the amount of water to the United States called for in the Treaty of 1944, which governed the division of the water in the Rio Grande. Texas farmers indignantly accused the Mexicans of hoarding water and pressed the U.S. government to force compliance. Although the U.S. State Department raised the issue in diplomatic talks, it did not take the aggressive stance demanded by the farmers. Mexicans justified noncompliance on the grounds of water insufficiency, pointing out that reservoirs in the Chihuahua border region had only 10–20 percent of normal capacity. Delivery of more water to the United States would make it impossible for local people to meet their basic water needs. When the drought ended in 2002 Mexico increased its water transfers and by 2004 had cut its water debt in half. That did not appease Texas farmers, however, who claimed that Mexico's withholding of water had seriously undermined their productivity for several years, and they demanded compensation in the amount of half a billion dollars. Wishing to get on with issues of greater importance in the U.S.–Mexico relationship, the two governments settled the water dispute in March 2005; Mexico agreed to deliver the balance of its water debt by September, and the United States pledged not to pursue the issue of compensation. Texas farmers felt betrayed by the agreement but had no choice but to accept it.[7]

One of the most complex resource issues is the allocation and use of water in aquifers shared by both countries. Extant treaties that cover apportionment of surface waters say nothing about groundwater deposits. Over the last half century serious depletion of various border aquifers has taken place, presenting the possibility that some border population centers will run out of water in the not too distant future if the two countries fail to institute an effective binational management plan.[8] The most acute groundwater problem exists in El Paso–Ciudad Juárez, where the combined population of the two cities grew from 253,000 in 1950 to over 2 million today. During that period the groundwater level declined significantly. As the area continues to experience rapid growth the reserves keep falling, leading to warnings that the main aquifer may one day be depleted.[9] One possible source of future local contention is the grossly unequal consumption of groundwater by the two cities. El Paso County, with its farms, golf courses, and large tract-home lawns, consumes about six times the amount of water used by the municipality of Ciudad Juárez, which has at least twice the population. Frequent water shortages south of the border heighten the awareness of the disadvantageous situation in which *juarenses* (residents of Ciudad Juárez) find themselves. Water lines do not reach many of the outlying *colonias* inhabited by the poor. As a result, crises erupt every summer in Ciudad Juárez when a large number of infants become seriously ill drinking contaminated water and some subsequently die from dehydration. One prominent local disease caused by impurities in the water is hepatitis A, which claims some 650 victims a year, a rate about ten times higher than in El Paso.[10]

Over many years water pollution has been an alarming problem along the California-Mexico border. Imperial Valley residents have complained for some time about the waste materials dumped at Mexicali into the New River, which flows northward into the Salton Sea. According to scientific studies, polluted water has threatened to spread diseases like hepatitis, typhoid, and encephalitis.[11] At San Diego–Tijuana raw sewage has flowed for decades into the United States via the Tijuana River, polluting the beaches and causing severe harm to agricultural lands and water wells. Tijuana built a plant in 1962 to treat the sewage, but frequent breakdowns occurred, forcing heavy dependence on facilities in San Diego. In 1987 Tijuana inaugurated a new twenty-million-dollar sewage plant, but within a short time it reached capacity and started dumping minimally treated sewage into the ocean.[12]

Apart from water contamination, some border communities suffer from high levels of air pollution. Although natural phenomena, such as temperature inversions that occur in the desert climate and topography that tends to trap polluted air in narrow spaces, partly explain the problem, human activities have a far more serious effect. Industrial waste, auto emissions, pesticide use, agricultural dust, open burning, and unpaved streets are some of the more significant contributors to the contamination of the air. Small communities such as Presidio, Ojinaga, and Del Rio–Ciudad Acuña attribute their relatively mild problems mostly to burning and dust, but at El Paso–Ciudad Juárez polluting practices of residents combine with natural causes to produce serious levels of pollution at various times during the year. Friction is often generated when one side of the border accuses the other of causing most of the problem. For example, El Paso is constantly blaming its inability to meet U.S. Environmental Protection Agency standards on the pollution that blows in from Mexico, which irritates juarenses.

Another environmental challenge at the border is the tendency of powerful interests to target remote, sparsely populated, politically weak areas for waste dumping and storage. Sierra Blanca, Texas, located about 86 miles east of El Paso, is one such community. Between 1992 and 2001 distant New

York City shipped over 200 tons of treated sewage sludge per day to Sierra Blanca on trains that became known as the "poo-poo choo-choos." The Sierra Blanca sludge dump, which had the approval of Texas officials, outraged local environmentalists, who pointed out the health risks, ecological damage, and foul odors endured by unprotected people. The project ended when New York City canceled the contract with Merco, the sludge company, as a "cost-saving" measure. In 1998, in the midst of the "poo-poo" episode, outsiders picked Sierra Blanca for another dump, this time a low-level radioactive refuse heap approved by the U.S. Congress and then–Texas governor George W. Bush. Incredibly, planners selected a spot vulnerable to seismic activity and only 17 miles from the Rio Grande. Environmentalists and other concerned citizens protested loudly, warning that the dump would pose a serious threat to the water table that feeds the river. Many on the Mexican side, including state governments, joined the dissent movement, increasing the pressure on U.S. politicians. Feeling the heat, Texas environmental officials abruptly denied the license to construct the dump, citing earthquake risks. That victory played a significant role in encouraging the people of Sierra Blanca to keep their fight against the sludge dump alive. When the dump closed in 2001 the rural west Texans, although permanently stuck with mountains of New York City's human waste piled over nearly a decade, could at least celebrate the end of the arrival of trains bearing unwanted, smelly, and revolting deliveries.[13]

The significance of environmental issues on the border did not escape the attention of both countries during the negotiations leading to NAFTA. When the agreement took effect in 1994, it provided for the creation of two new institutions, the Border Environment Cooperation Commission (BECC) and the North American Development Bank (NADBANK). The BECC's mission is to identify and certify environmental projects, while NADBANK provides the funds. Both institutions also extend technical assistance to communities in a binational strip that extends 62 miles into the United States and 186 miles into Mexico. As of March 2002 the BECC had certified thirty projects in Mexico and twenty-seven in the United States; twelve had been completed, and the rest were under construction or in the planning stage. Most of the projects concentrated on the treatment of wastewater and reclaimed water.[14]

Supporters of the BECC and NADBANK applauded the progress made, but critics charged that both institutions failed to appreciate the scope and urgency of the environmental challenges at the border. They called for stepped-up activity, pointing out that while hundreds of millions of dollars sat in the NADBANK coffers, many critical needs went unmet. Such complaints reached the highest levels of government in both countries, and proposals followed to merge the two agencies to achieve greater efficiency. President Vicente Fox of Mexico persuaded these agencies to extend their reach farther into the interior of Mexico. Such an extension worries border advocates who do not want to see the diversion of resources to areas distant from the international line. In their view that would constitute a fundamental change to objectives and policies enacted under NAFTA.[15]

The Border Flow

The suggestion that, for environmental purposes, the binational border zone be expanded to 248 miles is illustrative of the growing realization that international overlap is constantly increasing. Pronounced interdependence between northern Mexico and the U.S. Southwest is a fact of life, and the flow of people and products across the international boundary has long affected population centers near and far beyond the border zone.

Over the years the close economic links have made it essential that interruptions in the normal flow of people and trade across the boundary be avoided or at least kept to a minimum. Fronterizos/as in particular have sought to maintain an orderly and harmonious climate to prevent damage to the area's delicate economy and to existing neighborly relations. Yet historically, many controversial issues and incidents have arisen at the border, and many unwise policies have been implemented by government officials that have seriously disrupted movement across the boundary.

Economic rivalry between the two sides has been a major source of contention for generations. For example, the presence of the free trade zone on the Mexican side at various times during the late nineteenth century created antagonism in the United States and led to strained relations. U.S. merchants claimed that free trade gave Mexicans an unfair advantage and that attendant smuggling of merchandise into the United States harmed U.S. interests. The issue became a political football on both sides of the border and was not resolved until 1905, when the Porfirio Díaz government abolished the free trade zone in response to external and internal pressures.[16] With the economy of the Mexican side badly damaged by the absence of free trade, the U.S. side became the dominant partner in the area's binational commercial relations, triggering great resentment among Mexican merchants.[17]

As the two sides have competed for the border trade, the protectionism practiced by each, especially during hard times, has produced strife. During the Great Depression of the 1930s, for example, many people from El Paso vigorously urged the closing of the international bridges at an early hour to reduce the spending of dollars in Ciudad Juárez. This effort was only one of many previous borderwide attempts (some of which achieved temporary success) to close the gates to U.S. citizens who had frequented liquor and gambling establishments in the Mexican border towns since the start of Prohibition in 1920.[18]

An illustration of a local controversy integrally linked to border economics is the now "classic" transportation "war" between El Paso and Ciudad Juárez. For several years the two cities feuded over the reinstatement of the almost century-old international streetcar service that ended with a labor dispute in 1973. Many prominent Mexican border merchants objected to the streetcars because they transported large numbers of Mexican shoppers to El Paso but carried few U.S. consumers to Ciudad Juárez. Supporters of the streetcars, including El Paso officials and some Mexican leaders, generated considerable conflict when they bypassed the sentiments of influential juarenses by seeking to arrange for resumption of the service directly with Mexican state and federal officials. At one point the prostreetcar faction developed a plan to satisfy some objections, but Mexican merchants remained convinced that the total absence of the streetcars was necessary to reduce El Paso's traditional stronghold over the purchasing power of juarenses. Thus, because of lobbying efforts by the Ciudad Juárez Chamber of Commerce, former President Luis Echeverría reportedly "categorically refused renewal" of this transportation system. Even then, prominent El Pasoans remained determined to overcome the resistance of the Mexican merchants. Their efforts were in vain, however, and by the late 1970s hope vanished that the streetcars would ever return to the two cities.[19]

Seeing an opportunity to meet an obvious need for inexpensive public transportation between El Paso and Ciudad Juárez, a maverick Mexican businessman in 1974 started operating a fleet of aged, battered "red" buses along the old streetcar route, much to the delight of El Paso retailers and the dismay of merchants in Ciudad Juárez. Officials from the state of Chihuahua, under pressure from influential juarenses, stopped the buses temporarily by first fining the drivers and later impounding their vehicles. The troubles of the Mexican bus company were compounded by a series of challenges in El Paso to the routes used by the buses and to alleged infractions of U.S. transportation regulations. The bus company, however, overcame the opposition and continued to operate in both cities.

A related local issue that contributed to the strained relations of the 1970s was the confrontation over taxi service. The El Paso City Council, in part retaliating for the lack of cooperation in Ciudad Juárez over mass transportation, at one point required taxi liability insurance that few Mexican *taxistas* could afford. Municipal leaders in Ciudad Juárez responded by passing an anti–El Paso taxi ordinance that required U.S. drivers to obtain Mexican insurance as a condition for driving in Ciudad Juárez—practically an impossible condition, since Mexican insurance companies did not insure U.S. cabs.[20] Eventually, the two cities reached an agreement over the insurance matter, but the taxi controversy left a trail of negative feelings behind.

Throughout the duration of the conflict over the streetcars and taxis truces were declared, with each side backing off just enough to permit limited binational transportation. By 2005 the situation was only slightly improved. Even though the cities still desperately needed a modern, efficient international mass transit system, the prospects for bringing that about appeared very dim.

Another issue that has caused considerable problems at the border has been drug smuggling.[21] U.S. attempts to disrupt the flow of illegal narcotics through periodic rigid inspections of border crossers have played havoc on the border economy and have invited retaliation by Mexicans. In 1985, for example, one such operation caused traffic from Mexico to the United States to slow to a crawl. As trade transactions plummeted, a coalition of business, labor, and political organizations in Ciudad Juárez implemented Operación Respeto, which exhorted juarenses to boycott El Paso. Brigades of volunteers handed out flyers at the international bridges that carried the message: "*Juarense*: defend your dignity, don't go to El Paso; you do not deserve to be treated like a delinquent by North American officials."[22]

Over time, political demonstrations at the border stations have also caused interruptions in the transboundary flow. Immigration issues have been a major source of such demonstrations, often bringing together protesters from both sides of the border to show binational solidarity. In the 1980s, for example, activists from student, labor, and radical political groups on the Mexican side repeatedly disrupted the border traffic as a pressure tactic to realize demands made on local or federal officials. On numerous occasions student demonstrators in Ciudad Juárez blocked traffic to El Paso with parked buses or burning tires. Disputes over Mexican election results have also produced tension at the international bridges, as illustrated by violence in Piedras Negras in 1984 and repeated demonstrations in Ciudad Juárez in 1984, 1985, and 1986.[23]

Since the 1980s violence generated by the growing drug trade has also affected the border flow. The Mexican border cities became centers of great criminal activity with the emergence of Mexican drug cartels, and the worst consequence has been the creation of a climate of widespread violence, often extreme, in major centers like Tijuana and Ciudad Juárez (see chapter 7). Frequent street shootouts and periodic massacres have scared large numbers of U.S. border residents into refraining from crossing the border, resulting in a drastic decline in visits to commercial centers and an equally devastating drop in tourism on the Mexican side.

Yet, remarkably, despite all the disincentives, hurdles, and controversies, the level of cross-border traffic has remained high. This is illustrated in table 6.4, which shows trends between 1995 and 2003. All types of crossings had expanded greatly in the years leading up to 2000, but the terrorist attacks of September 11, 2001, altered that pattern, slowing down and, in some cases, diminishing the traffic. In 2003 49 million pedestrians, 194 million passengers in vehicles, and 3.7 million bus passengers crossed from Mexico into the United States; personal vehicles numbered 88 million, trucks 4.2 million, buses 319,000, and trains 7,774.

The number of trucks crossing the border could have been much higher from 1995 to 2003 had the U.S. government not blocked the entry of Mexican trucks into the United States beyond the immediate vicinity of the border. Although the policy of keeping the Mexican trucks out of the interior United States violated a provision of NAFTA, U.S. officials, under pressure from U.S.

Table 6.4 Crossings into the United States along the U.S.–Mexico Border

	1995	2000	2003
Pedestrians	33 million	47 million	49 million
Passengers in personal vehicles	169 million	240 million	194 million
Passengers in buses	1.5 million	3.5 million	3.7 million
Total	203.5 million	290.5 million	246.7 million
Personal vehicles	62 million	91.2 million	88 million
Trucks	2.9 million	4.5 million	4.2 million
Buses	108,000	271,000	319,000
Trains	9,432	7,108	7,774
Total	65 million	96 million	92.5 million

Source: U.S. Bureau of Transportation website, www.bts.gov.

trucking interests, kept insisting that safety and environmental concerns needed to be resolved. Mexico sued the United States, and in 2004 the U.S. Supreme Court ruled that the U.S. Department of Transportation needed to clear the hurdles keeping Mexican trucks from traveling on U.S. highways. The U.S. Congress then mandated rigid inspections to be conducted by U.S. mechanics and technicians in Mexico before allowing the long-haul Mexican trucks to cross the border. That requirement created an impasse because Mexico, citing sovereignty and protocol issues, refused to allow vehicle inspections by foreigners on its own soil.[24]

After September 11, 2001, with security concerns spawning more rigid inspections of vehicles, drivers and their passengers often experienced long, frustrating delays at the border crossings. To make commutes easier for frequent border crossers, officials opened "express lanes" at major crossings for those willing to undergo advance security checks and able to pay annual hefty fees for the privilege of not having to wait in long lines. Typically, businesspeople, professionals, and sundry affluent borderlanders acquired the coveted permits that allowed them to zip through the international bridges and inspection lines in a matter of minutes.

Summary and Conclusion

Since the mid-twentieth century explosive growth in the borderlands has produced innumerable problems and challenges. Population expansion has taxed the carrying capacity of a resource-scarce region, challenging the United States and Mexico to find effective means of preventing possible ecological disasters. The potential for serious conflict over environmental issues is most evident at the border, where "twin cities" have struggled to secure sufficient quantities of water to sustain their populations and to keep their environment clean in the face of ever-growing pollution problems. Issues such as immigration, drugs, economic competition, trade disagreements, and violence continue to strain binational relations. Cities adjacent to the border have suffered the greatest consequences stemming from unfavorable policies, controversies, disruptions, and incidents, the effects of which have been to interrupt and, in some instances, to diminish the normal flow of traffic across the border.

Despite the chronic instability, the area continues to grow and even prosper, at least in select sectors. Growth is explained by the opportunities that prevail in the region and the commitment that exists at the local level on both sides to manage conflict effectively. The efforts of fronterizos/as to maintain good neighborly relations have spanned a wide variety of arrangements, including the creation of binational organizations and alliances and the maintenance of international relations committees by municipal governments, chambers of commerce, and service clubs on both sides of the boundary. Additionally, health organizations, churches, and cultural, sports, and youth groups have maintained less formal but very significant contact. Finally, the daily trans-border contact stemming from the extensive routine movement of workers, businesspeople, students, shoppers, and tourists has fostered a wide network of positive relationships.

State-level efforts have also helped to promote favorable cross-border links. For example, Texas has long had a Good Neighbor Commission that has worked to smooth out problems between Texas and its bordering Mexican states. Similarly, California and Baja California and Arizona and Sonora have established commissions to coordinate matters of mutual concern. For several decades the governors of the border states in both countries have met regularly to promote good relations and to discuss ways of influencing federal policy making. Although these initiatives have certainly not solved major problems, they have helped considerably to maintain calm and a semblance of order along the border.

7 Migration, Drugs, and Violence

Migration and drugs have long dominated the agenda in the troubled border relationship between Mexico and the United States. In both cases the central point of contention has been illegal movement across the boundary, with one flow involving people who cross the border without authorization and the other flow encompassing the smuggling of banned substances. Conflict over both issues is hardly surprising.

Over the last century millions of documented and undocumented migrants from Mexico and other countries have entered the United States through the border ports and via well-established but unauthorized trails in the plains, deserts, and mountain areas of Texas, New Mexico, Arizona, and California. This unprecedented human movement has created chronic pressures and recurring controversies on both sides of the international line, but, as the receiving country, the United States has manifested the most anxiety, particularly over the illegal flow.

The massive influx into the United States of banned drugs such as marijuana, heroin, cocaine, and methamphetamine has likewise caused considerable consternation. While some of these drugs have originated in Mexico, others have made their way from other countries to the border communities for shipment as contraband to lucrative U.S. markets. Clearly, over the last half century there has been an overwhelming demand for drugs north of the boundary, and entrepreneurial mexicanos/as and other *latinoamericanos/as* have emerged as prominent suppliers for U.S. consumers. From an economic perspective, the presence of illegal drugs in Mexico and in the United States is simply a function of the law of supply and demand. Yet decision makers have been reluctant to accept this reality and to consider alternative policies to prohibition.

Apart from their international diplomatic ramifications, migration and drugs have had a profound impact on the development and functioning of border communities. The continuous influx of people has caused overpopulation and bred many social problems, while the influx of drugs has spawned lawlessness and insecurity for the border citizenry. This chapter considers both the local and international dimensions of these two troublesome and chronic problems.

International Migration and Border Relations

Between 1820 and 2002 6.6 million Mexicans migrated legally to the United States, and perhaps as many or maybe even more entered illegally.[1] Since the early twentieth century Mexico's border cities have not only acted as important way stations for Mexican migrants on their way to interior points in the United States but also provided a base from which many workers commute on a daily basis to jobs north of the border. During periods of economic recession and depression in the United States policy makers have taken measures to curb the flow, seriously affecting economic conditions on the Mexican side. Strained local relations in the twin city complexes on the border have been natural consequences of such actions.

Historically, hundreds of thousands of migrants have repeatedly found themselves stranded on the Mexican side when U.S. immigration officials have closed the border in response to anti-immigrant movements in the United States. Such actions have, predictably, upset Mexican municipal authorities because of the problems created by a "floating" population not native to the border cities. Human suffering was especially acute during the Great Depression, when the United States "repatriated" between 500,000 and 1 million Mexicans back to Mexico. A large portion of these migrants became stranded at the border waiting for transportation to the interior of Mexico. During those years of economic hardship both Mexican nationals and Mexican Americans encountered many problems when they attempted to cross the international bridges at the Texas border. Harassment and at times mistreatment of people by U.S. immigration officials were reported in the press and in personal testimonies.[2] Bridge inspectors who routinely asked embarrassing and insulting questions often prevented legally admitted Mexicans living north of the border from reentering the United States. At the time, U.S. labor unions escalated their efforts to prevent Mexicans who had jobs in the United States from crossing the Rio Grande. Many commuter workers were fired from their jobs and replaced by U.S. citizens, mostly European Americans. In Ciudad Juárez this practice prompted boycotts of U.S. commerce that lasted until tensions eased and the situation returned to normal.

One of the most serious migration incidents along the border occurred in El Paso–Ciudad Juárez in October 1948. That month thousands of people gathered on the Mexican side waiting to secure permits to cross into the United States under the auspices of the Bracero Program, a bilateral program that provided Mexican workers to U.S. employers on a yearly basis. As prolonged binational negotiations dragged on to settle a wage dispute between Texas growers and the Mexican government, the workers grew restless. The growers, anxious to get pickers for their already overripe crops, put pressure on U.S. immigration authorities to open the border. Clearly in violation of binational agreements with Mexico, the United States unilaterally allowed some seven thousand undocumented migrants to wade the Rio Grande for several days, "arresting" them at the river and immediately "paroling" them to growers who were waiting with trucks to take them to the fields. Upset by this blatant manipulation of its people, Mexico called a temporary halt to the Bracero Program.[3]

In the 1970s actions taken by the United States again gave rise to border incidents that took their toll on transboundary relations. During the recession of 1974–75 the U.S. Immigration and Naturalization Service (INS) carried out one of its periodic crackdowns on Mexican commuters "suspected" of holding jobs illegally in El Paso. Rigid and at times harassing inspections at the bridges led to charges that agents employed "Gestapo methods." Border crossings declined significantly, with an accompanying downturn in business in El Paso and in Ciudad Juárez. Both cities saw a repetition of practically the same scenario in 1979, except that this time the drama took a violent turn, catching U.S. officials by surprise. Mexican women who lost their crossing cards at the hands of abusive inspectors led demonstrations that effectively shut down the border traffic for two days. In the confusion and chaos that ensued, during which an American flag was torn down from its pole and thrown into the Rio Grande, one young girl died.

Officials worried that the altercations at the El Paso–Ciudad Juárez bridges might escalate into something far more serious, given the tensions that existed at the time over the construction of the "Tortilla Curtain," the much-publicized border fence intended to slow down the crossing of undocumented migrants. The Tortilla Curtain became a highly charged issue that triggered demonstrations along the border and angry commentary throughout Mexico. As originally proposed, the high wire fence would be topped with sharp blades intended to "cut the toes" of anyone attempting to scale it. Perhaps more than anything else, that feature in the design of the fence (which was later dropped) stirred the passions of Mexicans and Mexican Americans alike.[4]

The intensity of the reaction to the new fence took officials by surprise once again, but anyone familiar with the sentiments of border people toward highly visible border enforcement symbols and practices would have anticipated the resentment. Over the years many local residents had taken a dim view of horse-mounted Texas Rangers at the Rio Grande, border patrol observation towers, automated roving patrols, and wire fences. In an interview conducted in the 1970s, Ciudad Juárez ex-mayor René Mascareñas, who lobbied U.S. officials in the 1950s to remove the border patrol observation towers on the banks of the Rio Grande, expressed the feelings of many fronterizos/as regarding structures that divide the two cities.

> I don't like the idea of fences. We don't live between East and West Germany. The communist wall that is there is a slap in the face to any nation that boasts of being democratic. We want greater fluidity and communication between us. We don't want barriers; we don't want barbed wire fence. We brag we are two neighborly countries, two friendly nations, and that this is the longest border in the world where one does not see a single soldier, a single rifle, a single bayonet, or a single affronting or discriminatory sign. Besides, if a fence is put up, it won't last, because Mexicans have much ability to tear it down.[5]

Table 7.1 Border Patrol Apprehensions of Undocumented Immigrants in the Southwest Borderlands, 1993–95 and 2000–2003, in Thousands

	1993	1994	1995	2000	2001	2002	2003
Entire border	1,213	979	1,271	1,644	1,236	930	905
San Diego, CA	532	450	524	152	110	101	116
El Centro, CA	30	28	37	238	173	108	92
Yuma, AZ	24	21	21	109	78	43	57
Tucson, AZ	93	139	228	616	450	334	347
El Paso, TX	286	80	111	116	113	94	89
Marfa, TX	15	13	12	14	12	11	10
Del Rio, TX	42	50	76	157	105	67	50
Laredo, TX	82	73	93	109	87	82	70
McAllen, TX	109	124	169	133	108	90	78

Source: Statistical Yearbook, table 37.

Despite opposition from both sides of the border, in 1979 U.S. officials built the Tortilla Curtain in El Paso and in San Ysidro, California. But, as Mascareñas had predicted, the fence in El Paso became a victim of vandalism and chronic hole cutting. Nevertheless, a decade or so later, as the controversy over migration escalated, additional and much stronger fences went up in these and other U.S. border communities, making it more difficult for undocumented migrants to cross the border. The devastating impact of these new fences is discussed below.

The growing controversy over migration had its immediate origins in the expanded presence of undocumented workers in the United States. The greater visibility of foreign workers reflected both a growing demand for their labor and the passage in 1965 of a U.S. immigration law that made it impossible for most nonskilled laborers to obtain legal residency in the United States. A heated debate ensued, prompting lawmakers in Washington, D.C., to introduce a number of bills in the 1970s and early 1980s meant to stop unregistered migration. Each proposal, however, went down to defeat. Then in 1986 the U.S. Congress passed the Immigration Reform and Control Act (IRCA), which increased border enforcement, enacted sanctions against employers of undocumented persons, and granted amnesty to undocumented individuals who had lived in the United States continuously since January 1, 1982. This landmark legislation promised to resolve the illegal migration problem once and for all, but in reality it only diminished the flow temporarily. *Indocumentados/as* continued to enter the United States because strong U.S. demand for their services persisted and because employers found loopholes in the new law.

Along the border many indocumentados/as took advantage of the amnesty provision to legalize their status. Social agencies and community organizations assisted in the effort to identify people who qualified for amnesty and also helped with the required paperwork. Across the United States 2.7 million migrants received amnesty, most of them Mexicans. Without a doubt border people constituted a sizable percentage of that number.

Soon the restrictionist effects of the 1986 law dissipated, and by the early 1990s the levels of apprehension of undocumented migrants by the Border Patrol resembled those of the pre-IRCA period. Frustrated, the U.S. government turned to other strategies. The INS strengthened the infamous Tortilla Curtain and reinforced extant walls on the border. New barriers also went up, including formidable corrugated steel walls along the San Diego–Tijuana sector and the Arizona-Sonora border. More television cameras and electronic sensors guarded strategic points in the border cities, while powerful stadium lights illuminated the all-important San Diego–Tijuana crossing. The INS also dramatically increased the size of the Border Patrol and assigned more helicopters, land vehicles, and other equipment to border duty. The militarization of the border was in full swing.[6]

The greater presence and assertiveness of border law enforcement agents became evident in El Paso–Ciudad Juárez in 1993 with the implementation of Operation Blockade. Immigration officials sought to stop migrants from crossing the Rio Grande with an overwhelming show of force, positioning personnel and vehicles along the riverbank at close proximity to each other around the clock. When critics spoke out against this military-style campaign, the authorities changed its name to Operation Hold the Line in an effort to soften the image of the new strategy to halt unwanted migration. Few migrants could penetrate the line. In the first five months of the operation Border Patrol apprehensions in El Paso declined by 73 percent in comparison to the same period a year earlier. According to media accounts, most El Pasoans, including Mexican Americans, strongly supported the blockade, but residents of neighboring Ciudad Juárez made their outrage known in street demonstrations, international bridge shutdowns, and boycotts of U.S. stores.

The success of the blockade in El Paso prompted the INS to implement similar projects elsewhere. Operation Gatekeeper and Operation Safeguard followed along the California–Baja California and Arizona-Sonora borders, respectively. Collectively, the blockades, along with the new formidable walls, proved highly successful in deterring illegal crossings in urban centers.

As table 7.1 shows, in fiscal year 1993 the total number of apprehensions of undocumented immigrants along the entire border reached 1.2 million. A year later, following the implementation of the first blockade in El Paso, that number dropped to less than a million. As San Diego and other urban areas executed their own blockades, increasing numbers of migrants gravitated to remote, unpopulated, and less patrolled spaces such as the desert zones of Arizona and California and entered the United States in those areas.

With the new methods of crossing the border and the new desert corridors institutionalized, the overall number of apprehensions climbed again, reaching 1.6 million in 2000. Yet by 2003 that number had dropped to 905,000. What explains the decline in apprehensions during that three-year period? Perhaps migrants began staying longer in the United States in order to avoid the difficulties of crossing the border frequently, or perhaps after 2000 fewer migrants actually attempted to enter the United States. In any case, a by-product of the major shift in border-crossing patterns has been the drastic decline in apprehensions in the San Diego and El Paso Border Patrol sectors, made up mostly of urbanized spaces, and the dramatic increases in the Tucson and El Centro sectors, comprised largely of sparsely populated, remote, and dangerous desert areas.

Tragically, deaths became a common occurrence in desert zones, mountainous terrain, and treacherous stretches of the Rio Grande. Between 1993 and 2003 nearly three thousand border crossers lost their lives as a result of drownings, accidents, exposure, and homicide. On September 29, 2002, the *Arizona Daily Star* provided basic information on the identity of 163 individuals who had died from exposure to heat and cold in the southern Arizona desert during the previous year. The majority of the victims hailed from central and southern Mexico. Approximately 75 percent were men and 25 percent were women. Two thirds were under the age of forty, and nine were under the age of seventeen. One section of the newspaper report provided summaries of twelve significant events that stood out during a record-breaking year of border deaths on the desert. On June 6 the newspaper reported: "The high temperature reaches 108 degrees in Sells and border crossers begin dying across the area from Tucson to Lukeville. At least 16 people die over a four-day period. U.S. Border Patrol agents, Tohono O'odham police, Mexican consular officials and medical personnel scramble to confront the crisis."[7]

The human catastrophe on the border prompted a variety of responses from concerned citizens. Human rights and religious organizations, especially in southern Arizona, provided assistance to at-risk migrants by establishing water stations in the desert and conducting "Samaritan patrols" along trails used by the migrants. On the other hand, some ranchers and antimigrant groups engaged in vigilante activity as they attempted to stop undocumented people from entering the United States. Expressions of both sympathy and hostility could be found among the U.S. public at large, while in Washington, D.C., concern for the at-risk migrants failed to generate corrective legislation.

Underlying much of the contemporary negative reaction to Mexicans in the United States is the perception that undocumented workers have a pronounced deleterious impact on U.S. society. Over the last several decades anti-immigrant groups have charged repeatedly that Mexicans send money out of the United States, cause unemployment, depress wages, retard unionization, become welfare recipients, create social problems, and utilize costly educational, health, and other community services. Some critics have claimed that the expense to U.S. taxpayers is in the billions of dollars. Other detractors have stated that Mexicans, in contrast to European immigrants, will not assimilate into the U.S. mainstream, a situation that allegedly could lead to separatist tendencies in the Southwest, where most of the immigrants live.[8]

Such sentiments have driven voters to support anti-immigrant initiatives sponsored by organizations that have long sought to curtail the movement of Mexicans across the border. In 1994 Californians overwhelmingly approved Proposition 187, which denied welfare, health, and education benefits to undocumented persons and increased penalties for document fraud. A federal judge, however, struck down all provisions of the proposition except the parts pertaining to fraud. In 2004 Arizona voters passed Proposition 200, which imposed proof of U.S. citizenship as a requirement for obtaining public benefits and for becoming a registered voter. After certification by Arizona state officials and the U.S. Department of Justice, Proposition 200 became law in 2005, much to the dismay of proimmigrant groups, civil rights advocates, and the Mexican government.

The negative view of the economic impact of Mexican migrants has prevailed despite the fact that numerous field studies have produced different conclusions. Scholars have pointed out that the number of illegal aliens believed to be in the United States has been greatly exaggerated and that their presence has actually resulted in many benefits to the host society. In economic terms studies have demonstrated that Mexican migrants contribute far more to the United States than they take through payments sent abroad or as recipients of welfare and other social services.[9] Of course, the most significant contribution lies in the huge subsidy to U.S. consumers in the reduced prices of such goods as foodstuffs, clothing, and housing made possible by the low wages that are paid to foreign workers.

During the 1990s the Mexican government repeatedly asked the United States to consider the possibility of creating a new guest worker program as a way of channeling the undocumented migrants into a legal, safer means of crossing the border. Unfortunately, the terrorist attacks of September 11, 2001, and the subsequent acute U.S. concern for security on the border interrupted the migration negotiations. Finally, in January 2004 the Bush administration answered Mexico's long-expressed concerns by proposing a new Temporary Worker Program. The plan would allow undocumented workers in the United States (at the time of implementation only) as well as workers outside the United States to obtain work permits for a three-year period, with the possibility of renewal. All guest workers would be required to return to their home countries at the end of their work periods. The Bush plan generated substantial debate, but, as of spring 2005, no concrete action has been taken in the U.S. Congress. In the absence of a formal binational agreement to handle undocumented migration the border continues to be a very dangerous place for people on the move in search of a better life.

Drugs and Violence

The origin of drug trafficking as a law enforcement issue on the border can be traced to the smuggling of various narcotics during the late nineteenth and early twentieth centuries. At the time opium stood out globally as a drug that needed to be closely monitored and controlled. In 1912 the United States joined a dozen other nations in signing the Opium International Convention, which provided for the suppression of opium cultivation, manufacture of derivatives, and distribution. Mexico committed itself to these policies by ratifying the convention. In 1914 the U.S. government escalated the fight against opium by passing the Harrison Narcotics Act, a revenue measure to tax commerce in opium and its derivatives. The law's cumbersome bureaucratic requirements and restrictions made it very difficult even for doctors to prescribe morphine and effectively limited the availability of opium to the general public. Meanwhile, the Treasury Department began to make unauthorized possession of opium derivatives a crime, while the U.S. Supreme Court further strengthened the federal government's enforcement capacity in 1919 by declaring in *Webb v. United States* that doctors could not legally dispense prescription drugs to individuals addicted to narcotics. That drove addicts to the black market to obtain the substances they needed, giving birth to the underground drug trade that made the border area a prime distribution center.

To take advantage of new opportunities in the opium trade, Chinese, Mexican, and European Americans on the border formed rings, gangs, or partnerships. Such groups could not efficiently operate their nefarious businesses without the acquiescence of government officials and the police, so they resorted to bribery and graft to get the desired cooperation. During the 1910s, for example, the governor of Baja California granted concessions to Chinese entrepreneurs for the importation and sale of opium, while members of his extended family, in collaboration with U.S. Customs agents, smuggled the drug into California.[10]

Liquor prohibition in the United States, which had been enacted in many states in the early twentieth century and finally throughout the country in 1920, greatly increased the role of the Mexican border cities as centers of vice. Liquor produced in Mexico became much sought after in the United States, along with opium, marijuana, and cocaine. Smuggling proliferated as border bootleggers and drug traffickers stepped up their activities in defiance of Mexico's domestic antidrug laws and tight controls over the importation of narcotics from other countries. The government either could not or would not stop the expanding cultivation of marijuana, an old drug in Mexico, and opium, a newer drug, in the northern border states. Most of the illicit drugs wound up in the United States, causing alarm among U.S. officials. In 1923 the U.S. consul in Ciudad Juárez called that city a "plague spot," pointing out that "drugs are so easily and cheaply obtained in El Paso and Ciudad Juárez that thousands of addicts reside here on that account." In 1925 the consul reported that there were "huge stocks of narcotics in Ciudad Juárez ready for shipment to the U.S., some of which [will be] transported via airplane."[11]

As demand for drugs rose, suppliers and distributors expanded their operations. In 1931 an investigation in Ciudad Juárez by the Mexican government, aided by U.S. narcotics agents in El Paso, revealed widespread participation in drug trafficking of juarenses from many walks of life and from different nationalities. Loosely tied into a network led by Enrique Fernández, the list of suspects included politicians, bureaucrats, businesspeople, and workers in the service industry, including prostitutes. "La Nacha," a legendary figure for decades in the border drug trade, appeared on the list as well. The Fernández group dominated the local drug scene until 1932, when a similar collection of competitors led by the politically well connected Quevedo brothers began a challenge for control. Violence erupted in 1933–34, leaving twenty people dead, including Enrique Fernández. Thereafter the Quevedo group reigned supreme in the Ciudad Juárez drug trade.[12]

During the 1930s marijuana emerged as a thorny social problem in the United States when drug prohibitionists labeled users, especially poor Mexican migrants, as "decadent" people who corrupted youth and engaged in criminal activity. In 1937 the U.S. Congress passed the Marijuana Tax Act with the intent of stifling the distribution and consumption of marijuana rather than raising revenues. Anyone wishing to grow, sell, prescribe, or consume marijuana faced monumental bureaucratic obstacles and had to pay special fees. It is interesting that this law permitted the use of marijuana for medicinal purposes but banned nonmedicinal and unlicensed sale and use. Another purpose of the Marijuana Tax Act was to create pressures in society for bringing about a complete ban of marijuana. The federal strategy of stigmatizing users and making it extremely hard to legally obtain the drug worked; all the U.S. states banned marijuana that same year. Later, in the 1950s, the U.S. Congress dictated harsh, mandatory penalties for narcotics violations while giving greater powers to the police and to prosecutors. This was accomplished through the Boggs Act of 1951 and the Narcotics Act of 1956.

These increasingly tougher policies drove the United States to demand greater cooperation on the part of Mexico to eliminate the cultivation of opium and marijuana on its soil and to crack down on traffickers operating on the border. Mexico, of course, had long taken a legal stand against opium, and Article 202 of the nation's Health Code forbade the cultivation of hemp and made it illegal to sell, possess, or consume marijuana. Yet these laws proved impossible to enforce because a strong consumer demand for drugs guaranteed a supply, especially when the drug merchants stood to make a great deal of money. In reality Mexico and other countries could do little to stop the trafficking. A baffled United States, unwilling to accept the consequences of its own unrealistic drug prohibition policies, could only stand by as Mexico emerged as a leader in the international drug trade. By the 1940s the drug problem had created chronic friction between the two neighbors, a pattern that continues to the present.[13]

Drug abuse and drug trafficking escalated as major bilateral issues during the turbulent 1960s, when rebellious youth, particularly in the United States, popularized the use of marijuana and other substances. As demand for recreational narcotics among European Americans rose again, supply followed suit, much of it from Mexico. In 1969 the administration of Richard Nixon responded to the growing problem by declaring a "War on Drugs," and each subsequent U.S. government has not only followed but expanded on that policy. Since the 1970s the U.S. Congress has passed a series of laws that have greatly increased the size and power of enforcement agencies and significantly raised the penalties for drug violators. The amount of public revenues in the United States required to carry on the War on Drugs has grown exponentially in the last few decades. In 1981 the U.S. drug war budget stood at less than $2 billion; by 2005 it had increased to well over $20 billion.[14]

Yet the huge investment in resources and increased militarization of the border have yielded disappointing results, with increasing amounts of drugs constantly pouring into the United States. Mexico has borne much of the blame for this sad state of affairs. On various occasions Washington, D.C. has applied pressure on Mexico by slowing down the flow of pedestrian and vehicular traffic at the border, a strategy that has had important economic implications. For example, for nearly a month in 1969 U.S. authorities sustained a campaign known as Operation Intercept allegedly to curtail the entry of drugs onto U.S. soil. Rigid inspections at many crossing points caused tempers to flare and business on both sides to decline drastically. Mexican border communities in particular experienced the impact in a severe way as many U.S. shoppers and tourists stopped crossing into Mexico. Irritated border residents for the most part felt that the resulting negative economic and diplomatic effects far outweighed the seizure of limited amounts of drugs.[15]

In 1985 the drug problem once again prompted the U.S. government to institute tight inspections at the border for several weeks, predictably causing havoc in the border communities. The kidnapping and murder of a U.S. drug agent and numerous assaults on U.S. tourists in Mexico ostensibly served as the motive for taking that drastic action. U.S. officials apparently hoped that the interruption of trade and tourism at the border as well as in the interior of Mexico would put pressure on the Mexican government to become more aggressive in the fight against drugs. It also appears that the Reagan administration used the tightening of the border to accomplish broader policy objectives toward Mexico, that is, to pressure Mexicans to modify their position on Central American conflicts and other foreign policy questions where significant differences existed between the two nations. Mexico, however, continued to maintain its independent policy toward Central America and severely criticized Washington for failing to effectively address the root cause of the drug problem—insatiable demand and consumption in the U.S. population.

As the two countries feuded, drug trafficking increased and the border became more violent. Once again the United States responded with more enforcement, substantially beefing up the Border Patrol, the Drug Enforcement Agency, and the Customs Service. U.S. military personnel were also used selectively to patrol portions of the border and to help with inspections in the ports of entry. With the stepped-up militarization, more deadly confrontations erupted between enforcement personnel and smugglers. Tragically, innocent people, including migrants and residents of border towns, sometimes perished as they got caught in the deadly cross fire between agents and traffickers. For example, a widely publicized incident occurred in 1997 when a U.S. marine mistakenly shot young goatherd Esequiel Hernandez Jr. along the Texas border.

The tough, zero-tolerance policies followed by the United States in the past have had a profound effect on the Mexican border area. In many ways border society has been destabilized because of rising lawlessness associated with the drug trade. Before the escalation of the War on Drugs in the 1970s and 1980s major drug production and distribution states such as Sinaloa, Sonora, and Chihuahua and cities such as Ciudad Juárez and Tijuana certainly had their share of crime and corruption. But the transformation of these areas into global centers of criminality began when most of the drug trafficking shifted from Florida to the Mexican border as a result of a clampdown on Florida traffickers. Thereafter the 2,000-mile land border became the preferred launching pad for smuggling drugs into the United States. Apparently, the U.S. government underestimated or did not anticipate the difficulty of intercepting drugs along this porous border. Thus the combination of the increased significance of the Mexican border region as a prime corridor for the introduction of drugs into the United States, the subsequent U.S. militarization of the boundary, and the emergence of highly organized and well-financed Mexican criminal syndicates created mayhem throughout northern Mexico. It was a combustible and deadly formula guaranteed to profoundly disrupt the normal way of life in many Mexican border communities.

Ruthless criminals from within Mexico and elsewhere soon swarmed into Ciudad Juárez and Tijuana to take advantage of new lucrative opportunities, and this created an extremely dangerous local environment. With money to spare, the traffickers, now organized into large and sophisticated cartels, thoroughly corrupted the Mexican law enforcement system. The well-protected border syndicates have been able to do what they please in operating their deadly businesses and in fighting off competitors. One might say that life has been good for criminals, except, of course, for those traffickers shot, tortured, or executed by rival thugs. On the other hand, living conditions have taken a turn for the worse for ordinary residents of cities like Ciudad Juárez and Tijuana, as they have had to adjust to increasingly dangerous surroundings. The worst part for border people has been to have legions of unsavory characters share their living, public, and recreational spaces. Inevitably, juarenses and *tijuanenses* have been forced to alter their lifestyles as they have sought to stay away from potentially dangerous places, including theaters, restaurants, bars, and nightclubs patronized by traffickers. Many shootings and killings have occurred in such establishments, with innocent people often becoming collateral victims. Assaults, kidnappings, executions, and the discovery of often-mutilated bodies in empty urban lots or in the desert have become common occurrences. It is clear that criminals associated with the drug trade are heavily involved in these crimes.

Reliable data are very difficult to obtain to accurately trace historical trends pertaining to drug-related crime on a national or local level in Mexico. However, there is little doubt that the exponential growth in crime began when the Mexican drug cartels surfaced in the 1980s and that the bloodbath unleashed by the narco-criminals has taken a heavy toll. In Sinaloa an estimated sixteen thousand people died in drug-related crimes between 1980 and 2002, and thousands more perished in the other border states.[16] The *El Paso Times* has estimated that in the nine-year period from 1993 to 2002 the number of murders in Ciudad Juárez reached nearly two thousand, with men comprising about 83 percent of the victims and women 17 percent.[17] This is probably a conservative number, because the Ciudad Juárez newspapers for those years indicate that homicides occurred on an almost daily basis in this city. But two thousand homicides in a nine-year period is still shockingly high. Another measure of violence comes from statistics reported by local hospitals pertaining to the number of injured people seeking medical assistance. Between January and May 2001 nearly twelve thousand people received medical attention at the Ciudad Juárez Red Cross, the Instituto Mexicano del Seguro Social, and the Hospital General for injuries attributed to violence. This is an average of approximately eighty-six injured people per day.[18]

At times the violence in the border region has achieved savage proportions. For example, in 1998 in Ensenada, Baja California, 60 miles south of Tijuana, gunmen massacred twenty men, women, and children in a ferocious morning raid on three family homes.[19] Ciudad Juárez has witnessed similar atrocities. Over a period of six months in 1997 many shooting incidents took place in homes, the streets, and public places in Ciudad Juárez, with some of the attacks carried out by men armed with AK-47 assault rifles. Tragically, innocent people got caught in the cross fire. The worst calamities took place on August 3. In one episode several hit men burst into a popular restaurant-nightclub, killing six people who were having dinner. In a second incident, which happened just a short time later, three other people died at the hands of gunmen outside a bar. These murders shocked the people of Ciudad Juárez and initiated a period of acute fear of going out in public.[20]

The violence has continued unabated in Ciudad Juárez up to the present, with constant reports of shootouts, disappeared persons, and discoveries of mass graves. In 1999 investigators found six bodies in one grave on the outskirts of the city, and in 2004 they unearthed eleven bodies in several graves in the backyard of a centrally located urban residence. In early 2005 Ciudad Juárez's thoroughly tarnished reputation suffered two additional major blows when Mexico's top drug prosecutor branded that city's drug cartel as the strongest in the country, and the Secretaría de Desarrollo Social (Social Development Secretariat) labeled the border community as Mexico's most violent city.[21]

At about the same time the U.S. State Department issued a warning to U.S. citizens contemplating visits to northern Mexico, pointing out a sharp escalation in drug-related violence and acute security risks for travelers and tourists. A portion of the "Public Announcement" issued in February 2005 follows:

> Violent criminal activity along the . . . border has increased as a product of a war between criminal organizations struggling for control of the lucrative narcotics trade. . . . The leaders of several major criminal organizations have been arrested, creating a power vacuum. This has resulted in a wave of violence aimed primarily at members of those trafficking organizations and criminal justice officials. However, foreign visitors, including Americans, have been among the victims of homicides and kidnappings in the border region in recent months.

> Mexico's police forces suffer from lack of funds and training, and the judicial system is weak, overworked, and inefficient. Criminals, armed with an impressive array of weapons, know there is little chance they will be caught and punished. In some cases, assailants have been wearing full or partial police uniforms and have used vehicles that resemble police vehicles, indicating some elements of the police might be involved.[22]

The State Department warning, as well as a letter from the U.S. ambassador in Mexico that criticized the Mexican government for not doing enough about the lawlessness, prompted indignation south of the border. Mexican officials rejected the U.S. verbal assaults, labeling them as "interventionism" in Mexican internal affairs. Mexican officials reminded the United States that it too plays a role in fostering border lawlessness and that it needs to work constructively with Mexico in combating it. They further pointed out that it is weapons from the United States that are used almost exclusively to kill people on the border. The U.S. government has done little or nothing to curtail the illegal flow of powerful guns and rifles into Mexico that wind up in the hands of violent drug traffickers and other criminals. The resulting diplomatic squabble was mitigated by follow-up "explanations" and "clarifications" from U.S. officials as well as statements of "praise" for Mexico's overall cooperation in addressing major issues in the bilateral agenda of the two countries.

The crimes on the border that have attracted the most attention in recent years, both in Mexico and around the world, are the estimated over 400 women who have been murdered mysteriously in Ciudad Juárez, with many of their mutilated and decomposed bodies dumped in the desert. Many people have speculated that serial killers are responsible for the gruesome crimes against the women. However, sadistic criminals involved in the drug trade, their collaborators and protectors, gang members, sexual predators, and sundry deranged evildoers are more likely the perpetrators. The police have shown little inclination to solve these crimes, leading to speculation that they know where the trail might lead, and they do not want to go there. Numerous arrests of unlikely murderers and presumed serial executioners have only intensified cynicism toward law enforcement officials. A survey sponsored by *El Diario de Juárez* in early 2004 revealed that 73 percent of the local population did not trust the police. Embarrassed by such sentiments as well as the barrage of unfavorable publicity, officials escalated their efforts to get to the bottom of the brutal attacks on women. In a dramatic development a key federal investigator named some one hundred police officers as suspects. The public, however, remained extremely skeptical about the prospects for follow-up arrests and prosecutions.[23]

The Ciudad Juárez femicides illustrate the historic reality that, while many Mexican officials and law enforcement agents have frequently looked the other way when drug-related crimes have been committed, others have actually participated directly or indirectly in such criminal activity or have simply condoned it. At all levels of government many public servants have been arrested in recent years for their connections with drug traffickers. It is painfully clear that drug lords have used the carrot-and-stick strategy with politicians, military officers, and the police. The choice for these public servants has been to cooperate with the criminals and in return get lucrative payoffs or resist bribes and risk physical harm or death to themselves and their families. The extent of drug-related corruption at the highest levels of government in Mexico surfaced during the early 1990s, when Carlos Salinas de Gortari occupied the presidency. Those charged with crimes, such as taking bribes or laundering dirty money, included the president's own brother, the general who ran Mexico's "drug war," and the deputy attorney general.

Two examples of recent police corruption in Mexican border cities come from Ciudad Juárez and Nuevo Laredo. In May 2001 *El Diario de Juárez* reported connections between members of the Policía Judicial Federal (PJF) in Ciudad Juárez with organized crime. Allegedly, former PJF agents had become leaders of both the Ciudad Juárez and the Tijuana cartels. The PJF is part of the Procuraduría General de la República (Mexico's Department of Justice). In Nuevo Laredo in October 2002 the newspaper *El Mañana* reported widespread involvement of active as well as former police officers in violent crimes linked to the drug trade.[24]

Ordinary Mexicans from different walks of life have also been caught up in the illicit drug trade. In 1989 Chihuahua beauty queen María Dolores

Camarena was found guilty of laundering $1 million worth of drug money in many small deposits made in El Paso banks. In 1990 a propane tanker truck that formed part of a fleet of vehicles owned by a wealthy family, the Saragozas, from Ciudad Juárez was seized by U.S. Customs agents at a crossing near San Diego when it was discovered that it carried nearly 4 tons of cocaine.[25] From 1989 to 1995 Mennonites were involved in thirty drug seizures on the Mexican and Canadian borders. Canadian officials believe that what they called "the Mennonite ring" accounted for nearly 20 percent of the drugs smuggled into Canada.[26] In 2001 U.S. Customs reported the arrest of fifty-seven Mexican minors suspected of smuggling 700 kilos of marijuana between January and April of that year. Customs also reported "155 arrests of minors for 2000. These minors were caught with more than 5,600 kilograms of marijuana and 15 kilos of cocaine."[27]

The United States, of course, has not been immune to the corruptive influence of the drug trade. In the 1990s there were many reports of U.S. Border Patrol and Customs agents allowing drugs to enter the United States in exchange for bribes. One federal antidrug official estimated that 10–25 percent of the drugs smuggled into the United States from Mexico each year crossed the border with help from corrupt U.S. officials.[28] The number of law enforcement officials serving time in federal prisons increased from 107 to 548 between 1994 and 1998. These convicts included agents from local, state, and federal agencies, and most of their crimes were drug related.[29] In South Texas in 1994–95 a county judge, a county clerk, the sheriffs of three counties, a local district attorney, and a county jail administrator were convicted of drug crimes.[30] Drug corruption has even crept into the military. An example comes from San Diego, where, during the 1990s, at least fifty marines and sailors were investigated for smuggling marijuana and cocaine into California on behalf of Mexican drug rings. In 1998 alone the military launched twenty investigations of military personnel.[31]

Summary and Conclusion
Cross-border migration and drug trafficking have long been irritants in the U.S.–Mexico relationship, and the binational friction they have generated will continue into the foreseeable future. These two issues have transformed the border region's demographic and economic profile and have deeply affected the quality of life of its residents, particularly in large cities like Tijuana and Ciudad Juárez.

Continuous large-scale human movement since World War II from the interior of Mexico to the north has significantly expanded the population of the border communities. The fact that most of the migrants have been largely of humble origins has resulted in the creation of large, easily exploitable cheap labor pools and led to the establishment and institutionalization of sizable pockets of poverty at the border. Meeting the needs of the impoverished masses has posed great challenges for the border municipalities. For many decades now public agencies and private institutions have struggled to keep up with infrastructure requirements such as piped water, electricity, paved streets, and transportation and to provide basic necessities such as housing and schools.

In the U.S. border communities the presence of undocumented persons has brought many economic benefits, but such advantages have been tempered by certain negative consequences. Most U.S. borderlanders have expressed hostility to these migrants, and that hostility has translated into the passage of nativist initiatives such as California's Proposition 187 and Arizona's Proposition 200. Many have blamed the migrants for the region's economic problems. Indeed, all along the U.S. border there is a strong correlation between border overpopulation and a surplus of labor and the incidence of poverty, low wages, substandard working conditions, and low levels of unionization. Regional comparisons of wealth distribution in the United States also indicate that as one gets closer to the border, per capita income drops sharply and health and social problems increase. Are undocumented people to blame for these conditions? Perhaps to some degree, but certainly many other factors must be taken into account. The public at large, however, has been in no mood to consider the complexities of the issue, finding migrants to be convenient scapegoats.

With respect to the drug trade, the zero-tolerance policy followed by the United States has caused extraordinary damage to border communities. Terrible injustices have been inflicted on the area by a doctrinaire policy that has defined the production, sale, possession, and consumption of illegal drugs as criminal activity. Over several decades zealous enforcement of draconian drug laws has led to widespread violation of individual rights and imprisonment of massive numbers of people whose only guilt is consuming or possessing illegal drugs.

Drug trafficking has transformed cities like Tijuana and Ciudad Juárez into battlegrounds as cartels have fought each other as well as law enforcement agents for the privilege of conducting their nefarious activities without obstruction. Violence, crime, and corruption in high and low places have wreaked havoc on the citizenry. Important national institutions in Mexico have likewise been compromised, and the welfare and security of its people have been undermined.

Politicians in Washington, D.C., have long avoided admitting that the United States is the real source of the drug quagmire. Rather than seriously facing up to the voracious consumption of drugs in U.S. society and coming up with effective means to reduce demand, policy makers have instead heaped blame on Mexico and other countries as the perpetrators of the evils associated with the drug trade. The U.S. Congress's indifference to the reality of the difficulty that other countries face in stamping out drugs within their own borders or stopping drugs from being exported abroad is reflected in the unrealistic policy introduced during the 1990s of certifying "cooperative" partners and decertifying "uncooperative" ones. Those countries certified as "cooperative" have been rewarded with foreign aid, while those certified as "uncooperative" have lost that assistance. Such a policy is, in effect, an admission that drug consumption in the United States cannot be stopped or significantly curtailed, so the responsibility falls on the shoulders of the rest of the world to stop producing and exporting drugs. That mindset, astounding for a country that thrives on capitalism, ignores the natural workings of the law of supply and demand. Following years of complaints from Mexico regarding the humiliating certification policy, the U.S. Congress in 2003 exempted Mexico from such a requirement.

The call for reform of the drug policy in the United States has grown louder in recent years. Judges, law enforcement officials, scholars, and many other knowledgeable observers have pointed out the ineffectiveness of the "War on Drugs" as well as its destructive nature. Recently, some states have implemented some minor changes, but the zero-tolerance approach remains the law of the land. Thus, for years to come the drug problem will remain one of the major social challenges confronting the U.S.–Mexico border.

Conclusion

The historical record reveals an evolving border relationship between Mexico and the United States. Turbulence dominated during the nineteenth and early twentieth centuries, with serious conflict erupting repeatedly over issues such as the delimitation and maintenance of the boundary, filibustering, Indian raids, banditry, revolutionary activities, and ethnic strife. Continuous clashes led to a full-scale war between the two nations and frequently verged on an outbreak of hostilities on other occasions. This pattern did not change until after the Mexican Revolution, when a region weary of violence and destruction began to experience stability. Border problems continued to trouble binational relations, but after 1920 the two sides sought solutions within a framework of peaceful negotiation and diplomacy, thus keeping tension levels well in check. Even though issues such as undocumented migration today continue to engender controversy, disagreements are unlikely to lead to violent confrontation, as they did a few generations ago.

The recent relative stability along the U.S.–Mexico border contrasts sharply with conflicts in certain other border zones in the world. In the Middle East, for example, the difficulties involved in fixing boundaries recognized by all nations in the region has embroiled Jews and Arabs in continuous bloodshed and interethnic struggles. India faces enormous difficulties in its efforts to achieve true national integration owing to religious, linguistic, and cultural fragmentation in many areas. Countless African nations continue to struggle with the problem of ethnic populations partitioned by artificial boundaries. In the Western Hemisphere unresolved territorial disputes periodically disrupt peaceful relations between a number of neighboring nations. Thus, when viewed in a global context, the troubles faced by the United States and Mexico along their common border appear to be much less threatening and well within the range of resolution—or at least to approach acceptable accommodation.

To their credit, therefore, the United States and Mexico have made significant progress in managing border conflict. On the other hand, they have fallen short of the accomplishments of a number of Western European nations whose border zones have become focal points for meaningful interchange and cooperation.[1] Increased binational integration has spurred Europeans to enter into pacts to facilitate joint planning and to promote economic development along frontiers. Old fears pertaining to territorial security have given way to concerns over solving transborder problems, especially those of a social and environmental character. A prime example of transborder cooperation is found in the trinational region that overlaps France, Germany, and Switzerland. Through a unique body known as the Regio Basiliensis, the former Swiss canton Basel, the German state Baden-Württemberg, and the French region Alsace-Lorraine coordinate regional planning and smooth out border problems.[2]

Unfortunately, the United States and Mexico seem distantly removed from negotiating an agreement that would establish a binational commission modeled after the Regio Basiliensis. Nationalistic feelings and mutual suspicions remain strong enough to block such an eventuality. Of the many border issues that continue to stir nationalism in the United States, migration is the most compelling. A large percentage of the U.S. population perceives the heavy influx of Mexicans across the border as a security threat, especially since the terrorist attacks of September 11, 2001. That explains the recent strong support for federal legislation for border walls and "blockades" and for state initiatives that deny benefits to undocumented people. Many in the United States fear that terrorists will infiltrate the country if the southern border is not properly secured. Further, Mexicans and other Latin Americans will continue to pour across the line and eventually become a political force in the United States, a situation that many feel could lead to the destabilization of U.S. society. This notion is based on the perception that Mexican Americans, Puerto Ricans, Cuban Americans, and others of Latin American extraction tend not to assimilate into the U.S. mainstream but to maintain close ties and loyalties to their countries of origin, which often are at odds with U.S. foreign policy.[3]

The belief that U.S. Hispanics lack commitment to the U.S. way of life rests largely on lack of information, misunderstanding, and biases in European American society. That Hispanics wish to preserve at least some of their culture, language, and traditions is a well-established fact. Yet it does not follow that they reject U.S. culture. The outspoken objection of many Mexican Americans to what they believe are discriminatory immigration policies does not mean that they wish to have an open border with Mexico. For Mexican Americans, the major issue in the migration debate has been the protection of basic rights of migrants as well as those of long-term U.S. residents of Hispanic heritage.

The heated controversies generated in recent years over migration and the related issue of bilingual education are to some extent a product of the large-scale internal movement of people from the European American–dominated Frost Belt to the heavily Hispanic Sun Belt. Many newcomers unacquainted with the Spanish Mexican antecedents in the Southwest resent the Hispanic presence in the area. They believe the large Hispanic population stems from unwise, lenient immigration policies of the past, and they deeply dislike expenditure of public funds for social and educational programs that they perceive benefit a "foreign" group. The widespread use of the Spanish language in the area is a constant irritant to these European Americans. They feel left out when they cannot understand what is being said, and, more fundamentally, they deem it "un-American" for anyone to speak a language other than English on U.S. soil. The growth of the "English only" movement and increased attacks on bilingual education have deepened ethnic divisions in some areas.

If ethnic harmony between Hispanics and non-Hispanics is to prevail, European Americans who live in the Southwest, especially those along the border, will need to become more fully informed about the peoples, cultures, and history of the region. They will need to recognize that the Spanish language and Mexican culture in the area go back several centuries and that the human interaction across the border is long-standing and a contemporary fact of life. Above all, cultural differences must be respected, not denigrated.

More and more European Americans of retirement age have come to realize that the integration between the Southwest and the Mexican borderlands works in their favor. Older people in the United States face dwindling resources and rising health-related expenses, and many retirees will not be able to afford a comfortable lifestyle in the United States. Northern Mexico, with its cheaper cost of living, warm climate, and bilingual population, has become very attractive to that population cohort as a retirement destination. Already hundreds of thousands of U.S. retirees have made that choice, living along the coasts of Baja California and Sonora and in various sites in the Mexican interior. In the Tijuana area, where almost two hundred thousand U.S. expatriates now reside, local entrepreneurs have announced plans to build new, affordable retirement housing for fifty thousand additional U.S. retirees. Other localities throughout northern Mexico are bound to follow suit.

With regard to perceptions in Mexico about the border, the view of many Mexicans that their northern frontier is "drifting away" from the rest of the nation is also in need of modification. Concern over the pronounced U.S. economic presence in the region is understandable, but such is the nature of remote zones in close proximity to wealthier neighbors. Despite their ties to the U.S. side, there is no evidence to suggest that the people of the north wish to be something other than loyal Mexicans. The recent political revolt against the ruling party is a product of dissatisfaction with government inefficiency, corruption, and policies harmful to the region's economy, not a reflection of foreign influences present in the polity of the north. Existing misconceptions and stereotypes about fronterizos/as and their unique relationship with the United States serve only to promote internal divisiveness and retard needed solutions to pressing border problems.

Thus both nations need to rethink their perceptions of what the border zone is, how it functions, and how it relates to national interests. The prevailing notion that each country ends at the boundary is certainly accurate from a political point of view, but it is incorrect in many other respects. Demographically, economically, linguistically, and culturally, the U.S. border area is, functionally, an extension of Mexico, and, in a similar fashion, the

Mexican border zone is an extension of economic, social, and cultural influences from the United States. The massive movement of people and products across the border and the sharing of resources, jobs, and space make clear that the sharp division implied by the line of demarcation does not mirror reality. It is more meaningful to visualize the border as a zone of "overlapping territoriality," as Ellwyn R. Stoddard has observed. "This concept of overlapping territoriality reflects the functional interrelationship which exists along both sides of the binational border and seeks to replace the erroneous structural model which characterizes the international boundary line as a point at which two distinct nations touch."[4] Recognition of the "overlap" concept necessitates putting aside nationalistic sentiments that cause people to see the border as an untouchable and impenetrable barrier.

Stoddard's suggestion that both countries adopt a "doctrine of mutual necessity" as a framework for tackling border problems is worthy of serious consideration.[5] Under such a policy, both countries would allow problem-solving mechanisms and institutions to function on both sides of the boundary with minimum restrictions. For example, in addressing the air pollution problem, the two parties would be prepared to create a binational body that would utilize resources from both nations and would implement measures to improve the environment on *both* U.S. and Mexican soil. The recent experience of El Paso and Ciudad Juárez demonstrates that it is absurd to attempt to clean up the air of one city without doing the same on the opposite side of the Rio Grande. "Twin city" complexes along the boundary need to be treated as unified metropolitan areas sharing single "airsheds."

On the question of undocumented migration, the United States, as the initiator and implementer of major policy initiatives, should accept the issue as a bilateral matter that requires transboundary coordinated planning and mutually determined courses of action. Recent U.S. laws spring from a process that in essence has ignored Mexico's views and ideas for lasting solutions. As with air contamination, policies to curb migration that are formulated unilaterally and directed at only one side of the border are doomed to fail. Short of sealing the border with troops from the Gulf to the Pacific, nothing will stop economically desperate Mexicans from crossing into the United States in search of job opportunities. Besides, the labor provided by these migrants is badly needed by the U.S. economy; thus anything done in Washington to interrupt the flow of workers damages U.S. interests, particularly along the border.

The other intractable binational problem, drug trafficking, can only be resolved by ending or drastically diminishing demand in the United States, legalizing or decriminalizing drugs, or implementing the right combination of these different approaches. Given the U.S. government's long, stubborn adherence to the disastrous policy of zero tolerance, along with its exceedingly feeble, ineffective educational effort to discourage the use of drugs, reform remains but a dream. That means the Mexican border cities will continue to bear the brunt of the criminal activity that is required to sustain the illegal distribution system that services the insatiable U.S. market. It means more frequent shootouts, kidnappings, tortures, killings, femicides, massacres, and mass burial graves involving not only traffickers but innocent people as well. It means more corruption of the Mexican police, judges, and politicians and, dreadfully, less protection for the people whom these public servants are supposed to serve. It means an intensification of the reputation of cities like Tijuana and Ciudad Juárez as extremely violent places. It means an inevitable further decline of border tourism and jobs tied to this important economic sector. Although other factors play a role in these horrendous problems, by far it is the misguided and callous War on Drugs that bears the major responsibility. Truly, the drug quagmire is one of the great tragedies in the history of the border region.

As we look back on the enormous scientific breakthroughs and great improvements in people's material well-being in the past several generations, it is disturbing to realize that the progress achieved in international relations has been relatively unimpressive. The current condition of the world, including the state of the relationship between the United States and the countries south of the Rio Grande, suggests that many historical lessons have not been learned and that much remains to be done to achieve an acceptable international climate. Certainly, the U.S.–Mexico border has made advances. But progress has come about largely through an evolutionary process and through the efforts of the people of the region rather than as a product of deliberate planning and action on the part of high-level policy makers. A new approach for conducting U.S.–Mexico transboundary relations is essential if pressing issues are to be addressed successfully. It is in the best interests of both nations as well as of the borderlands population to make that commitment.

Notes

Preface

1. See Fernández, *United States–Mexico Border*; House, *Frontier on the Rio Grande*; Kearney and Knopp, *Border Cuates*; Lorey, *The U.S.–Mexican Border*; Metz, *Border*; Ruiz, *On the Rim of Mexico*; Torrans, *Forging the Tortilla Curtain*; and Weber, *Mexican Frontier*.

Introduction

1. See, for example, the following books: Clendenen, *Blood on the Border*; Demaris, *Poso del Mundo*; Dunn, *Militarization of the U.S.–Mexico Border*; Myers, *Border Wardens*; Ruiz, *On the Rim of Mexico*; Utley, *International Boundary*. Newspaper citations in the chapters that follow provide a good idea of the extensive coverage that the press has given border problems and conflicts.

2. The portrayal in Strieber and Kunetka's novel *Warday* of an independent Mexican American country known as "Aztlán" emerging in the southwestern United States in the aftermath of a nuclear war illustrates the fears about the alleged separatist tendencies at the border. El Paso, the largest U.S. city directly on the border, appropriately becomes the capital of Aztlán, a socialist nation unfriendly to Americans.

3. This is a constant theme on U.S. cable television talk shows, especially *The O'Reilly Factor* (Fox) and *Lou Dobbs Tonight* (CNN).

4. See Kristof, "Nature of Frontiers and Boundaries," 271–73; and Lattimore, "Frontier in History," 374.

5. Neuberger, "Natural and Artificial Borders," 99; Jones, "Boundary Concepts," 251.

6. For views on the arbitrary division of ethnic groups in Africa see Asiwaju, *Partitioned Africans*; Saadia, *Boundary Politics of Independent Africa*; and Widstrand, *African Boundary Problems*. China, India, and the United States are among the many countries that have experienced problems as a result of the absorption of ethnic groups against their will.

7. When using Spanish terms that refer to groups I follow the rule of gender inclusiveness by adding a slash and the letter *a* (female singular) or the letters *as* (female plural) at the end of words like *norteño*, *fronterizo*, Chicano, *tejano*, gringo, and so on.

8. Leonard, "Southwestern Boundaries," 40, 42.

Chapter 1. Whither the Boundary?

1. Nasatir, "Shifting Borderlands," 4–5, 7.

2. *American Museum* 3 (1786): 434–35, quoted in Fidler, *Movement for the Acquisition*, 12–13.

3. Ibid., 7–13.

4. The most thorough study of the Louisiana-Texas border question was conducted by Father José Antonio Richardo, who completed an authoritative treatise of over five thousand sheets in 1812. His findings supported the Spanish position and appear to have been influential in subsequent negotiations with the United States. See Hackett, *Richardo's Treatise*.

5. Nasatir, "Shifting Borderlands," 14–15.

6. Binkley, *Expansionist Movement in Texas*, 8. On the Adams-Onís Treaty see Brooks, *Diplomacy and the Borderlands*.

7. Weber, *Mexican Frontier*.

8. García Cantú, *Invasiones norteamericanas en México*, 17–18.

9. Quotes from Rippy, *United States and Mexico*, 2.

10. Medina Castro, *Gran despojo*, 12, 17, 20; Binkley, *Expansionist Movement in Texas*, 13; Zorrilla, *Historia de las relaciones*, 1:67.

11. Historian Justin H. Smith, who wrote the classic defense of the role of the United States in the outbreak of the U.S.–Mexico War, used the following terms in his devastating characterization of Butler: "a national disgrace," "bully," "swashbuckler," "ignorant," "shamefully careless," "scandalous in conduct," "a cantankerous, incompetent rascal" (*War with Mexico*, 1:62–63).

12. Because it was bankrupt Mexico had defaulted on payments, and Polk made this a major grievance. The sum outstanding was $3.25 million, which was small compared to the contemporary default of American states and corporations on bonds in British possession, amounting to $220 million (Merk, "Dissent in the U.S.–Mexico War," 36).

13. For guides to the literature on the U.S.–Mexico War see Benjamin, "Recent Historiography"; Tutorow, *Mexican-American War*; Vásquez de Knauth, *Mexicanos y norteamericanos*; Zavala, "Historiografía americana." See also the annotated bibliography in Connor and Faulk, *North America Divided*.

14. The legality of the Treaty of Velasco, the document signed by Santa Anna with the Texans, is discussed in Escoto Ochoa, *Integración y desintegración*, 77–84.

15. Binkley, *Expansionist Movement in Texas*, 9; Cox, "Southwest Boundary of Texas," 97–98; Merk, *Monroe Doctrine*, 147–48.

16. Even Justin H. Smith, who blamed Mexico for the war, rejected Polk's claim that the Rio Grande was the Texas boundary. However, Smith buried that opinion in a footnote after giving the impression in the text of his *War with Mexico* that he agreed with Polk (1:138–39, 2:448–49).

17. Only a few historians have defended Polk's policies that led to the war with Mexico. Smith's *War with Mexico* holds that Polk acted aggressively only as a last resort, after Mexico had insulted the United States and refused to negotiate. A modern variation of Smith's interpretation is found in the following works: Connor and Faulk, *North America Divided*; and Faulk and Stout, *U.S.–Mexico War*.

18. Merk, "Dissent in the U.S.–Mexico War," 38–40, 43, 46, 48; Ruiz, "American Imperialism," 221.

19. Texas, of course, had been acquired through annexation in 1845.

20. Miller, *Treaties and Other Acts*, 5:263, 288, 325.

21. On the "all Mexico" movement see Fuller, *Movement for the Acquisition*.

22. Merk, "Dissent in the U.S.–Mexico War," 51–52.

23. Billington, *Westward Expansion*, 586–87; Fuller, *Movement for the Acquisition*, 81; Weisberg, *Manifest Destiny*, 160. Paul F. Lambert disagrees on the inevitability of the annexation of all Mexico had the treaty not been negotiated by Trist or had it been rejected by Polk. Lambert points out that a strong peace movement had developed to counter the "all Mexico" drive ("'All-Mexico' Movement," 171–72).

24. Quote appears in Montejano, "Why Commemorate," 65.

25. For the story of the surveying and marking of the boundary as well as the negotiations that led to the signing of the Gadsden Treaty see Faulk, *Too Far North*; Garber, *Gadsden Treaty*; Goetzmann, "United States–Mexican Boundary Survey"; Schmidt, "Manifest Opportunity."

26. Washington deemed Tehuantepec of great importance for a railroad route that would connect the Atlantic with the Pacific and would be readily accessible to U.S. citizens. The proposal to acquire U.S. rights became complicated when U.S. private interests clashed with the Mexican government over claims they had obtained in the area.

27. Zorrilla, *Historia de las relaciones*, 1:343–44. For a detailed record of the Gadsden Treaty negotiations see Miller, *Treaties and Other Acts*, 6:342–91.

28. Garber, *Gadsden Treaty*, 91–93; Rippy, *United States and Mexico*, 141–42.

29. Garber, *Gadsden Treaty*, 103–4.

30. The United States retained rights in Tehuantepec until 1937, when Mexico convinced the U.S. government to do away with that anachronistic and burdensome part of the Gadsden Treaty. Miller, *Treaties and Other Acts*, 6:432–33; Sepúlveda, *Frontera norte de México*, 78.

31. Zorrilla, *Historia de las relaciones*, 1:377, 379–80. Forsyth's "we will take it" statement is found in Rippy, *United States and Mexico*, 216.

32. Rippy, *United States and Mexico*, 217–19, 223; Webb, *Texas Rangers*, 197–215. Houston's amendment is found in U.S. Congress, Senate, S. Misc. Doc. 241.

33. Schmitt, *Mexico and the United States*, 83–85.

34. Rippy, *United States and Mexico*, chap. 13, quote on p. 231.

35. The story of the Chamizal dispute is told in Liss, *Century of Disagreement*.

36. Pretreaty discussions established that jurisdiction over Morteritos rightfully belonged to the United States. Mueller, *Restless River*, 40–42.

37. In 1944 the commission was renamed the International Boundary and Water Commission to indicate the added responsibility of finding solutions to water problems along the border.

38. Zorrilla, *Historia de las relaciones*, 2:139–41.

39. Ibid., 2:145–46; Mueller, *Restless River*, 53–57.

40. Zorrilla, *Historia de las relaciones*, 2:147; Friedkin, "International Boundary and Water Commission," 3.

41. U.S. State Department, *Chamizal Settlement*, 2.

42. Ibid.; Mueller, *Restless River*, 69–73.

43. Friedkin, "International Boundary and Water Commission," 5; Mueller, *Restless River*, 75, 86–90.

44. Discussions of the 1970 treaty appear in Sepúlveda, *Frontera norte de México*, 145–53; and Mueller, *Restless River*, 105–20.

Chapter 2. Marked Frontier

1. Pike's edited journals and correspondence appear in Jackson, *Zebulon Montgomery Pike*.

2. Warren, *Sword Was Their Passport*, chaps. 1–3; Zorrilla, *Historia de las relaciones*, 1:39.

3. Warren, *Sword Was Their Passport*, chap. 11. Other significant filibustering ventures prior to 1820 include the following: 1806: Aaron Burr plans an invasion of Florida, Texas, and other Spanish territories with the intention of combining them with Louisiana and Mississippi to form a new nation. Abandoned by fellow plotters, Burr is arrested by U.S. authorities and tried for treason but is acquitted. 1810: Following the seizure of the Spanish fort at Baton Rouge, Louisiana, U.S. settlers in West Florida seek and receive annexation to the United States during the James Madison administration. A detachment of U.S. troops from Mississippi then occupies the area. At the time the United States claimed a portion of West Florida as part of the Louisiana Territory. 1812: Backed by the James Madison administration, expansionist George Matthews leads two hundred U.S. volun-

teers in a temporary occupation of East Florida. 1818: Proclaiming their sympathies with Mexican independence fighters, French and British sailors attack Monterey, California. They encounter strong resistance in other coastal cities. 1818: Gen. Andrew Jackson, who has a notorious ambition to seize the Floridas from Spain, claims approval of the James Monroe administration as he invades West Florida with a force of three thousand men. Jackson destroys Indian settlements, captures Pensacola, and metes out frontier justice during his raid.

4. Ibid., 255–56.

5. Horgan, *Great River*, 559–69.

6. Kendall, *Narrative*; Loomis, *Texas–Santa Fe Pioneers*.

7. Price, *Origins*.

8. Ibid., chap. 3.

9. See Stenberg, "Polk and Fremont"; Tays, "Fremont Had No Secret Instructions"; Hawgood, "John Charles Fremont."

10. Rippy, *United States and Mexico*, 85.

11. Stout, *Liberators*, chap. 1.

12. Wyllys, *French in Sonora*, 8. See also Stevens, "Forsaken Frontier."

13. Faulk, "Colonization Plan," 300.

14. Ibid., 295.

15. Stout, *Liberators*, 29.

16. Comisión Pesquisadora, *Reports of the Committee*, 182–214.

17. See, for example, U.S. Congress, Senate, S. Rept. 39, and U.S. Congress, House, H. Rept. 343.

18. Carvajal later became an important government official in Tamaulipas when the Liberals assumed political power in that state. He also distinguished himself against the French during the occupation of Mexico in the 1860s. Zorrilla, *Historia de las relaciones*, 1:298, 301, 302; Rippy, *United States and Mexico*, 89–90; Utley, *International Boundary*, 64.

19. Wyllys, *French in Sonora*, chap. 3.

20. Ibid.; Stout, *Liberators*, chaps. 4–5. Other significant contemporary French expeditions into Mexico include the following: 1851–52: Charles de Pindray leads over 150 Frenchmen in a colonization effort in Sonora that initially has the permission of Mexican officials. Suspicious of Pindray's motives, however, the government subsequently withholds support, leading to the disintegration of the colony. 1855: Apparently intending to revolutionize Mexico's northwestern frontier, Adm. Jean-Napoléon Zerman leads a band of Frenchmen and Americans to Baja California but is unsuccessful.

21. Walker managed to get elected president of Nicaragua in 1856 and was backed by U.S. Southerners who wished to see Nicaragua become another U.S. slave state. He stayed in power until 1857. He returned to the United States and in 1860 made two other attempts to invade Central America. He was executed in Honduras that same year. See Green, *Filibuster*; Brown, *Agents of Manifest Destiny*, chaps. 8–19.

22. Forbes, *Crabb's Filibustering Expeditions*.

23. *U.S. Statutes at Large*, sec. 6.

24. Zorrilla, *Historia de las relaciones*, 1:310–13.

25. Rippy, *United States and Mexico*, 96, 102, 171–72.

26. Rippy, "Anglo-American Filibusters," 180.

27. Webb, *Texas Rangers*, chap. 10.

28. McPherson, "Plan of William McKendree Gwin."

29. Rippy, *United States and Mexico*, 249–51; Ellison, "Anglo-American Plan," 51–52.

30. Webster, "Intrigue on the Rio Grande."

31. Rolle, "Futile Filibustering," 160.

32. Ibid.

33. Frémont's statement appears in the *San Diego Union*, May 26, 1890, cited in ibid., 165.

34. Martínez, *Border Boom Town*, 19–21.

35. Blaisdell, *Desert Revolution*, 21–37; Chamberlain, "Mexican Colonization," 44.

36. Gerhard, "Socialist Invasion," 295, 302.

37. Cited in Blaisdell, "Was It Revolution or Filibustering?" 150. Seeing the prospect of a rebel victory, two Imperial Valley newspapers urged U.S. acquisition of Baja California.

38. *San Diego Sun*, June 23, 1911, cited in Blaisdell, *Desert Revolution*, 181.

39. Blaisdell, *Desert Revolution*, 199, 202.

40. Ibid., 148, 203–4.

41. Works that present the filibustering thesis include Gerhard, "Socialist Revolution"; González and Figueroa Domenech, *Revolución y sus héroes*; and Ponce de León, *Interinato presidencial de 1911*. Revisionist works that look favorably on the Liberal Party include Blaisdell, "Was It Revolution or Filibustering?"; Blaisdell, *Desert Revolution*; and Martínez, *Historia de Baja California*.

42. Blaisdell, "Harry Chandler," 388.

43. Ibid., 386–93. In *Historia de Baja California* Martínez flatly accuses Chandler of initiating the attempted coup with the intention of detaching Baja California from Mexico in the tradition of earlier filibusters (531).

44. Chamberlain, "Mexican Colonization," 46–49; Price, *Tijuana*, 52–56.

45. Chamberlain, "Mexican Colonization," 51–53, quote on p. 52.

46. Ibid., 53–55.

47. See Piñera Ramírez, *Panorama histórico*, chap. 11.

Chapter 3. Border Indians

1. Spicer, *Cycles of Conquest*, 12–16.

2. Bannon, *Spanish Borderlands Frontier*, 76–77, 167–89.

3. Spicer, *Cycles of Conquest*, 239–40.

4. Newcomb, *Indians of Texas*, 349.

5. Comisión Pesquisadora, *Reports of the Committee*, 245–50.

6. Dale, *Indians of the Southwest*, 21.

7. Rippy, *United States and Mexico*, 68–69.

8. Zorrilla, *Historia de las relaciones*, 1:276.

9. Rippy, *United States and Mexico*, 69–70.

10. Comisión Pesquisadora, *Reports of the Committee*, 253–56; Zorrilla, *Historia de las relaciones*, 1:290.

11. Bailey, *Indian Slave Trade*, 41–42; Zorrilla, *Historia de las relaciones*, 1:284.

12. Rippy, *United States and Mexico*, 76. See also Bancroft, *History of Arizona and New Mexico*, chap. 26.

13. Webb, *Texas Rangers*, 127–28.

14. Zorrilla, *Historia de las relaciones*, 1:285; Rippy, *United States and Mexico*, 72.

15. Zorrilla, *Historia de las relaciones*, 1:284, 286; Rippy, *United States and Mexico*, 74–75.

16. Garber, *Gadsden Treaty*, 36–38; Rippy, *United States and Mexico*, 76.

17. Zorrilla, *Historia de las relaciones*, 1:283, 279–80; Rippy, *United States and Mexico*, 79–80.

18. Zorrilla, *Historia de las relaciones*, 1:288–89; Garber, *Gadsden Treaty*, 35–40.

19. The detailed record of the Gadsden Treaty negotiations is found in Miller, *Treaties and Other Acts*, 6:293–437. See also Rippy, *United States and Mexico*, 148, 152–53.

20. Rippy, *United States and Mexico*, 192, 279–80, 282.

21. U.S. Congress, Senate, S. Rept. 39.

22. Comisión Pesquisadora, *Informe de la Comisión*.

23. Comisión Pesquisadora, *Reports of the Committee*.

24. Cosío Villegas, *Porfiriato*, 271–74.

25. Rippy, "Some Precedents," 313–15; Zorrilla, *Historia de las relaciones*, 2:75.

26. If a sense of "mission" existed in the European American approach, it is detected in the desire to make farmers out of the Indians and to improve their lives through technology, yet those policies developed slowly and did not have much impact until the late nineteenth century. See Spicer, *Cycles of Conquest*, 343–44.

27. Garner, "Treaty of Guadalupe Hidalgo," 10–13.

28. Dale, *Indians of the Southwest*, 83, 89.

29. Comisión Pesquisadora, *Reports of the Committee*, 406–16; Rippy, "Border Troubles," 100; Porter, "Seminole in Mexico."

30. Webb, *Texas Rangers*, 135–36.

31. Newcomb, *Indians of Texas*, 341–42.

32. Webb, *Texas Rangers*, 55.

33. Newcomb, *Indians of Texas*, 350–53.

34. Webb, *Texas Rangers*, 161–72; Comisión Pesquisadora, *Reports of the Committee*, 309.

35. Beck and Haase, *Historical Atlas of New Mexico*, 22; Walker and Bufkin, *Historical Atlas of Arizona*, 22; Richardson and Rister, *Greater Southwest*, 276–77.

36. For a detailed narrative of events connected with the Long Walk see Bailey, *Long Walk*.

37. Lamar, *Far Southwest*, 438, 446–49.

38. Walker and Bufkin, *Historical Atlas of Arizona*, 42–43; Lamar, *Far Southwest*, 449.

39. The Navajo reservation had been established in 1868. See Hollon, *Southwest: Old and New*, 304; Beck and Haase, *Historical Atlas of New Mexico*, 38; Walker and Bufkin, *Historical Atlas of Arizona*, 42–45.

40. Richardson and Rister, *Greater Southwest*, 323–24; Dale, *Indians of the Southwest*, 111; Spicer, *Cycles of Conquest*, 255–56.

41. Bailey, *Indian Slave Trade*, 59–69.

42. Garner, "Treaty of Guadalupe Hidalgo," 12–13.

43. Dale, *Indians of the Southwest*, 82–89.

44. Dana and Krueger, *California Lands*, 52–53.

45. For surveys of Kickapoo and Yaqui history see Gibson, *Kickapoos*; Latorre and Latorre, *Mexican Kickapoo Indians*; Hu-DeHart, *Missionaries, Miners, and Indians*; and Spicer, *Yaquis*.

46. Latorre and Latorre, *Mexican Kickapoo Indians*, 9, 11–12, 24; U.S. Congress, Senate, S. Rept. 97-684, 13.

47. Latorre and Latorre, *Mexican Kickapoo Indians*, 17–18.

48. Ibid., 24–28.

49. Ibid., 12, 22.

50. Ibid., 24–25.

51. Ibid., 13–14, 25; Jamail, "Indians on the Border," 34–37; Miller, *On the Border*, chap. 6.

52. Public Law 97-429 (H.R. 4496, January 8, 1983), *U.S. Code Congressional and Administrative News*.

53. *San Antonio Express-News*, February 11, 2001, 1A, and October 29, 2004, 1A.

54. Hu-DeHart, *Missionaries, Miners, and Indians*, 28; Spicer, *Yaquis*, 236.

55. Spicer, *Yaquis*, 236.

56. In 1917 eight Yaquis from Tucson attempted to cross into Mexico intent on fighting the Sonora government, but on the way U.S. cavalry troops intercepted them. Accused of violating U.S. neutrality laws, they were tried in court but were released on condition that they not repeat the action. See Spicer, *Pascua*, 21–22.

57. Spicer, *Cycles of Conquest*, 83; Spicer, *Yaquis*, 236.

58. Spicer, *Yaquis*, 235; Spicer, *Pascua*, 18–20.

59. Hu-DeHart, "Resistance and Survival," iii; Hu-DeHart, *Missionaries, Miners, and Indians*, 2.

60. Hu-DeHart, *Missionaries, Miners, and Indians*, 2.

61. Ibid. Aside from the Yaquis, many other indigenous groups in the U.S.–Mexico borderlands have successfully resisted assimilation into the white man's world, but of course none have remained culturally intact. Groups like the Mayos, Ópatas, Seris, Pimas, Tarahumaras, Mescaleros, Pueblos, Navajos, Hopis, and Tohono O'odham have a relatively autonomous existence, although historically they have been afflicted by economic marginalization, poverty, and other social problems. Of course, those tribes that have embraced gaming operations have increased their exposure to the outside world.

62. *Christian Science Monitor*, March 4, 1998, 4; *Arizona Daily Star*, May 16, 2000, and May 30, 2001.

63. The account of Tigua history that follows is reprinted, with some modifications, from my booklet *The First Peoples*.

64. *Washington Post*, September 26, 2004; *USA Today*, September 30, 2004.

65. U.S. Commission on Civil Rights, *Southwest Indian Report*, 2, 53.

66. Ibid., 2–3.

67. *El Paso Herald Post*, May 5, 1983, 1; *El Diario de Juárez*, June 2, 1983, 1, 8.

68. *New York Times*, October 31, 1994, A4, and June 2, 1995, A1.

Chapter 4. Mexican Americans, Ethnic Conflict, and Identity Issues

1. U.S. Congress, House, *El Paso Troubles*, 51, 78.

2. See statement of Paso del Norte priest Ramón Ortíz in ibid., 68–69.

3. Bowden, "Magoffin Salt War"; U.S. Congress, House, *El Paso Troubles*, 68; Sonnichsen, *El Paso Salt War*, 7–8.

4. U.S. Congress, House, *El Paso Troubles*, 14–15, 132–34, 137. Determining the citizenship of people who lived in the U.S. border communities often presented problems, as indicated by Capt. Thomas Blair of the Fifteenth Infantry: "The citizenship of some of the [participants in the disturbance] seems to be rather uncertain, as they sometimes live on one side of the border, sometimes on the other, and had resided for some time previous to the riot in Texas and in New Mexico" (58). Recognition of the strong bonds that linked Mexicans across the border is underscored by the following statements: "The people of one [side of the Rio Grande] are bound to those of the other by more than the ordinary obligation of race and hospitality. They have married and intermarried; their interests are in many respects identical; their wants and fears spring from the same source and hold them in sympathy; for time out of mind they have reciprocally enjoyed the same feasts and festivities; they are invited by the same religion, and have all the passions and prejudices common to an ignorant [sic] people" (statement of J. P. Hague, 50). "Having lived here over 25 years, ever since I have been here, the Mexicans have claimed this country [the El Paso area] as belonging to the Republic of Mexico. I have never been able to prevent or keep the Mexicans of El Paso, Mexico, from herding my lands" (statement of Joseph Schutz, 54).

5. Ibid., 143, 153, 115, 120, 137, 140–41, 146, 152.

6. Sonnichsen, *El Paso Salt War*, 4.

7. Martínez, *Fragments of the Mexican Revolution*, 137–40, 145–48.

8. Crisp, "Anglo-Texan Attitudes," 90–92, 96.

9. Ibid., 325–26.

10. Ibid., 340, 392, 396; Tijerina, "Tejanos and Texas," 319–20.

11. Tijerina, "Tejanos and Texas," 318.

12. *Morning Star* (Houston), May 28, 1942, cited in Crisp, "Anglo-Texan Attitudes," 387–88.

13. *Personal Memoirs of John N. Seguín*, 1, 8, 10–11.

14. Ibid.; Crisp, "Anglo-Texan Attitudes," 368–69, 399–403.

15. The unique characteristics of the Lower Rio Grande Valley as a closely integrated and independent-minded region are discussed in Rosenbaum, *Mexican Resistance*, 35–39.

16. Goldfinch, "Juan N. Cortina," 23–24, 37; Webb, *Texas Rangers*, 193.

17. Acuña, *Occupied America*, 34.

18. Goldfinch, "Juan N. Cortina," 25; Canales, *Juan N. Cortina*, 6; U.S. Congress, House, *Southwestern Frontier*, 72.

19. U.S. Congress, House, *Difficulties*, 82.

20. Ibid., 71–72.

21. Goldfinch, "Juan N. Cortina," 62–63; Acuña, *Occupied America*, 37.

22. The defamation of the Mexican character by U.S. fiction writers as well as the print and visual media has been well documented. See Paredes, "Image of the Mexican"; De León, *They Called Them Greasers*; Pettit, *Images of the Mexican American*; Robinson, *With the Ears of Strangers*; Robinson, *Mexico and the Hispanic Southwest*; and Martínez, "Advertising and Racism."

23. Additional terms used by Mexican Americans to refer to themselves have included "Spanish American," "Latin American," "Hispano/a," and "Latino/a." Some regional variants are "Tejano/a," "Nuevo Mexicano/a," and "Californio/a."

24. *New York Times*, May 4, 1969, 78; U.S. Supreme Court, *Saxbe v. Bustos*.

25. *El Paso Herald Post*, November 22, 1974, A1.

26. The following incident is an example of Chicano/a contempt for Mexican currency. As I prepared to pay the donation at a community fundraiser in El Paso in mid-1983, a prominent Chicano elected official boasted that the event was raising lots of money, that among the bills stuffed in the collection box there was even "uno de cien bolas" (one one hundred–denomination bill). He then asked the person in charge of taking the money to show me the big bill. She dug into the box and produced a one hundred–peso note, and they both smiled wryly. At the time Mexican currency was experiencing frequent devaluations.

27. Mexico's problems, of course, are a product of complex forces frequently not understood or deliberately ignored by many people. Just as European Americans in general fail to appreciate worldwide drops in oil prices, recurring recessions in the global economy, and other external factors that account largely for Mexico's misfortunes, so do many Chicanos/as. Critics fall back instead on negative stereotypes to explain conditions in the neighboring country.

28. One example is Ruben Bonilla, chairman of the Texas Mexican American Democrats and ex-LULAC national president, who called on the Mexican government to annul the 1986 Chihuahua elections.

29. The feelings of Chicanos/as toward Mexico are explored in de la Garza, "Chicano Perspective of Mexico."

30. De la Garza, "Chicanos and U.S. Foreign Policy." See also Juan N. Vásquez, "Mexico-Chicano Political Dialogue Fades," *Los Angeles Times*, August 12, 1983.

Chapter 5. Norteños/as, Fronterizos/as, and Foreign Dependence

1. The literature on northern Mexico is vast, but few efforts have been made to seriously examine the history of the region and its relationship to the rest of Mexico. The recent outpouring of works on border problems by Mexican writers clearly illustrates Mexico's preoccupation with conditions in the border states. Helpful sources for the understanding of the north include Bannon, *Spanish Borderlands Frontier*; Escoto Ochoa, *Integración y desintegración*; Flores Caballero, *Evolución de la frontera norte*; Gonzáles Salazar, *Frontera del norte*; León-Portilla, "Norteño Variety of Mexican Culture"; Martínez, *Border Boom Town*; Martínez, *Fragments of the Mexican Revolution*; Martínez, *Historia de Baja California*; Mora-Torres, *The Making of the Mexican Border*; Ojeda, *Administración del desarrollo*; Saragoza, *The Monterrey Elite and the Mexican State*; Sepúlveda, *Frontera norte de México*; Weber, *Mexican Frontier*.

2. Details of how the PRI rigged the elections in Sonora are given in the *Financial Times of London*, July 16, 1985, 34.

3. The strategy formulated by the PRI to recapture Chihuahua is detailed in *Proceso*, July 7, 1986, 6–10. Interestingly, this article was published a few days *before* the elections (held on July 6), which gave voters advance notice of what the ruling party would do to "win." The widespread evidence of fraud gathered by civic groups during the elections is contained in Comité de la Lucha por la Democracia, *Chihuahua '86*.

4. *El Diario de Juárez*, July 14, 1986, 2, and August 10, 1986, 1.

5. For reports on the demonstrations and the bridge takeovers see the *El Paso Herald Post*, July 12, 1986, A1; *El Paso Times*, August 4, 1986, A1; *El Diario de Juárez*, August 10, 1986, 1, and August 18, 1986, A2.

6. Their stay in El Paso lasted two weeks, after which they returned to Parral upon being assured that they would not be arrested. See *El Paso Herald Post*, August 21, 1986, A1; *El Diario de Juárez*, August 31, 1986, 1.

7. *El Paso Times*, July 6, 2004, B1.

8. Meyer and Sherman, *Course of Mexican History*, 446–47.

9. Martínez, *Border Boom Town*, 10–13. The historical background of the border communities presented in this section is based largely on *Border Boom Town*.

10. *Programa Nacional Fronterizo*; Secretaría de Industria y Comercio, *Estudio del desarrollo comercial*; *Proceso*, October 11, 1982; *Dallas Morning News*, February 27, 1983, sec. A.

11. *El Paso Times*, June 22, 2003 (special report, "10 Years of NAFTA").

12. Martínez, *Border Boom Town*, 29–31.

13. *Kansas City Star*, July 21, 1930.

14. The role of the Mexican border cities in providing cheap labor for the U.S. borderlands is explained in Martínez, "Chicanos and the Border Cities."

15. *Washington Post*, April 20, 1986.

16. El Paso Chamber of Commerce, *El Paso Area Fact Book*, 12:1.

17. The history of Mexican migration to the United States is treated in the following works: Cardoso, *Mexican Emigration*; Corwin, *Immigrants and Immigrants*; Cross and Sandos, *Across the Border*; Reisler, *By the Sweat of Their Brow*; Samora, *Los Mojados*.

18. Cited in Weber, *Mexican Frontier*, 207.

19. *Revista Novedades*, February 14, 1948.

20. *A Toda Máquina*, March 1954.

21. *Norte*, August 31, 1957.

22. On North American cultural influences in the Mexican border region and suggested strategies for dealing with the "problem" see Castellanos Guerrero and López y Rivas, "Influencia norteamericana"; Mendoza Berrueto, "Algunos aspectos socioeconómicos," esp. 58–67.

23. Hidalgo, *Language Attitudes*, 8–9.

24. Ibid. An interesting project at the state level is former Chihuahua Governor Manuel Ornelas's creation of a Centro de Estudios Musicales (Center for the Study of Music) in Chihuahua City to facilitate the learning of Mexican classical music. By elevating the taste of youth for national forms, the governor hoped to counteract the constant onslaught of rock music from the United States. See *El Diario de Juárez*, June 8, 1984.

25. Bustamante, "Identidad nacional."

26. *Wall Street Journal*, May 27, 1986.

Chapter 6. Growth, the Environment, and the Border Flow

1. Rice and Bernard, *Sunbelt Cities*, 11–15.

2. Ibid., 16–20.

3. I thank the late Larry McConville, former research associate at the Center for Inter-American and Border Studies, University of Texas at El Paso, for his contributions to this section.

4. To provide the energy for the enormous consumption of electricity for air conditioners in the Phoenix area, large parts of Arizona and New Mexico have been mined for coal. The extraction of coal from the Four Corners area and the Colorado Plateau has had considerable impact upon the landscape.

5. The standard work on this subject is Hundley, *Dividing the Waters*.

6. The Colorado River water dispute is discussed in Sepúlveda, *Frontera norte de México*, 129–44. See also *Arizona Daily Star*, June 3, 2001, A6–7.

7. *San Antonio Express-News*, August 28, 2004, 1A; *Los Angeles Times*, March 11, 2005, 7A.

8. *Symposium on U.S.–Mexican Transboundary Resources*; Ross, *Ecology and Development*, chap. 4.

9. Experts disagree on the amount of water left in the aquifer and how long it will last, yet all strongly urge conservation. See Day, "International Aquifer Management"; *El Paso Herald Post*, December 5, 1983; Jamail and Mumme, "Disputing Hidden Waters"; interview, Nestor Valencia, El Paso Community Foundation, March 18, 2005.

10. The seriousness of the water problem in Juárez is reflected in the following headlines from *El Diario de Juárez*: "Grave escasés de agua amenaza a 42 colonias" (Grave scarcity of water threatens 42 neighborhoods), April 15, 1985; "Crece la tensión social por falta de agua" (Social tension rises as a result of lack of water), June 8, 1985; "Mueren deshidratados dos niños cada día" (Two children die from dehydration daily), June 9, 1985; "Sin gota de agua las partes altas" (The high areas are without a drop of water), June 11, 1985. The press has continued to report such problems in recent years.

11. Undated article from the *Washington Post*, reprinted in *Estudios Fronterizos*, 83–84.

12. *Los Angeles Times*, September 26, 1983, and February 22, 1987; Ganster, "Environmental Issues."

13. *New York Times*, July 27, 2001, A12; *Financial Times of London*, October 24, 1998, 3.

14. Nitze, "Meeting the Water Needs," 9–11; *El Paso Times*, June 23, 2003.

15. *San Diego Union-Tribune*, December 16, 2001, A1.

16. Bell and Smallwood, *Zona Libre*.

17. Martínez, *Border Boom Town*, 27–30.

18. Ibid., 66, 78–82.

19. Ibid., 124–25.

20. Ibid.

21. See Lupsha and Schlegel, "Drug Trafficking," and Walker, *Drugs in the Western Hemisphere*, for background on the drug trade.

22. *El Diario de Juárez*, February 21, 1985.

23. Ibid., January 15, 1984, and May 30, 1984; *El Paso Herald Post*, December 31, 1984; *El Paso Times*, July 15, 1985, and July 26, 1986.

24. *San Antonio Express-News*, December 18, 2004, 10.

Chapter 7. Migration, Drugs, and Violence

1. *Statistical Yearbook*, tables 1–2. Excellent books on the history of Mexican migration to the United States include Balderrama and Rodríguez, *Decade of Betrayal*; Gamio, *The Life Story of the Mexican Immigrant*; García, *Operation Wetback*; Gutiérrez, *Walls and Mirrors*; and Reisler, *By the Sweat of Their Brow*.

2. Martínez, *Border Boom Town*, 80–82. The Institute of Oral History at the University of Texas at El Paso has an extensive collection of tape-recorded interviews that document many problems encountered by Mexicans crossing the border.

3. Kristein, "Anglo over Bracero," 145–49.

4. The "Tortilla Curtain" incident is discussed in Stoddard, Martínez, and Martínez Lasso, *El Paso–Ciudad Juárez Relations*.

5. Martínez, "Frontera vista por René Mascareñas Miranda," 287–88.

6. For background on the militarization of the border see Dunn, *Militarization of the U.S.–Mexico Border*.

7. *Arizona Daily Star*, September 29, 2002, and June 6, 2002. Over the last decade the Center for Immigration Research at the University of Houston has kept track of the number of migrants who have died attempting to cross the border. See www.uh.edu/cir/.

8. See, for example, Buchanan, *Death of the West*, chap. 6; and Huntington, *Who Are We?* chap. 9.

9. For concise reviews of the research on the impact of immigrants see Center for Immigration Studies, "The Cost of Immigration," and González Baker, Cushing, and Haynes, "Fiscal Impacts."

10. Robinson, "Vice and Tourism," 25–28.

11. Quoted in Mottier, "Organised Crime," 17–18.

12. Ibid., 27–45.

13. See Walker, *Drugs in the Western Hemisphere*.

14. Gray, *Why Our Drug Laws Have Failed*, 42.

15. Cruz Soto, "Efectos económicos."

16. Getty, "Mexico's Forgotten Disappeared," as reported in Frontera, www.nmsu.edu/~frontera/.

17. *El Paso Times*, June 23, 2002.

18. *El Diario de Juárez*, May 16, 2001, as reported in Frontera, www.nmsu.edu/~frontera/.

19. *New York Times*, September 18, 1998, A6.

20. *El Paso Times*, January 1, 1998.

21. Ibid., December 1, 1999, January 29, 2004, and January 6, 2005; *Arizona Daily Star*, December 3, 1999, and February 13, 2005.

22. The U.S. State Department Public Announcement was issued on February 4, 2005. See http://travel.state.gov/travel. The resulting diplomatic flap was well covered in the press.

23. *El Diario de Juárez*, January 18, 2004; *Arizona Daily Star*, October 26, 2004; Washington Valdez, *Cosecha de mujeres*, 211, 237, app. 2.

24. *El Diario de Juárez*, May 18, 2001, and May 23, 2001; *El Mañana*, October 9, 2002, as reported in Frontera, www.nmsu.edu/~frontera/.

25. *El Paso Herald Post*, November 25, 1989, and October 6, 1990.

26. *Arizona Daily Star*, July 9, 1995.

27. *El Diario de Juárez*, June 29, 2001, as reported in Frontera, www.nmsu.edu/~frontera/.

28. *Washington Post*, November 3, 1997.

29. Gray, *Why Our Drug Laws Have Failed*, 74.

30. *Washington Post*, November 3, 1997.

31. *Los Angeles Times*, December 13, 1998.

Conclusion

1. Hansen, "Comparative Perspective," 9.

2. Briner, "The Regio Basiliensis."

3. Huntington, *Who Are We?* chap. 9.

4. Stoddard, "Northern Mexican Migration," 64.

5. Ibid.

Bibliography

Newspapers and Magazines
Albuquerque Journal
Arizona Daily Star
A Toda Máquina
Christian Science Monitor
Dallas Morning News
El Diario de Juárez
El Fronterizo
El Paso Herald Post
El Paso Times
Financial Times of London
Hispanic Monitor
Kansas City Star
Los Angeles Times
Monitor (McAllen, Texas)
Morning Star (Houston)
New York Times
Norte (Ciudad Juárez, Mexico)
Proceso (Mexico City)
Revista Novedades (Ciudad Juárez, Mexico)
San Antonio Express-News
San Diego Union-Tribune
USA Today
Wall Street Journal
Washington Post

Acuña, Rodolfo. *Occupied America: A History of Chicanos*. 2d ed. New York: Harper and Row, 1981.
Alisky, Marvin. "Mexican Border Conflicts and Compromises." *Southeastern Latin Americanist* 17, no. 2 (1973): 1–5.
Andreas, Peter. *Border Games: Policing the U.S.–Mexico Divide*. Ithaca, N.Y.: Cornell University Press, 2000.
Anzaldúa, Gloria. *Borderlands, La Frontera: The New Mestiza*. San Francisco: Aunt Lute Book Co., 1987.
Aramburo, Guillermo. *Encuesta sobre transmigración en la frontera norte*. Mexicali: IIS-UABC, 1988.
Arreola, Daniel D., and James R. Curtis. *The Mexican Border Cities: Landscape Anatomy and Place Personality*. Tucson: University of Arizona Press, 1993.
Asiwaju, Anthony I., ed. *Partitioned Africans: Studies in Ethnic Relations across Africa's International Boundaries, 1884–1984*. London: C. Hurst and Co., 1984.
Bailey, Lynn R. *Indian Slave Trade in the Southwest*. Los Angeles: Westernlore Press, 1966.
———. *The Long Walk: A History of the Navajo Wars, 1846–1868*. Pasadena, Calif.: Socio-Technical Books, 1970.

Balderrama, Francisco E., and Raymond Rodríguez. *Decade of Betrayal: Mexican Repatriation in the 1930s.* Rev. ed. Albuquerque: University of New Mexico Press, 2006.

Bancroft, Hubert Howe. *Works.* Vol. 27, *History of Arizona and New Mexico, 1530–1888.* San Francisco: History Co., 1889.

Bannon, John Francis. *The Spanish Borderlands Frontier, 1513–1821.* New York: Holt, Rinehart and Winston, 1970.

Bartlett, John Russell. *Personal Narrative of Explorations and Incidents in Texas, New Mexico, California, Sonora, and Chihuahua.* 2 vols. New York and London: D. Appleton and Co., 1854.

Beck, Warren A., and Ynez D. Haase. *Historical Atlas of New Mexico.* Norman: University of Oklahoma Press, 1969.

Bell, Samuel E., and James M. Smallwood. *The Zona Libre, 1858–1905: A Problem in American Diplomacy.* Southwestern Studies Monograph no. 69. El Paso: Texas Western Press, 1982.

Benjamin, Thomas. "Recent Historiography of the Origins of the U.S.–Mexico War." *New Mexico Historical Review* 54, no. 3 (1979): 169–81.

Benjamin, Thomas, and William McNellie, eds. *Other Mexicos: Essays on Regional Mexican History, 1876–1911.* Albuquerque: University of New Mexico Press, 1984.

Billington, Ray Allen. *Westward Expansion: A History of the American Frontier.* New York: Macmillan, 1960.

Binkley, William C. *The Expansionist Movement in Texas.* Berkeley: University of California Press, 1925.

Blaisdell, Lowell J. *The Desert Revolution: Baja California, 1911.* Madison: University of Wisconsin Press, 1962.

———. "Harry Chandler and Mexican Border Intrigue." *Pacific Historical Review* 35, no. 4 (November 1966): 385–93.

———. "Was It Revolution or Filibustering? The Mystery of the Flores Magón Revolt in Baja California." *Pacific Historical Review* 23, no. 2 (May 1954): 147–64.

Bowden, Charles. *Juárez: The Laboratory of Our Future.* New York: Aperture Foundation, 1998.

Bowden, J. J. "The Magoffin Salt War." *Password* (El Paso County Historical Society) 8, no. 3 (Summer 1963): 95–121.

———. *Spanish and Mexican Land Grants in the Chihuahuan Acquisition.* El Paso: Texas Western Press, 1971.

Briner, Hans. "The Regio Basiliensis: A Model of Transfrontier Cooperation." In *Across Boundaries: Transborder Interaction in Perspective,* edited by Oscar J. Martínez, 45–53. El Paso: Texas Western Press, 1986.

Brooks, Philip C. *Diplomacy and the Borderlands: The Adams-Onis Treaty, 1819.* Berkeley: University of California Press, 1939.

Brown, Charles H. *Agents of Manifest Destiny: The Lives and Times of the Filibusters.* Chapel Hill: University of North Carolina Press, 1979.

Buchanan, Patrick J. *The Death of the West: How Dying Populations and Immigrant Invasions Imperil Our Country and Civilization.* New York: St. Martin's Press, 2002.

Bustamante, Jorge. "Identidad nacional en la frontera forte de México: Hallazgos preliminares." Centro de Estudios Fronterizos del Norte de México, Tijuana, Mexico, 1983.

Call, Frank J. "A Survey of Environmental Problems along the U.S.–Mexico Border." In *Air Quality Issues in El Paso–Cd. Juarez Border Region,* edited by Willard P. Gingerich, 1–3. Center for Inter-American and Border Studies, Occasional Paper no. 5. El Paso: University of Texas at El Paso, 1980.

Canales, José T. *Juan N. Cortina Presents His Motion for a New Trial.* San Antonio: Artes Gráficas, 1951; New York: Arno Press, 1974.

Cardoso, Lawrence A. *Mexican Emigration to the United States, 1877–1931.* Tucson: University of Arizona Press, 1980.

Castellanos Guerrero, Alicia, and Gilberto López y Rivas. "La influencia norteamericana en la cultura de la frontera norte de México." In *La frontera del norte: Integración y desarrollo*, edited by Roque González Salazar, 68–84. Mexico City: El Colegio de México, 1981.

Ceballos Ramírez, Manuel, coordinator. *Encuentro en la frontera: Mexicanos y norteamericanos en un espacio común.* Mexico City: El Colegio de México, 2001.

Censos generales de población. Mexico City: Dirección General de Estadística, 1950–2000. www.inegi.gob.mx.

Center for Immigration Studies. "The Costs of Immigration: Assessing a Conflicted Issue." *Backgrounder*, no. 2-94 (September 1994): 1–21.

Chamberlain, Eugene Keith. "Mexican Colonization versus American Interests in Lower California." *Pacific Historical Review* 20, no. 1 (February 1951): 43–55.

Clendenen, Clarence C. *Blood on the Border: The United States Army and the Mexican Irregulars.* New York: Macmillan, 1969.

Coerver, Don M. "From Morteritos to Chamizal: The U.S.–Mexican Boundary Treaty of 1884." *Red River Valley Historical Review* 2, no. 4 (1975): 531–38.

Comisión Pesquisadora de la Frontera del Norte. *Reports of the Committee of Investigation Sent in 1873 by the Mexican Government to the Frontier of Texas.* New York: Baker and Goodwin, 1875. (Translation of original report: *Informe de la Comisión Pesquisadora de la Frontera del Norte al Ejecutivo de la Union.* Mexico City, 1874.)

Comité de la Lucha por la Democracia. *Chihuahua '86. ¿Vencedores del desierto o asesinos de la democracia?* 1986.

Community Research Associates. *Undocumented Immigrants: Their Impact on the County of San Diego.* San Diego, Calif.: Community Research Associates, 1980.

Connor, Seymour V., and Odie B. Faulk. *North America Divided: The U.S.–Mexico War, 1846–1848.* New York: Oxford University Press, 1971.

Conover, Ted. *Coyotes: A Journey Through the Secret World of America's Illegal Aliens.* New York: Random House, 1987.

Cornelius, Wayne A. *Mexican Migration to the United States: Causes, Consequences and U.S. Responses.* Cambridge: Massachusetts Institute of Technology Center for International Studies, 1978.

Corwin, Arthur F. "America's Immigration Dilemma; with Special Reference to Mexico." June 1975.

Corwin, Arthur F., ed. *Immigrants and Immigrants: Perspectives on Mexican Labor Migration to the United States.* Westport, Conn.: Greenwood Press, 1978.

Cosío Villegas, Daniel. *Historia moderna de México.* Vol. 6, *El Porfiriato: La vida política exterior.* Mexico City: Editorial Hermes, 1955–70.

Cox, I. J. "The Southwest Boundary of Texas." *Quarterly of the Texas State Historical Association (Southwestern Historical Quarterly)* 6, no. 2 (October 1902): 81–102.

Crisp, James Ernest. "Anglo-Texan Attitudes toward the Mexican, 1821–1845." Ph.D. diss., Yale University, 1976.

Cross, Harry E., and James E. Sandos. *Across the Border: Rural Development in Mexico and Recent Migration to the United States.* Berkeley: Institute of Government Studies, University of California–Berkeley, 1981.

Cruz Soto, Gustavo. "Efectos económicos de la Operación Interceptación en Ciudad Juárez." Thesis, Universidad Nacional Autónoma de México, 1972.

Cue Canovas, Agustín. *Los Estados Unidos y el México olvidado.* Mexico City: B. Costa-Amic, 1970; New York: Arno Press, 1976.

Dale, Edward E. *The Indians of the Southwest: A Century of Development under the United States.* Norman: University of Oklahoma Press, 1949.

Dana, Samuel Trach, and Myron Krueger. *California Lands: Ownership, Use, and Management*. Washington, D.C.: American Forestry Association, 1958.

Day, J. C. "International Aquifer Management: The Hueco Bolson and the Rio Grande River." *Natural Resources Journal* 18 (January 1978): 168–69.

De la Garza, Rodolfo O. "A Chicano Perspective of Mexico." Author's files, n.d.

———. "Chicanos and U.S. Foreign Policy: The Future of Chicano-Mexican Relations." *Western Political Quarterly* 33, no. 4 (December 1980): 571–82.

———. "Texas Land Grants and U.S.–Mexican–Chicano Relations: A Study in Linkage Politics." Paper presented at the meeting of the Latin American Studies Association, Mexico City, October 1, 1983.

De la Garza, Rudolph O., Z. Anthony Kruszewski, and Tomás A. Arciniega. *Chicanos and Native Americans: The Territorial Minorities*. Englewood Cliffs, New Jersey: Prentice-Hall, 1973.

De León, Arnoldo. *The Tejano Community, 1836–1900*. Albuquerque: University of New Mexico Press, 1982.

———. *They Called Them Greasers: Anglo Attitudes toward Mexicans in Texas, 1821–1900*. Austin: University of Texas Press, 1983.

Demaris, Ovid. *Poso del Mundo*. New York: Pocket Books, 1971.

Dunn, Timothy J. *The Militarization of the U.S.–Mexico Border, 1978–1992: Low-Intensity Conflict Doctrine Comes Home*. Austin: Center for Mexican American Studies, University of Texas at Austin, 1996.

Dwyer, Augusta. *On the Line: Life on the U.S.–Mexico Border*. London: Latin American Bureau, 1994.

Ellison, Simon J. "An Anglo-American Plan for the Colonization of Mexico." *Southwestern Social Science Quarterly* 16, no. 2 (1935–36): 42–52.

El Paso Chamber of Commerce. *El Paso Area Fact Book, 1981–1982*. El Paso, 1982.

Escoto Ochoa, Humberto. *Integración y desintegración de nuestra frontera norte*. Mexico City: Universidad Nacional Autónoma de México, 1949.

Estudios Fronterizos. Mexico City: ANUIES, 1981.

Faulk, Odie B. "A Colonization Plan for Northern Sonora, 1850." *New Mexico Historical Review* 44, no. 4 (October 1969): 293–314.

———. *Too Far North, Too Far South*. Los Angeles: Westernlore Press, 1967.

Faulk, Odie B., and Joseph A. Stout Jr., eds. *The U.S.–Mexico War: Changing Interpretations*. Chicago: Sage Books, 1973.

Fernández, Raúl A. *The United States–Mexico Border: A Politico-Economic Profile*. Notre Dame, Ind.: University of Notre Dame Press, 1977.

Flores Caballero, Romeo. *Evolución de la frontera norte*. Monterrey, Mexico: Universidad Autónoma de Nuevo León, 1982.

Forbes, Robert H. *Crabb's Filibustering Expeditions into Sonora, 1857: A Historical Account*. Tucson: Arizona Silhouettes, 1952.

Friedkin, J. F. "The International Boundary and Water Commission, United States and Mexico." Paper presented at the UCLA Chicano Studies Center Symposium on U.S.–Mexico Border Relations, Santa Monica, California, April 24, 1981.

Fuller, John D. P. *The Movement for the Acquisition of All Mexico*. Baltimore, Md.: Johns Hopkins University Press, 1936.

Gamio, Manuel. *The Life Story of the Mexican Immigrant: Autobiographic Documents*. New York: Dover, 1971.

Ganster, Paul. "Environmental Issues of the California–Baja California Border Region." *Border Environmental Reports* 1 (June 1996).

———, ed. *The U.S.–Mexican Border Environment: A Road Map to a Sustainable 2020*. San Diego, Calif.: San Diego State University Press, 2000.

Ganster, Paul, and David E. Lorey, eds. *Borders and Border Politics in a Globalizing World*. Lanham, Md.: Rowan and Littlefield, 2005.

Garber, Paul Neff. *The Gadsden Treaty*. Philadelphia: University of Pennsylvania Press, 1923.

García, Juan Ramon. *Operation Wetback: The Mass Deportation of Mexican Undocumented Workers in 1954*. Westport, Conn.: Greenwood Press, 1980.

García Cantú, Gastón. *Las invasiones norteamericanas en México*. Mexico City: Ediciones Era, 1971.

Garner, Van Hastings. "The Treaty of Guadalupe Hidalgo and the California Indians." *Indian Historian* 9, no. 1 (Winter 1976): 10–13.

Gerhard, Peter. "The Socialist Invasion of Baja California, 1911." *Pacific Historical Review* 15, no. 3 (September 1946): 295–304.

Getty, Mark. "Mexico's Forgotten Disappeared: The Victims of the Border Narco Bloodbath." Frontera NorteSur, http://frontera.nmsu.edu. Accessed February 2004.

Gibson, Arrell M. *The Kickapoos: Lords of the Middle Border*. Norman: University of Oklahoma Press, 1963.

Gibson, Lay James, and Alfonso Corona Rentería, eds. *The U.S. and Mexico: Borderland Development and the National Economies*. Boulder, Colo.: Westview Press, 1985.

Goetzmann, W. H. "The United States–Mexican Boundary Survey, 1848–1853." *Southwestern Historical Quarterly* 62 (1958–59): 164–90.

Goldfinch, Charles W. "Juan N. Cortina, 1824–1892: A Re-Appraisal." Master's thesis, University of Chicago, 1949; New York: Arno Press, 1974.

González, Antonio P., and J. Figueroa Domenech. *La Revolución y sus héroes*. Mexico City, 1911.

González Baker, Susan, Robert G. Cushing, and Charles W. Haynes. "Fiscal Impacts of Mexican Migration to the United States." In *At the Crossroads: Mexico and U.S. Immigration Policy*, edited by Frank D. Bean et al. Lanham, Md.: Rowan and Littlefield, 1997.

González Salazar, Roque, ed. *La frontera del norte: Integración y desarrollo*. Mexico City: El Colegio de México, 1981.

Gray, Judge James P. *Why Our Drug Laws Have Failed and What We Can Do About It: A Judicial Indictment of the War on Drugs*. Philadelphia: Temple University Press, 2001.

Gray, Mike. *Drug Crazy: How We Got into This Mess and How We Can Get Out*. New York: Random House, 1998.

Green, Lawrence. *The Filibuster: The Career of William Walker*. Indianapolis: Bobbs-Merrill Co., 1937.

Gregg, Robert D. *The Influence of Border Troubles on Relations between the United States and Mexico, 1876–1910*. Baltimore, Md.: Johns Hopkins Press, 1937.

Griswold del Castillo, Richard. "La Frontera and the Border: Mexican and American Historical Views of the Mexican American Frontier." Paper presented at the Border Governors' Conference, Tijuana, Mexico, September 20–21, 1982.

Gutiérrez, David G. *Walls and Mirrors: Mexican Americans, Mexican Immigrants, and the Politics of Ethnicity*. Berkeley: University of California Press, 1995.

Hackett, Charles W., ed. *Richardo's Treatise on the Limits of Louisiana and Texas*. 3 vols. Austin: University of Texas Press, 1931–34.

Hansen, Niles. "Comparative Perspective on Border Region Development in Western Europe and in the U.S.–Mexico Borderlands." In *Across Boundaries: Transborder Interaction in Perspective*, edited by Oscar J. Martínez, 31–44. El Paso: Texas Western Press, 1985.

Hawgood, J. A. "John Charles Fremont and the Bear Flag Revolution: A Reappraisal." *Southern California Quarterly* 44, no. 5 (1962): 67–96.

Herzog, Lawrence A. "Border Commuter Workers and Transfrontier Metropolitan Structure along the United States–Mexico Border." *Journal of Borderlands Studies* 2 (Fall 1990): 1–20.

———. *Where North Meets South: Cities, Space, and Politics on the U.S.–Mexico Border*. Austin: Center for Mexican American Studies, University of Texas at Austin, 1990.

Heyman, Josiah McC. *Life and Labor on the Border: Working People of Northeastern Sonora, Mexico, 1886–1986*. Tucson: University of Arizona Press, 1991.

Hidalgo, Margarita. *Language Attitudes and Language Use in Ciudad Juárez, México.* Center for Inter-American and Border Studies, Border Issues and Public Policy Reports, no. 17. El Paso: University of Texas, October 1984.

Hinojosa, Gilberto Miguel. *A Borderlands Town in Transition: Laredo, 1755–1810.* College Station: Texas A & M University Press, 1983.

Hollon, William Eugene. *The Southwest: Old and New.* New York: Knopf, 1961.

Horgan, Paul. *Great River: The Rio Grande in North American History.* 2 vols. New York: Rinehart, 1954.

House, John W. *Frontier on the Rio Grande: A Political Geography of Development and Social Deprivation.* New York: Oxford University Press, 1982.

Hu-DeHart, Evelyn. *Missionaries, Miners, and Indians: Spanish Contact with the Yaqui Nation of Northwestern New Spain, 1533–1820.* Tucson: University of Arizona Press, 1981.

———. "Resistance and Survival: A History of the Yaqui People's Struggle for Autonomy, 1533–1910." Ph.D. diss., University of Texas at Austin, 1976.

Hundley, Norris, Jr. *Dividing the Waters: A Century of Controversy between the United States and Mexico.* Berkeley: University of California Press, 1966.

———. *Water and the West: The Colorado River Compact and the Politics of Water in the American West.* Berkeley: University of California Press, 1976.

Huntington, Samuel P. *Who Are We? The Challenges to America's National Identity.* New York: Simon and Schuster, 2004.

Jackson, Donald, ed. *Zebulon Montgomery Pike, 1779–1813. Journals, with Letters and Related Documents.* Norman: University of Oklahoma Press, 1966.

Jamail, Milton H. "Indians on the Border." *Indian Historian* 10, no. 3 (1977): 34–37.

Jamail, Milton H., and Stephen H. Mumme. "Disputing Hidden Waters: Groundwater along the U.S.–Mexico Border." *New Scholar* 9 (1984): 215–30.

Jones, Stephen B. "Boundary Concepts in the Setting of Place and Time." *Annals* (of the Association of American Geographers) 46, no. 3 (September 1959): 241–55.

Kearney, Milo, and Anthony Knopp. *Border Cuates: A History of the U.S.–Mexican Twin Cities.* Austin: Eakin Press, 1995.

Kendall, George W. *Narrative of the Texas Santa Fe Expedition.* 2 vols. Edited by Milo M. Quaife. London, 1848; Chicago: University of Chicago Press, 1929; Austin: University of Texas Press, 1935.

Kristein, Peter N. "Anglo over Bracero: A History of the Mexican Worker in the United States from Roosevelt to Nixon." Ph.D. diss., St. Louis University, 1973.

Kristof, K. D. "The Nature of Frontiers and Boundaries." *Annals* (of the Association of American Geographers) 49 (September 1959): 269–82.

Lamar, Howard Roberts. *The Far Southwest, 1846–1912.* New York: Norton, 1970.

Lambert, Paul F. "The 'All-Mexico' Movement." In *The U.S.–Mexico War: Changing Interpretations,* edited by Odie B. Faulk and Joseph A. Stout Jr., 163–72. Chicago: Sage Books, 1973.

Latorre, Dolores L., and Felipe A. Latorre. *The Mexican Kickapoo Indians.* Austin: University of Texas Press, 1976.

Lattimore, Owen D. "The Frontier in History." In *Theory in Anthropology: A Sourcebook,* edited by Robert A. Manners and David Kaplaw, 374–86. Chicago: Aldine, 1968.

Leonard, Glen M. "Southwestern Boundaries and the Principles of Statemaking." *Western Historical Quarterly* 8 (January 1977): 39–53.

León-Portilla, Miguel. "The Norteño Variety of Mexican Culture: An Ethnohistorical Approach." In *Plural Society in the Southwest,* edited by Edward H. Spicer and Raymond H. Thompson, 77–114. New York: Weatherhead Foundation, 1972.

Liss, Sheldon. *A Century of Disagreement: The Chamizal Conflict, 1864–1964.* Washington, D.C.: University Press, 1965.

Loomis, Noel M. *The Texas–Santa Fe Pioneers.* Norman: University of Oklahoma Press, 1958.

Lorey, David E. *The U.S.–Mexican Border in the Twentieth Century*. Wilmington, Del.: Scholarly Resources, 1999.

Los Angeles Times. Poll No. 65 (Latinos). February 1983.

Lupsha, Peter A., and Kip Schlegel. "Drug Trafficking in the Borderlands: Its Impact on North/South Relations." Paper presented at the meeting of the Latin American Studies Association, Pittsburgh, April 5–9, 1979.

MacLachlan, Colin M., and William H. Beezley. *El Gran Pueblo: A History of Greater Mexico*. 3rd ed. Upper Saddle River, N.J.: Prentice-Hall, 2004.

Martínez, Orlando. *The Great Land Grab: The Mexican-American War, 1846–1848*. London: Quartet Books, 1975.

Martínez, Oscar. *Border Boom Town: Ciudad Juárez since 1848*. Austin: University of Texas Press, 1978.

———. *Border People: Life and Society in the U.S.–Mexican Borderlands*. Tucson: University of Arizona Press, 1994.

———. "Chicanos and the Border Cities: An Interpretive Essay." *Pacific Historical Review* 46 (February 1977): 85–106.

———. *The First Peoples: A History of Native Americans at the Pass of the North*. El Paso: El Paso Community Foundation, 2000.

———. "La frontera vista por René Mascareñas Miranda: Entrevista de historia oral." Institute of Oral History, University of Texas at El Paso.

Martínez, Oscar, ed. *Across Boundaries: Transborder Interaction in Perspective*. El Paso: Texas Western Press, 1986.

———, ed. *Fragments of the Mexican Revolution: Personal Accounts from the Border*. Albuquerque: University of New Mexico Press, 1983.

———, ed. *U.S.–Mexico Borderlands: Historical and Contemporary Perspectives*. Wilmington, Del.: Scholarly Resources, 1996.

Martínez, Pablo L. *Historia de Baja California*. Mexico City: Editorial Baja California, 1956.

Martínez, Tomás M. "Advertising and Racism: The Case of the Mexican American." In *Voices*, edited by Octavio L. Romano-V., 48–58. Berkeley, Calif.: Quinto Sol, 1971.

McPherson, Hallie M. "The Plan of William McKendree Gwin for a Colony in North Mexico, 1863–1865." *Pacific Historical Review* 2, no. 2 (December 1933): 357–86.

McWilliams, Carey. *North from Mexico*. New York: Greenwood Press, 1968.

Medina Castro, Manuel. *El gran despojo (Texas, Nuevo Mexico, California)*. Mexico City: Editorial Diógenes, 1971.

Meinig, Donald W. *Southwest: Three Peoples in Geographical Change, 1600–1970*. New York: Oxford University Press, 1971.

Mendoza Berrueto, Eliseo. "Algunos aspectos socioeconómicos de la frontera norte de la república mexicana." In *La frontera del norte: Integración y desarrollo*, edited by Roque González Salazar, 46–67. Mexico City: El Colegio de México, 1981.

Merk, Frederick. "Dissent in the U.S.–Mexico War." In *Dissent in Three American Wars*, edited by Samuel Eliot Morrison, Frederick Merk, and Frank Freidel, 35–63. Cambridge, Mass.: Harvard University Press, 1970.

———. *The Monroe Doctrine and American Expansionism, 1843–1849*. New York: Knopf, 1967.

Metz, Leon C. *Border: The U.S.–Mexico Line*. El Paso: Mangan Books, 1989.

Meyer, Michael, and L. Sherman. *The Course of Mexican History*. New York: Oxford University Press, 1979; 7th ed., 2003.

Miller, Hunter, ed. *Treaties and Other Acts of the United States of America*. Vols. 5 and 6. Washington, D.C.: U.S. Department of State, 1937, 1942.

Miller, Tom. *On the Border: Portraits of America's Southwestern Frontier*. New York: Harper and Row, 1981.

———. *Writing on the Edge: A Borderlands Reader*. Tucson: University of Arizona Press, 2003.

Miranda, Mario, and James W. Wilkie, eds. *Reglas del juego y juego sin reglas en la vida fronteriza*. Mexico City: ANUIES/PROFMEX, 1985.

Montejano, David. "Why Commemorate the Treaty of Guadalupe Hidalgo?" In Yolanda C. Padilla, ed., *Reflexiones 1998: New Directions in Mexican American Studies*. Austin: Center for Mexican American Studies, University of Texas at Austin, 1999.

Mora-Torres, Juan. *The Making of the Mexican Border: The State, Capitalism, and Society in Nuevo León, 1848–1910*. Austin: University of Texas Press, 2001.

Mottier, Nicole. "Organised Crime, Political Corruption, and Powerful Governors: Drug Gangs in Ciudad Juárez, Mexico, 1928–1937." M.Phil. thesis, Oxford University, 2004.

Mueller, Jerry E. *Restless River: International Law and the Behavior of the Rio Grande*. El Paso: Texas Western Press, 1975.

Myers, John. *The Border Wardens*. Englewood Cliffs, N.J.: Prentice-Hall, 1971.

Nance, Joseph Milton. *After San Jacinto: The Texas-Mexican Frontier, 1836–1841*. Austin: University of Texas Press, 1963.

Nasatir, Abraham P. *Borderland in Retreat: From Spanish Louisiana to the Far Southwest*. Albuquerque: University of New Mexico Press, 1976.

———. "The Shifting Borderlands." *Pacific Historical Review* 34, no. 1 (February 1965): 1–20.

Neuberger, Benjamin. "Natural and Artificial Borders: The African View." *International Problems* (Israel) 17, no. 1 (1978): 95–102.

Nevins, Joseph. *Operation Gatekeeper: The Rise of the "Illegal Alien" and the Making of the U.S.–Mexico Boundary*. New York: Routledge, 2002.

Newcomb, W. W., Jr. *The Indians of Texas, from Prehistoric to Modern Times*. Austin: University of Texas Press, 1961.

Nitze, William A. "Meeting the Water Needs of the Border Region: A Growing Challenge for the United States and Mexico." *Policy Papers on the Americas* 13, study 1. Washington, D.C.: CSIS, 2002.

Nostrand, Richard L. *Los Chicanos: Geografía histórica regional*. Mexico City: SepSetentas, 1976.

Ojeda, Mario, ed. *Administración del desarrollo de la frontera norte*. Mexico City: El Colegio de México, 1982.

Paredes, Raymund. "The Image of the Mexican in American Literature." Ph.D. diss., University of Texas at Austin, 1974.

Park, Joseph F. "The Apaches in Mexican-American Relations, 1848–1861: A Footnote to the Gadsden Treaty." *Arizona and the West* 3, no. 2 (Summer 1961): 129–46.

Peña, Devon G. *The Terror of the Machine: Technology, Work, Gender, and Ecology on the U.S.–Mexico Border*. Austin: Center for Mexican American Studies, University of Texas at Austin, 1997.

Perrigo, Lynn Irwin. *The American Southwest: Its People and Cultures*. New York: Holt, Rinehart and Winston, 1971.

Personal Memoirs of John N. Seguín, from the Year 1834 to the Retreat of General Woll from the City of San Antonio, 1842. San Antonio, Tex.: Ledger Book and Job Office, 1852. Typescript in Barker Texas History Center, University of Texas at Austin.

Peters, Donald W. "The Rio Grande Boundary Dispute in American Diplomacy." *Southwestern Historical Quarterly* 54, no. 4 (April 1951): 412–29.

Pettit, Arthur G. *Images of the Mexican American in Fiction and Film*. College Station: Texas A & M University Press, 1980.

Piñera Ramírez, David, ed. *Panorama histórico de Baja California*. Tijuana: Centro de Investigaciones Históricas UNAM-UABC, 1983.

Pletcher, David M. *The Diplomacy of Annexation: Texas, Oregon, and the U.S.–Mexico War*. Columbia: University of Missouri Press, 1973.

Ponce de León, Gregorio. *El interinato presidencial de 1911*. Mexico City: n.p., n.d.

Porter, Kenneth W. "The Seminole in Mexico, 1850–1861." *Hispanic American Historical Review* 31, no. 1 (February 1951): 1–36.

Prescott, John R. V. *Boundaries and Frontiers*. Totowa, N.J.: Rowan and Littlefield, 1978.

Price, Glenn W. *Origins of the War with Mexico: The Polk-Stockton Intrigue*. Austin: University of Texas Press, 1967.

Price, John A. *Tijuana: Urbanization in a Border Culture.* Notre Dame, Ind.: University of Notre Dame Press, 1973.

Profitt, T. D., III. *Tijuana: The History of a Mexican Metropolis.* San Diego, Calif.: San Diego State University Press, 1994.

Programa Nacional Fronterizo. Mexico City, 1961.

Reeves, T. Zane. *The U.S.–Mexico Border Commissions: An Overview and Agenda for Further Research.* Center for Inter-American and Border Studies, Border Issues and Public Policy Reports, no. 13. El Paso: University of Texas at El Paso, March 1984.

Reich, Peter L., ed. *Statistical Abstract of the United States–Mexico Borderlands.* Los Angeles: University of California, Los Angeles, Latin American Center Publications, 1984.

Reisler, Mark. "Always the Laborer, Never the Citizen: Anglo Perceptions of the Mexican Immigrant during the 1920's." *Pacific Historical Review* 45 (May 1976): 231–54.

———. *By the Sweat of Their Brow: Mexican Immigrant Labor in the United States, 1900–1940.* Westport, Conn.: Greenwood Press, 1976.

Rice, Bradley R., and Richard M. Bernard, eds. *Sunbelt Cities: Politics and Growth since World War II.* Austin: University of Texas Press, 1983.

Richardson, Chad. *Batos, Bolillos, Pochos, and Pelados: Class and Culture on the South Texas Border.* Austin: University of Texas Press, 1999.

Richardson, Rupert Norval, and Carl Coke Rister. *The Greater Southwest.* Glendale, Calif.: Arthur H. Clark Co., 1934.

Rippy, J. Fred. "Anglo-American Filibusters and the Gadsden Treaty." *Hispanic American Historical Review* 2 (May 1922): 155–80.

———. "Border Troubles along the Rio Grande, 1848–1860." *Southwestern Historical Quarterly* 23 (October 1919): 91–111.

———. "The Indians of the Southwest in the Diplomacy of the United States and Mexico, 1848–1853." *Hispanic American Historical Review* 2 (August 1919): 363–96.

———. "Some Precedents of the Pershing Expedition into Mexico." *Southwestern Historical Quarterly* 24, no. 2 (April 1921): 292–316.

———. *The United States and Mexico.* New York: Knopf, 1926.

Rister, Carl Coke. *The Southwestern Frontier, 1865–1881.* Cleveland, Ohio: Arthur H. Clark Co., 1928.

Ritzenthaler, Robert E., and Frederick A. Peterson. *The Mexican Kickapoo Indians.* Westport, Conn.: Greenwood Press, 1970.

Robinson, Cecil. *Mexico and the Hispanic Southwest in American Literature.* Tucson: University of Arizona Press, 1977.

———. *With the Ears of Strangers: The Mexican in American Literature.* Tucson: University of Arizona Press, 1963.

Robinson, Robin E. "Vice and Tourism on the U.S.–Mexico Border: A Comparison of Three Communities in the Era of U.S. Prohibition." Ph.D. diss., Arizona State University, 2002.

Rolle, Andrew F. "Futile Filibustering in Baja California, 1888–1890." *Pacific Historical Review* 20, no. 2 (May 1951): 159–66.

Rosenbaum, Robert J. *Mexican Resistance in the Southwest: The Sacred Right of Self-Preservation.* Austin: University of Texas Press, 1981.

Ross, Stanley R., ed. *Ecology and Development of the Border Region.* Mexico City: ANUIES/PROFMEX, 1983.

Ruiz, Ramón Eduardo. "American Imperialism and the U.S.–Mexico War." In *American Vistas, 1607–1877,* edited by Leonard Dinnerstein and Kenneth T. Jackson, 217–28. 3rd ed. New York: Oxford University Press, 1979.

———. *On the Rim of Mexico: Encounters of the Rich and Poor.* Boulder, Colo.: Westview Press, 1998.

Ruiz, Vicki L., and Susan Tiano, eds. *Women on the U.S.–Mexico Border: Responses to Change.* Boston: Allen and Unwin, 1987.

Saadia, Touval. *The Boundary Politics of Independent Africa.* Cambridge, Mass.: Harvard University Press, 1972.

Salazar, Robert J., et al. *Asociación de Reclamantes v. The United Mexican States: Texas Land Grants Heirs Seek Justice.* 1981.

Samora, Julian. *Los Mojados: The Wetback Story.* Notre Dame, Ind.: University of Notre Dame Press, 1971.

Saragoza, Alex M. *The Monterrey Elite and the Mexican State, 1880–1940.* Austin: University of Texas Press, 1988.

Schmidt, Louis Bernard. "Manifest Opportunity and the Gadsden Purchase." *Arizona and the West* 3, no. 3 (Autumn 1961): 245–64.

Schmitt, Karl M. *Mexico and the United States, 1821–1973: Conflict and Coexistence.* New York: Wiley, 1974.

Secretaría de Industria y Comercio. *Estudio del desarrollo comercial de la frontera norte.* Mexico City, 1972.

Sepúlveda, César. *La frontera norte de México: Historia, conflictos, 1762–1975.* Mexico City: Editorial Porrúa, 1976.

———. "Historia y problemas de los limites de México." *Historia Mexicana* 8 (1958): 1–34, 145–74.

———. *Tres ensayos sobre la frontera septentrional de la Nueva España.* Mexico City: Editorial Porrúa, 1977.

Sierra, Carlos J. *Los indios de la frontera.* Mexico City: Ediciones de la Muralla, 1980.

Smith, Justin H. *The War with Mexico.* 2 vols. New York: Macmillan, 1919.

Smith, Ralph A. "Indians in American-Mexican Relations before the War of 1846." *Hispanic American Historical Review* 43, no. 1 (February 1963): 34–64.

Sonnichsen, C. L. *The El Paso Salt War (1877).* El Paso: Carl Hertzog and the Texas Western Press, 1961.

Spicer, Edward H. *Cycles of Conquest: The Impact of Spain, Mexico, and the United States on the Indians of the Southwest, 1533–1960.* Tucson: University of Arizona Press, 1962.

———. "Highlights of Yaqui History." *Indian Historian* 7, no. 2 (1974): 2–9, 53.

———. *Pascua: A Yaqui Village.* Chicago: University of Chicago Press, 1940.

———. *The Yaquis: A Cultural History.* Tucson: University of Arizona Press, 1980.

Statistical Yearbook of the Immigration and Naturalization Service, 2003. Washington, D.C.: Government Printing Office, 2003. www.uscis.gov.

Staudt, Kathleen. *Free Trade? Informal Economies at the U.S.–Mexico Border.* Philadelphia: Temple University Press, 1998.

Staudt, Kathleen, and Irasema Coronado. *Fronteras no más: Toward Social Justice at the U.S.–Mexico Border.* New York: Palgrave Macmillan, 2002.

Stenberg, R. R. "Polk and Fremont, 1845–1846." *Pacific Historical Review* 7 (September 1938): 211–27.

Stevens, Robert C. "Forsaken Frontier: A History of Sonora, Mexico, 1821–1851." Ph.D. diss., University of California, Berkeley, 1963.

Stoddard, Ellwyn R. "The Adjustment of Mexican American Barrio Families to Forced Housing Relocation." *Social Science Quarterly* 58, no. 4 (March 1973): 749–59.

———. *Borderlands Trilogy.* Vol. 1, *U.S.–Mexico Borderlands Issues: The Bi-National Boundary, Immigration and Economic Policies.* El Paso: Promontory, 2001.

———. *Borderlands Trilogy.* Vol. 2, *U.S.–Mexico Borderlands Studies: Multidisciplinary Perspectives and Concepts.* El Paso: Promontory, 2002.

———. *Maquila: Assembly Plants in Northern Mexico.* El Paso: Texas Western Press, 1987.

———. "Northern Mexican Migration and the United States–Mexican Border Region." *New Scholar* 9 (1984): 51–72.

———. *Patterns of Poverty along the U.S.–Mexico Border.* Center for Inter-American and Border Studies, University of Texas at El Paso, 1978.

Stoddard, Ellwyn R., Oscar J. Martínez, and Miguel Angel Martínez Lasso. *El Paso–Ciudad Juárez Relations and the Tortilla Curtain. A Study of Local Adaptation to Federal Border Policies.* El Paso: Council on the Arts and Humanities, 1979.

Stout, Joseph Allen, Jr. *The Liberators: Filibustering Expeditions into Mexico, 1848–1862, and the Last Thrust of Manifest Destiny.* Los Angeles: Westernlore Press, 1973.

Strieber, Whitley, and James W. Kunetka. *Warday.* New York: Holt, Rinehart and Winston, 1984.

Symposium on U.S.–Mexican Transboundary Resources. Special issues, *Natural Resources Journal* 17, no. 4 (October 1977): 543–634 and 18, no. 1 (January 1978): 1–212.

Tays, George. "Fremont Had No Secret Instructions." *Pacific Historical Review* 9 (June 1940): 157–71.

Tijerina, Andrew Anthony. "Tejanos and Texas: The Native Mexicans of Texas, 1820–1850." Ph.D. diss., University of Texas at Austin, 1977.

Timmons, W. H. "The El Paso Area in the Mexican Period, 1821–1848." *Southwestern Historical Quarterly* 84, no. 1 (July 1980): 1–28.

Tinker Salas, Miguel. *In the Shadow of the Eagles: Sonora and the Transformation of the Border during the Porfiriato.* Berkeley: University of California Press, 1997.

Torrans, Thomas. *Forging the Tortilla Curtain: Cultural Drift and Change along the United States–Mexico Border from the Spanish Era to the Present.* Fort Worth: Texas Christian University Press, 2000.

Tuett, Samuel, and Elliot Young, eds. *Continental Crossroads: Remapping U.S.–Mexico Borderlands History.* Durham, N.C.: Duke University Press and the William P. Clements Center for Southwest Studies, 2004.

Tutorow, Norman E., comp. *The Mexican-American War: An Annotated Bibliography.* Westport, Conn.: Greenwood Press, 1981.

U.S. Bureau of the Census. *Census of Population: General Social and Economic Characteristics,* United States Summary and State Reports, 1950–2003.

U.S. Code Congressional and Administrative News, 9th Cong., 2d sess., vol. 2. St. Paul: West Publishing Co., 1982.

U.S. Commission on Civil Rights. *Socio-economic Profile of American Indians in Arizona and New Mexico.* Washington, D.C., 1972.

———. *The Southwest Indian Report.* Washington, D.C., 1973.

U.S. Congress. House. *Difficulties on the Southwestern Frontier.* 36th Cong., 1st sess., 1860. H. Exec. Doc. 52.

———. *El Paso Troubles in Texas.* 45th Cong., 2d sess., 1878. H. Exec. Doc. 93.

———. H. Rept. 343. Serial 1709. 44th Cong., 1st sess., 1876.

———. *Troubles on the Texas Frontier.* 36th Cong., 1st sess., 1860. H. Exec. Doc. 81.

U.S. Congress. Senate. S. Misc. Doc. 241. 35th Cong., 1st sess., 1858.

———. S. Rept. 39. Serial 1565. 42d Cong., 3rd sess., 1872.

———. S. Rept. 97-684. 97th Cong., 2d sess., 1982.

U.S. Immigration and Naturalization Service. Statistical reports. Author's files.

U.S. National Archives. Selected correspondence and documents.

U.S. State Department. *The Chamizal Settlement.* Washington, D.C., 1963.

U.S. Supreme Court. *Saxbe v. Bustos.* 419 U.S. 65 (1974).

Utley, Robert. *The International Boundary, United States and Mexico: A History of Frontier Dispute and Cooperation, 1848–1963.* Santa Fe, N.M.: U.S. Department of the Interior, National Park Service, 1964.

Vásquez de Knauth, Josefina. *Mexicanos y norteamericanos ante la guerra del 47.* Mexico City: Secretaría de Educación Pública, 1972.

Velázquez, María del Carmen. *Establecimiento y pérdida del Septentrión de Nueva España.* Mexico City: El Colegio de México, 1974.

Vila, Pablo. *Crossing Borders, Reinforcing Borders: Social Categories, Metaphors, and Narrative Identities on the U.S.–Mexico Frontier.* Austin: University of Texas Press, 2000.

Villalpando, M. Vic, et al. *A Study of the Socioeconomic Impact of Illegal Aliens on the County of San Diego.* San Diego, Calif.: County of San Diego Human Resources Agency, 1977.

Voss, Stuart F. *On the Periphery of Nineteenth-Century Mexico: Sonora and Sinaloa, 1810–1877*. Tucson: University of Arizona Press, 1982.

Walker, Henry P., and Don Bufkin. *Historical Atlas of Arizona*. Norman: University of Oklahoma Press, 1979.

Walker, William O., III, ed. *Drugs in the Western Hemisphere: An Odyssey of Cultures in Conflict*. Wilmington, Vt.: Scholarly Resources, 1996.

Warren, Harris Gaylor. *The Sword Was Their Passport: A History of American Filibustering in the Mexican Revolution*. Baton Rouge: Louisiana State University Press, 1943.

Washington Valdez, Diana. *Cosecha de mujeres: Safari en el desierto mexicano*. Mexico City: Oceano, 2005.

Wasserman, Mark. *Capitalists, Caciques, and Revolution: The Native Elite and Foreign Enterprise in Chihuahua, Mexico, 1854–1911*. Chapel Hill: University of North Carolina Press, 1984.

Webb, Walter Prescott. *The Texas Rangers: A Century of Frontier Defense*. Austin: University of Texas Press, 1965.

Weber, David J. *The Mexican Frontier, 1821–1846. The American Southwest under Mexico*. Albuquerque: University of New Mexico Press, 1982.

Webster, Michael G. "Intrigue on the Rio Grande: The *Rio Bravo* Affair, 1875." *Southwestern Historical Quarterly* 74, no. 2 (October 1970): 149–64.

———. "Texas Manifest Destiny and the Mexican Border Conflict, 1865–1880." Ph.D. diss., Indiana University, 1972.

Weeks, John R., and Roberto Ham-Chande, eds. *Demographic Dynamics of the U.S.–Mexico Border*. El Paso: Texas Western Press, 1992.

Weintraub, Sidney, and Gilberto Cárdenas. *Use of Public Services by Undocumented Aliens in Texas*. Austin: Lyndon B. Johnson School of Public Affairs, 1983.

Weisberg, Albert K. *Manifest Destiny*. Baltimore, Md.: Johns Hopkins University Press, 1935.

Widstrand, Carl Gosta, ed. *African Boundary Problems*. Uppsala, Sweden: Scandinavian Institute of African Studies, 1969.

Williams, Edward J., and Mitchell A. Seligson. *Maquiladoras and Migration: Workers in the Mexico–United States Border Industrialization Program*. Austin: Mexico–U.S. Border Research Program, University of Texas, distributed by the University of Texas Press, 1981.

Wood, Andrew Grant, ed. *On the Border: Society and Culture between the United States and Mexico*. Lanham, Md.: Rowan and Littlefield, 2001.

Wyllys, Rufus Kay. *The French in Sonora (1850–1854): The Story of French Adventurers from California into Mexico*. Berkeley: University of California Press, 1932.

Xirau Icaza, Joaquín. *Nuestra dependencia fronteriza*. Mexico City: Fondo de Cultura Económica, 1976.

Zavala, Silvio. "La historiografía americana sobre la guerra del '47." *Cuadernos Americanos* 38, no. 2 (March–April 1948): 190–206.

Zorrilla, Luis G. *Historia de las relaciones entre México y los Estados Unidos de América, 1800–1958*. 2 vols. Mexico City: Editorial Porrúa, 1977.

Index

About the Author

Oscar J. Martínez is a Regents' Professor of History at the University of Arizona. He earned his B.A. at California State University, Los Angeles, M.A. at Stanford University, and Ph.D. at the University of California at Los Angeles.

He has taught at Foothill Community College in Los Altos Hills, California (1970–71), Cal State Hayward (1970), the University of Texas at El Paso (1975–88), Yale University (fall 1995), New Mexico State University (spring 2003), and the University of Arizona (1988–present). While at the University of Texas at El Paso he directed the Institute of Oral History (1975–82) and the Center for Inter-American and Border Studies (1982–87). He also served as interim director of the Latin American Area Center at the University of Arizona during 1994–95. He spent the academic year 1981–82 as a fellow at the Center for Advanced Study in the Behavioral Sciences at Stanford, California.

Martínez has authored and edited eight books and many articles, book chapters, and reviews. His most recent works include *Mexican-Origin People in the United States: A Topical History* (University of Arizona Press, 2001), *Border People: Life and Society in the U.S.–Mexico Borderlands* (University of Arizona Press, 1994), and *U.S.–Mexico Borderlands: Historical and Contemporary Perspectives* (Scholarly Resources Press, 1995). Currently, he is conducting research on two projects, "Ethnicity and the American Dream: A Mexican American Perspective" and "Why Mexico Is Poorer than the United States."

Martínez has served on the boards of several journals and professional associations. He is a former president of the Association of Borderlands Scholars.

LaVergne, TN USA
07 January 2010
169045LV00006B/5/P